Fractured Identities

Changing Patterns of Inequality

HARRIET BRADLEY

Polity Press

First published in 1996 by Polity Press in association with Blackwell Publishing Ltd.

Reprinted 1997, 2002, 2003

Editorial office:
Polity Press
65 Bridge Street, Cambridge CB2 1UR, UK

Marketing and production:
Blackwell Publishing Ltd
108 Cowley Road, Oxford OX4 1JF, UK

Published in the USA by
Blackwell Publishing Inc.
350 Main Street, Malden MA 02148, USA

A CIP catalogue record for this book is available from the British Library.

Library of Congress Cataloging-in-Publication Data

Bradley, Harriet.
Fractured identities : changing patterns of inequality / Harriet Bradley.
p. cm.
Includes bibliographical references and index.
ISBN 0–7456–1083–8 (hc). — ISBN 0–7456–1084–6 (pbk.)
1. Equality. 2. Social classes. I. Title.
HM146.B79 1996
305—dc20 95–40291
CIP

Typeset in 10 on 11½ pt Times
by Graphicraft Typesetters Ltd, Hong Kong
Printed in Great Britain by TJ International, Padstow, Cornwall
This book is printed on acid-free paper.

For further information on Polity, visit our website: http:www.polity.co.uk

Fractured Identities

In memory of Michael Martindale
who dedicated his life to the ideal of a better life
for all in the community

Contents

Acknowledgements

This book arose out of some work written for the Open University course D203 *Understanding Modern Societies*. I wish to thank David Held of Polity Press for offering me the chance to expand on my exploration of 'interacting dynamics'.

At times it has seemed an act of sheer hubris to write a book dealing with four different aspects of social inequality. I have drawn on the advice of people more expert than myself in specific areas. I would like to thank the following for their help and suggestions for reading, for lending me books and for discussions around aspects of the book: Kay Adamson; Rohit Barot; Steve Fenton; Ruth Levitas; Tony Maltby; Allen Maunders; Parita Mukta; Peter Rushton; Sylvia Walby; Jackie West. Thanks also to three anonymous reviewers for useful comments.

Above all I would like to thank Irving Velody for the patience with which he has listened to me working through the debates and dilemmas aired in the book. Although he would not agree with the conclusions reached in it, the direction of the book has been shaped by his insights and perceptions. It could not have been written without him.

The ideas in the book are, of course, my own responsibility, as are any mistakes. None of the above-named is to blame!

The author and publishers would like to thank the following for permission to reproduce material in the book:

Sage Publications for Table 3.2 (based on G. Esping-Andersen, *Changing Classes*, 1993, pp. 24–5), and for Table 6.1 (from Arber and Ginn, *Gender and Later Life*, 1991, Table 1.3). Crown copyright (Tables 5.1 and 5.2) is reproduced with the permission of the Controller of HMSO.

The author wishes to acknowledge the help of the Department of Employment in providing latest figures for these two tables.

Every effort has been made to trace all copyright holders, but if any has been inadvertently overlooked the publishers will be pleased to make the necessary arrangement at the first opportunity.

Tables

Introduction

A crisis in stratification theory

Inequality has long been a central concern within sociology. Unequal distribution of wealth, privilege and power has been a major focus of analysis and research. Although at times some sociologists have suggested that resources are being distributed more equally as societies develop, there appears to be a consensus emerging in the 1900s that the contrary is true. The development of a global capitalist economy has brought sharper disparities between those at the top and the bottom of the social hierarchy. Old people, young people, ethnic minority members, the unemployed, low-paid women workers are among those who are losing out as a result of current processes of social and economic change. The losers are increasingly marginalized and excluded from the prosperous life-style enjoyed by the elite groups. Study of inequality is still, then, a key sociological task. However, the focus in the study of inequality has dramatically changed in the past two decades.

When I was an undergraduate student in the late 1970s, study of inequality hinged on the concept of class. Certainly, there was no agreement over exactly *what* class was or *how* it could best be conceptualized. The disagreements were vigorous, involving a longstanding debate between neo-Marxists and neo-Weberians, with a brief and fairly dismissive nod at the functionalist account of Davis and Moore, seen as a kind of transatlantic naivety. The debates were explored in a number of central texts, among them Giddens's *The Class Structure of the Advanced Societies* (1973), Parkin's *Class, Inequality and Political Order* (1972), Westergaard's and Resler's *Class in a Capitalist Society* (1975) and Crompton's and Gubbay's *Economy and Class Structure* (1977). However, all parties agreed that Britain was a society stratified by class. By contrast, much less attention was paid to other sources of social inequality and division such as gender or 'race' and ethnicity; and it was characteristically suggested that class theory could be extended and reconstructed to cover these other dimensions.

Now, less than twenty years later, the primacy of class has been challenged in a number of ways. One critic, Peter Calvert, has even suggested that the concept of class is so problematic that it should be discarded (1982, p. 216). Michael Mann argued that the recognition of the crucial importance of gender domination by feminist sociologists had led to a 'serious theoretical crisis' for stratification theory (1986, p. 41). Class has not yet been totally displaced from its central position in British sociology: the Emperor has not been deposed; but it has been suggested that his apparel is scanty and that he stands in desperate need of new clothes.

These challenges to class theory come from many quarters, but we can discern three major strands among them:

(1) It has been argued that in the post-war period, and most especially in the past twenty years, the class structure has changed so rapidly and radically that the old frameworks for thinking about class are now no longer applicable. A new set of concepts is needed.
(2) A second and more fundamental critique has come from theorists of gender and of race and ethnicity who question the idea that traditional class theory can be adapted to explain gender and ethnic differences. Gilroy has spoken of the theoretical challenges to class-based analysis posed by

> Writers and thinkers from radical traditions struggling against forms of subordination which are not obviously or directly related to class. These may be based on gender, race, ethnicity or age and are often found in political locations removed from the workplace. (1987, p. 18)

Although there is still considerable debate about the relationship between class, 'race' and gender, it has emerged as a new orthodoxy that other forms of social inequality are not reducible to those of class. Each needs to be considered in its own right, while an awareness and understanding of their interaction is retained.

(3) An even more fundamental challenge comes from the intellectual movement known as postmodernism. This is a bundle of new approaches (discussed further in chapter 2) within the social sciences and humanities, which reject traditional forms of general theory, predominantly that of Marx, as invalid. Such 'grand narratives' are seen to embody unacceptable views of historical development in terms of progress to a stated goal, in the case of Marxism that of a class-free socialist Utopia. Such theories must be replaced with accounts which focus only on specific limited local contexts. Postmodernism has thus focused attention on the diversity of social experience in a way that, at the

least, endorses new forms of pluralism through its focus on the specific positions of different groups, and, at its most extreme, can undermine all notions of collectivities, such as classes, promoting a view of society as made up of atomized individuals.

Postmodernist thinking has also been accompanied by an interest in 'deconstructing' linguistic categories such as 'class' or 'women'. For deconstructionists such collective terms are socially constructed concepts which have no necessary 'real' basis beyond our use of them. The use of such concepts only serves to put limits on people who are forced to accept polarized identities, such as those of 'man' or 'woman'. Classes and genders are denied existence outside of the way we choose to apply such labels. This contention is accompanied by an interest in how such terms are used in various verbal and written linguistic and conceptual frameworks or 'discourses'. Such approaches, which draw particularly on the work of Derrida, Foucault and Lacan and are very influential within feminism, are often described as 'post-structuralist'. Indeed the postmodern approach within sociology has turned away from the analysis of social *structures* to a study of social *meanings* and the way they are embodied in *cultures*.

Such an approach does not necessarily imply an abandonment of the study of class, gender and ethnicity, since at the very least they can be studied as examples of discourses or of social constructs. But postmodern approaches sit uneasily with study of material factors such as inequality and deprivation, and those influenced by the ideas of postmodernism have tended to avoid these topics. Indeed, it is not quite clear whether such study can legitimately be carried out, certainly within existing frameworks, since postmodernism opposes itself to 'foundationalist' accounts of society (that is, accounts which seek to identify the bases or underlying structures upon which society is founded and which generate specific patterns of social behaviour), and to 'totalizing' narratives about society. Marx's analysis of the way in which economic relations form the 'base' on which the whole superstructure of society depends is a classic example of a foundationalist and totalizing theory. Postmodernist theorists would identify the theories both of capitalism and of patriarchy as examples of foundationalist thinking, a position which seriously undermines classic approaches to class and gender.

In this book I explore the way stratification theory is now evolving in response to these challenges. Throughout the book, I try to integrate some empirical evidence of inequalities in society with discussion of the range of theories developed to explain them. A key objective is to pull together classical or modernist approaches to understanding inequalities with the newer perspectives inspired by postmodernism and post-structuralism. In this way I hope to provide a broad overview of the current 'state of play' in theorizing inequality, as well as considering whether sociology can move beyond the critiques of class theory.

Beyond the crisis: new approaches to stratification

Over the past decade many writers on inequality have grappled with the first two sets of challenges outlined above. Within class theory there has been a focus on the way old class alignments are breaking up and discussion of new class groupings such as the 'underclass'. While the classic framework of Karl Marx had posited the idea of class polarization, newer approaches stress the multiplication of class groupings and the evolution of new types of class cleavages, for instance those based on different patterns of consumption. Classes are seen as 'fragmenting' rather than polarizing. This idea of fragmentation has been echoed in other areas of stratification theory. While early approaches to 'race' centred on a major divide between 'black' and 'white' groupings in Britain and America, recent work has focused on the different social positions of a plurality of racially and ethnically defined groups in Britain, for example, Afro-Caribbeans, Indians, Pakistanis, Jews, Chinese and Irish. Rather than the single category of 'race', sociology now concerns itself also with the interconnecting categories of ethnicity, nationality, culture and religion and the way these serve to fragment a country's population. Analysis of gender, too, has moved away from the view that women as a group are unified by a common experience of male domination, and has started to explore the situations of different groups of women.

Such new feminist approaches focus particularly on the diverse experiences of women of different ethnic groups. Theorists of 'race', too, have taken the lead in exploring the way in which different aspects of inequality interrelate. Pioneering studies, such as those of Phizacklea (1990) and Anthias and Yuval-Davis (1992), have explicitly set out to examine the way racial inequality is structured by class and gender relations. Class theory has perhaps had more of a struggle to adapt itself to these new perceptions. But a pioneering meeting of the Cambridge Social Stratification Seminar involved debates between theorists of class and of gender leading to the publication of 'Gender and Stratification' (Crompton and Mann, 1986). These moves can be taken as pointing to the way ahead for stratification theory and they are discussed in subsequent chapters in this book.

The challenge from postmodernism has been the hardest to accommodate. It has been more or less ignored in recent texts on class (Saunders, 1990; Scase, 1992; Edgell, 1993). Rosemary Crompton in her recent study acknowledges that 'class analysis might be viewed as a particular example of a "totalizing discourse" which postmodernist thinking might reject' (1993, p. 178), but fails to explore fully the consequences of such a view. However, the challenge has been taken up by many theorists of 'race' and ethnicity and gender, who utilize the techniques of deconstruction in their analysis (for example, Riley, 1988; Donald and Rattansi, 1992). The postmodern stress on diversity and pluralism sits easily with the interest in fragmentation and the interaction of class, gender and ethnicity, as outlined above. Kobena Mercer states that 'like "identity" difference, diversity and fragmentation are keywords in the postmodern vocabulary' (1990, p. 49). Within feminism a growing interest in the study of 'discourses' has meant a greater involvement in the study of literary and cultural texts and how the categories of gender are displayed within them, with a consequent move away from studying the economic manifestations of gender inequality. Such moves can be seen to reflect a growing unease as to how material inequalities should be analysed in the face of the anti-foundationalist stance of postmodernism.

Analysing inequalities: fluidity and stability

Today's postmodern challenge to the structural theories of class and gender elaborated in the 1960s and 1970s can be seen as the latest manifestation of a schism which has always been present in sociology. Alan Dawe (1970) pointed to the existence of 'the Two Sociologies': the sociology of action and agency, as exemplified by Weber and Simmel, and the sociology of structure and system as exemplified by Marx and Durkheim. Dawe speculated, like many before and after him, as to how this seeming chasm could be bridged. One influential recent attempt to integrate the analysis of structures and of actors and meanings is Giddens's theory of 'structuration' (1976; 1984). Seeking to overcome the dualism of structure and action, he speaks of the duality of structure: structures are seen both as the *means* through which social practices are enabled and their *outcome*. In this vision, structures are constituted by the actions of agents, but action itself is organized within the parameters of existing structures.

The difficulty with which generations of sociologists have struggled, and which Giddens's concept of structuration attempts to encapsulate, is that social reality presents two faces. One perception of it emphasizes chaos and confusion, the limitless welter of apparently unique events. In this view society is fluid and social behaviour and relationships are inherently unstable, endlessly changing. Each piece of interaction is unique, never to be replicated. Human beings are unique individuals and the diversity of human experience is infinite. The other perception is that, despite the surface confusion of events, society is ordered. Patterned regularities of social behaviour emerge and persist over time, as manifested in statistical rates. Social institutions may change gradually but also show remarkable stability; there are marked resemblances among institutions of the same kind in any given society and indeed across different societies and in different historical periods. In given situations human beings are likely to behave in similar ways and social action is thus, at least to a degree, predictable.

The paradox is that *both* these apparently contradictory views of society are correct! Societies are chaotic, but also orderly; behaviour is infinitely variable, but also regular and predictable; social relations change, but are also stable and persistent. The problem of sociology is that it has found it remarkably hard to develop a perspective that can encompass both sets of truths. The history of sociology shows regular swings between the ascendancy of one or other perspective.

Those who emphasize fluidity and chaos have often been drawn to the study of interaction between individuals. They explain the apparent orderliness of society as a social construct: order has to be constantly renegotiated through interaction processes. The stress on fluidity is also linked to the study of meaning and the way meanings are embedded in cultural practices or discourses. Language, meaning, social action and culture are the key concepts which reappear in these kinds of approaches. The most radical versions, such as that of ethnomethodology, deny any validity to notions of social structure; ethnomethodologists suggest that sociology should confine itself to the study of actors' accounts of social interaction, a position which comes remarkably close to the postmodernist stress on language and discourse. Ethnomethodology instructs us to talk about how people talk about inequality, not about inequality itself. Postmodernism can be seen as the latest phase in this sociological strand. It is described by one of its most influential commentators, David Harvey, as displaying 'total acceptance' of 'ephemerality, fragmentation, discontinuity and the chaotic' (1989, p. 44).

By contrast, those who emphasize order have made structure their key concept. They have focused on discernible regularities in social relationships, often using statistical sources as evidence. Such regularities may be considered as structures in themselves or be taken as manifestations of underlying mechanisms or 'deep structures', such as 'the capitalist mode of production', which are seen to regulate society. In structural approaches, societies are frequently conceptualized as systems in which parts work together to provide an integrated whole. Individual behaviour is seen as constrained by social structures. While the concepts of culture, meanings and action may be employed by sociologists who emphasize order, they tend to see them as circumscribed by prevailing structures or at least enmeshed in a circle of causality with them: 'men make history, but they make it under circumstances not of their own choosing'. At its radical extreme such a position, as in various forms of Marxist structuralism, may deny the validity of the concept of the individual or the human agent. Postmodernism evolved partly as a challenge to the various types of Marxism that had become theoretically dominant in the 1960s and 1970s.

The framework employed within this book is one that tries to retain the concept of structured inequalities while at the same time accepting some aspects of the postmodern framework. In this way it is acknowledged that societies are both stable and fluid, both variable and orderly. Marshall Berman has argued that in the twentieth century sociological theorizing of change has become more rigid and inflexible, as compared to the 'classical' approach of the nineteenth-century thinkers who were ready to acknowledge the ambiguous and contradictory nature of society: 'open views of modern life have been supplanted by closed ones, Both/And by Either/Or' (Berman, 1983, p. 24). This book seeks to recapture a 'both/and' view.

On the one hand, class, gender, 'race' and age are all viewed as social constructs, categories used to define, explain and justify the various forms of social differentiation. As social categories they are inherently unstable and indeed contestable. Even where they may have some basis in biological and physical differences, these categories are seen to have substantial social aspects and thus to be socially and historically variable. For example, age as a biological fact refers to the amount of time that has passed since an individual was born and to certain physical signs and developments that accompany the ageing process. But age as a sociological category refers to differential power relations between individuals of differing ages, different access to economic resources and to social privileges, different rules governing behaviour seen as suitable for different age-groups. In this sense age is socially defined and culturally variable. Moreover Donna Haraway's work has alerted us to the fact that even biological facts, such as reproduction, seen to be immutable, are in fact susceptible to social construction through new technologies (1990). The writings of William Gibson and the cyberpunks play with the idea that with the development of the cyborg the ageing process may be overcome, by means of technologies involving the replication and replacement of body parts, although such technologies are as yet in the realms of fantasy.

At the same time these socially constructed categories derive from lived sets of social relationships which are orderly and persist over time, although they may be subject to longer-term processes of change and shorter-term fluctuations. These sets of relationships *lie outside of the way in which we categorize them*, although the processes of categorization will affect the ways in which the relationships evolve. They are in fact what the sociologists of order have called structures. However, the metaphor 'structure', borrowed from natural and mechanical sciences (as in the structures of an atom, a leaf or a bridge), may be an inappropriate one in over-emphasizing the element of fixity. Rather, in this book I have chosen to employ the metaphor 'dynamic' to convey the sense that these relationships are constantly evolving. I hope by the use of this term to convey the notion of the two faces of social reality outlined above: continuity within change, order within variability, fixity within fluidity.

These sets of relationships, then, are the structures or dynamics which work together to produce and perpetuate inequalities and social hierarchies. The four sets of relationships considered in this book, class, 'race' and ethnicity, gender, and age are all seen as having different bases – 'different existential locations', in the phrase of Anthias and Yuval-Davis (1992, p. 17). Mannheim (1952) used the term 'social location' to indicate the common placing of certain individuals within the power structure of a society, citing class and age as two types of social location. These different locations are sketched out in chapter 1.

The remainder of this book explores these two elements: the changing social categories of class, 'race'/ethnicity, gender and age; and the changing lived relationships which these categories attempt to encompass. I suggest there is no contradiction between seeing social phenomena as social constructs and seeing them as objectively existing lived relationships, as long as the mutual and circular relationship between these two aspects is acknowledged.

Chapter 1 provides an overview of current patterns of inequality and the way sociological approaches to them have been changing in the post-war decades; particular attention is given to the notions of polarization, fragmentation and identity.

In chapter 2, ways are considered in which societies have been categorized, and it is argued that to have some view of the nature of society as a whole is necessary in order to understand fully the operation of particular social institutions. The notions of industrialism, capitalism, modernity, post-industrialism and postmodernism are briefly outlined and discussed.

Chapters 3 to 6 constitute the heart of this study. Each deals with one dynamic of inequality: class, gender, 'race'/ethnicity and age. Each follows approximately the same format, dealing first with classic approaches; newer conceptualizations are then discussed. Each chapter also explores the interaction with other dynamics of inequality and considers the consequences of changes in terms of social identity.

These four chapters are designed to be accessible to undergraduate students. Each can be read as a self-contained unit. I have tried to avoid the excessive use of sociological jargon and technical language and to simplify complex ideas to make them comprehensible; it is my experience as a teacher that many students are deterred by the complicated styles in which some more recent texts, especially those influenced by postmodernism and deconstruction, are couched. More advanced readers may find these chapters somewhat oversimplified; moreover, inevitably the attempt to compress such wide fields of analysis into one single chapter means it is impossible to do justice to the complexities and nuances of debates. Each chapter, then, is to be viewed strictly as an introduction to the area and each concludes with a short bibliography designed for students who wish to explore the topic in more depth.

Chapter 7 provides a brief comparative perspective. It highlights similarities and variations in the dynamics of inequality in a range of industrial societies. These are viewed in light of the debate over the validity of local or of 'grand' narratives of social development.

The concluding chapter returns to the theme of fragmentation and polarization in relation to the debates reviewed in preceding chapters and repeats the call for a 'both/and' approach. The need to study the interaction of the four dynamics is stressed and related to the issue of identity in a changing world.

Throughout the book the theme of change, both in terms of social categories and the lived relations they seek to represent, is stressed. While persistent patterns of inequality are identified, it is emphasized that the structures of stratification are volatile. My hope is that this may indicate how some of the difficulties associated with structural analysis, which the postmodern critique has illuminated, may be resolved through the development of a 'both/and' approach to social reality.

A 'both/and' approach: materiality and meaning

It would be nice if the social world were no more than a contestation of meanings, so that, merely by renaming the world, we could change it. Thus, for example, Pringle and Watson, working within a post-structuralist feminist framework, argue that what various diverse groups of women have in common is the experience of 'discursive marginality': that is, the fact that prevailing discursive frameworks are constructed by men around men and have at their centre the assumption of the male subject as the norm (Pringle and Watson, 1992, p. 68). It would follow, then, that if women were able to rewrite these discourses and relocate themselves at the centre the balance of power between the sexes would alter in women's favour. While there is no doubt that such a discursive transformation would be beneficial to women, my argument would be that this underestimates the multi-dimensionality of gendered power, which has both cultural and material aspects. Why do some discourses stick and others not? After all, the wealth of feminist writing which has been carried out both outside and inside the academic world has certainly contributed to the project of rewriting history from female points of view; yet it must be acknowledged to have had as yet rather little effect on the massive exploitation of women by entrepreneurs around the world, nor does it prevent many male academics from continuing to work with the assumption of male experience as the norm.

Our everyday engagement with the process of defining the world takes place within relationships of power which involve differential control of and access to a range of resources, material, political, cultural and symbolic, including the utilization of means of force and violence. Power relationships put constraints upon our ability to remake the world, even at the level of our own small personal 'life-worlds' (Luckmann, 1978). We may, for example, be firmly committed to the idea of equal sharing within marriage but find ourselves quite unable to work out equitable arrangements about housework with our partners within our own relationships.

Class, 'race'/ethnicity, gender and age are all aspects of these power relationships. While symbolic aspects of power, such as those highlighted in discourse theory, are extremely important, they are only one aspect of the power relationships which are embodied in social inequalities. To return to Pringle's and Watson's post-structuralist arguments, men are able to dominate women not only by marginalizing them in discourse, but also by controlling the distribution of social wealth (economic power), by confining them to lower-rated positions in the division of labour, subjecting them to male authority and keeping them out of some social functions altogether (positional and political power), and by using violent tactics, such as rape and assault to keep them in place (physical power). Now, clearly all these forms of power are tightly interlocked together and discursive frameworks are part of the social processes which enable men to exclude women economically and politically, and legitimate to individual men their use of physical violence. Pringle and Watson, in fact, seem to me to acknowledge this 'under the counter', by slipping in 'inequalities at every level' as an accompaniment to the 'discursive marginality' which might unite women (p. 69). It is not, after all, clear whether 'inequalities' can be elided with 'discourse'.

In other words, I am arguing that materiality and meaning ('things' and 'words' in Michèle Barrett's (1992) phrase) are different but can hardly be separated. Approaches which seek to prioritize one to the exclusion of the other, be it Marxism on the one hand or post-structuralism on the other, are distorting social reality. The need to consider both is a key assumption of this book, as is the fact that both materiality and meaning are aspects of constraining power relations. The remainder of this book can be seen as an exploration both of processes of 'renaming' and of power constraints.

1

Inequality, Fragmentation and Identity

Virtually all contemporary societies are marked by notable social inequalities, as most past societies have been. Only in small, localized tribal societies do we find that there are few differences in wealth and power and that most members of society share a common lifestyle. In urban industrial societies, with a complex division of labour, sharp gulfs emerge between the richer and poorer members. Those at the top of the social hierarchy are able to procure for themselves privileges and power and a disproportionate share of the social wealth. Such social hierarchies may be based on military conquest, ownership of property, occupation, family background, ethnic origin, religious affiliation, educational qualifications, gender and age. Characteristically, in modern societies they rest on a complex mixture of many of these factors.

Those inequalities which are related to the production, distribution and exchange of wealth we have come to know by the complex and rather controversial shorthand term of *class*. Karl Marx linked the emergence of class to the notion of a social surplus: that is, the pool of wealth left over once the subsistence needs of society's members have been met. As societies grow richer, it follows that the potential for social inequalities increases. In contemporary Britain John Scott has estimated that the 200 top families have fortunes of £50 million pounds each (Scott, 1991). The Duke of Westminster, considered to be one of Britain's richest men, is said to own property worth £750 million. At the other end of the scale, many claim that the 1980s and 1990s witnessed the emergence of an 'underclass' made up of the very poor whose main source of subsistence was social security benefits. Surveys suggested that around one fifth of families in Britain lived below the poverty line. In 1993, such families could expect to earn around £1000 a year on average; with benefits their final disposable income would be just less than

£5500 (Social Trends, 1995). The income share of the bottom fifth of households has fallen steadily since 1982 and the gap between rich and poor is the greatest since the Second World War (Rowntree Report, 1995).

Even in the USA, popularly seen as a society of affluence and classlessness, poverty was demonstrated to be widespread during the 1980s; the Carnegie Corporation reported in 1994 that nearly a quarter of America's children aged under three were living in poverty (*Guardian*, 13 April 1994). In 1989 1 per cent of the American population owned 37 per cent and 10 per cent owned 86 per cent of the wealth (West, 1994). In Britain the gap between the richest and the poorest grew steadily through the 1980s; between 1980 and 1993 the average annual income of the top 1 per cent of British earners rose from £35,407 to £129,365, an increase of 265 per cent, while that of the bottom 50 per cent rose from £3780 to £7794, an increase of 106 per cent. Despite this, there was a perception, aired frequently in the media, that Britain was on the way to becoming a classless society.

The idea of 'classlessness' is not a new one. Indeed, it seems that as soon as forms of inequality such as class are 'discovered' by social investigators people start to proclaim their disappearance! The uncovering by feminists in the 1970s and 1980s of all sorts of inequalities between the sexes in modern society has rapidly been followed by proclamations that we now live in a 'post-feminist' society in which gender inequality is a thing of the past. The imminent death of class has often been pronounced. In the Victorian era this was linked to faith in the now unfashionable idea of 'progress'. The Victorians believed that the advances of science, technology and knowledge, linked to economic growth, were leading to a steady improvement in the social condition which would usher in a 'new age' of equality and prosperity. Similarly in the twentieth century the period of economic expansion and affluence after the Second World War led some sociologists to develop the notion of 'embourgeoisement': that is, the idea that the working classes were being absorbed into the middle classes and adopting middle-class lifestyles. While there might be a small powerful economic elite at the top and a small disadvantaged group at the bottom, the majority of the British populace, it was argued, could be seen as a homogenized mass living in relative affluence.

Although the embourgeoisement theory fell into disrepute during the 1970s, with the advent of mass unemployment, the idea of classlessness resurfaced in the 1980s. This time the focus was less on equalization of living standards, but more on the idea that economic opportunities were open to all, regardless of birth, background or educational qualifications. John Major's election to Prime Minister was seen to symbolize this trend, as Major came from an unorthodox family background (his father was said once to have been a circus artiste), had attended a state school and had not been to university. Major himself frequently proclaimed his own attachment to the notion of a classless society and his government's attempts to promote it. What was at issue here was not really a society without classes but a meritocracy, a society in which access to social rewards is determined by the talents and achievements of individuals, not their background.

The idea of classlessness is rejected by most sociologists who point to the evidence, such as that presented above, of persistent inequalities of wealth. These inequalities in Western societies can be seen as part of a system of social stratification: that is, the division of society into unequal groups or strata which share a common situation. While in the 1960s and 1970s this system of stratification was analysed mainly in terms of class, from the 1980s there has been a growing recognition of the importance of other forms of inequality, such as gender and ethnicity. Mann, discussing the crisis of stratification theory, indicated a need to explore the interrelations of different social actors, what he called 'stratification nuclei', which for him included classes, genders and nations. He concluded that 'a more complex form of stratification is now emerging' (1986, p. 56).

Aspects of inequality: class, gender, 'race' and ethnicity, and age

As was mentioned earlier, social hierarchies can be formed on a number of bases. Sociologists are now interested in exploring many of these aspects of inequality, such as gender, age, 'race' or ethnicity, nationality, religious affiliation, sexual orientation (heterosexual, gay or lesbian, bisexual, trans-sexual) and dis/ability, all of which are seen to affect the lifestyle and life chances of individuals and the differential distribution of social rewards and privileges. This book deals with four of these aspects of inequality: class, gender, 'race'/ethnicity and age.

These have been chosen partly because they have received the most sustained exploration within sociology: class has long been central to the agenda of sociological research and the other three have now become so. But also all are currently implicated in important processes of social change, both national and international. As subsequent chapters will show, the spread of a globally based capitalist economy has built upon existing hierarchies of class, gender, 'race' and age, promoting new patterns of social and economic inequality. No complete account of contemporary social development can overlook these factors.

This is not to deny that other less-studied aspects of inequality, such as disability or sexual orientation, are important: they may become more so. The post-structuralist critiques detailed in this book suggest that we could evolve quite new ways of categorizing inequalities, which would allow unacknowledged aspects of differentiation to emerge as objects of study. However, class, gender, ethnicity and age are currently the categories which occupy both public and academic attention, although they may not do so in the future. At the present time they are all viewed as being at the heart of processes of social change.

Class

As has already been suggested, class is the form of social inequality that has received the most attention in sociology. The interest in class goes right back to the roots of sociology and the nineteenth-century thinkers who produced what we now refer to as classical sociological theory. Class plays a major role in the theories of Marx and Weber. Even Durkheim, who is associated with a more harmonistic vision of industrial societies, believed that a meritocratic society could not be achieved unless inherited privileges were abolished. The strongest assertion of the importance of class came from Marx, who argued that inequalities of wealth and power were increasing as the capitalist system developed: tendencies which he saw as inherent in capitalism would serve to widen the gap between the two major classes, the property-owning bourgeoisie and the working class or 'proletariat':

> The epoch of the bourgeoisie, possesses . . . this distinctive feature: it has simplified the class antagonisms. Society as a whole is more and more splitting into two great hostile camps, into two great classes directly facing each other – bourgeoisie and proletariat. (Marx and Engels, 1934, p. 10)

In post-war British sociology class theorists themselves divided into two 'hostile camps', broadly known as neo-Marxists and neo-Weberians (see chapter 3). During the 1950s and 1960s class and poverty were perhaps the major topics of sociological research. Gordon Marshall's book *In Praise of Sociology* includes five texts dealing with class and poverty among his chosen 'top ten' influential British sociological studies (1990). However, the study of class seems to have fallen from favour. A recent account of inequalities among young people refers to 'the silence gathering round class' (Bates and Riseborough, 1993, p. 1). The authors argue that 'class analysis, for over a century central to progressive social thought and political organization, has come to seem anachronistic' (p. 2). In the 1980s interest switched to other aspects of inequality.

Gender

Perhaps the most trenchant challenge to class theory came from feminists concerned with the exploration of gender differences and inequalities. The study of gender within sociology has a much shorter history than that of class. The 'classical' theorists acknowledged inequalities of gender but did not explore them to any great extent, partly because they shared the view, widespread in the nineteenth century, that gender differences were 'natural', arising ultimately from biology. Sydie (1987) has argued that Marx, Durkheim and Weber could not escape from the prevailing gender ideologies of their time. For example, in his classic study of suicide, first published in 1897, Durkheim argued that widows were less likely to commit suicide than widowers because women were less involved in social life:

> Society is less necessary to her, because she is less impregnated with sociability. She has few needs in this direction and satisfies them easily. With a few devotional practices and some animals to care for, the old unmarried woman's life is full. (1952, p. 215)

Following a nineteenth-century trend, Durkheim considered men to be 'almost entirely the product of society', while women 'remained to a far greater extent the product of nature' (p. 385).

Within post-war sociology, gender issues only made their appearance in areas of study such as the family, which reflected prevailing norms about 'women's sphere'. In other areas, such as work, deviance or youth cultures, the existence and experiences of women were largely overlooked. This marginalizing of women's experience was epitomized in class theory. Major research projects on class, such as those carried out at Nuffield College by Goldthorpe, Halsey and others, were based upon men only. It was argued that women took their class from husbands or fathers, that to include women would make it difficult to compare findings with earlier studies which had also omitted women, or that since women's social roles were primarily domestic, occupational class was not relevant to women. Feminists claim that, when women appeared not to fit into the models and theories of class (or work, or deviance, or youth subculture), rather than discarding those models and theories as incorrect or inadequate, sociologists simply stated that women were 'abnormal' and continued to leave them out.

The view of gender as a major source of social division developed in the late 1970s with the spread of 'second-wave' feminism as a political movement (see Banks, 1981). This stimulated an immense interest in the uncovering of women's lost and hidden experience. Different strands of political feminism, often known as liberal, socialist and radical feminism, inspired different theoretical approaches to the explanation of gender differences, which are explored in chapter 4.

In Britain in the early 1980s Marxism was still a particularly strong influence and many feminists tried to build an analysis of gender into existing theories of capitalism. Others, however, preferred to see gender relations as an autonomous system and developed the key concept of 'patriarchy' to explore the origins and operation of such a system (see chapter 4). Gradually, feminism has moved away from its links with Marxism and class theory. Attention has shifted to the relationship of gender with other aspects of social inequality, especially ethnicity and sexual orientation.

Initial attempts to combine class and gender analysis proved difficult because gender is a much more diffuse source of inequality and differentiation than class; while class divisions are conceptualized as deriving from economic aspects of social relations, gender differentiation is not confined to a single sphere. Gender plays a part in every aspect of social and cultural life (from sexual relations to politics, from leisure to art and literature). Ulrich Beck has described this as the 'omni-dimensionality of inequality between men and women' (1992, p. 103). Indeed gender is a fundamental way in which we organize every facet of our experience; it is a key category by which we make sense of the natural and social world, which is not true of class. Feminists have never been able to agree where exactly the basis of gender divisions can be found and this has necessitated a much more flexible approach to studying gender than the relative rigidities of class theory.

'Race' and ethnicity

The same is to some extent true of the third dimension of inequality studied in this book, 'race' and ethnicity, for racial and ethnic inequalities are also spread across the spectrum of social life. The study of 'race' in sociology has a longer history than that of gender. Race relations became an important area of academic research in America in the 1940s (Stanfield, 1993). It was firmly established in Britain by the early 1960s. Its popularity as a topic for research, however, was linked to the emergent view that relations between different racial groups in Britain were becoming a widespread 'social problem' as a result of post-war immigration from the commonwealth countries. Similarly in America the sociological study of 'race' was linked to the perception of black Americans as a social problem. The early research on race, therefore, dealt with prejudice, discrimination and conflict and was focused on groups who were defined in terms of skin colour: the descendants of the slave populations in America and in Britain immigrants from the Caribbean colonies (also descended from slaves) and from India, Pakistan and East Africa.

Research has documented the persistent discrimination faced by these groups in all areas of social life, especially in employment, education and housing (for example, Smith, 1977; Brown, 1984). In America Wilson has described the black inhabitants of the urban ghettoes as 'the truly disadvantaged' (W. Wilson, 1987), and evidence suggests that British of Afro-Caribbean and Asian origin have suffered particularly in the recessions of the past decades. For example, a TUC report revealed that in 1993 unemployment among ethnic minority workers was 22 per cent as compared to 10 per cent among white workers: black and Asian workers were seven times more likely to lose their jobs than whites (TUC, 1994).

Sociologists have challenged the notion that the concepts of 'race' and racial origin have any real scientific basis. Nineteenth-century scientists had developed the idea of distinct racial groups, with a differing genetic inheritance which produced differing patterns of behaviour, personality traits, levels of intelligence and so forth. Such ideas, which we would now categorize as racist, were used to justify white supremacy and the domination of indigenous populations by Western colonial nations. However, modern science suggests that there is little validity in these attempts to root 'race' in biological difference, especially in view of the centuries of migration and miscegenation which have passed since Europeans first made contact with the populations of Africa, Asia, Australasia and the Americas. Sociologists argue that the idea of 'race' is a social construct, used to justify discrimination and exclusionary practices. For that reason, some have suggested that the use of the term should be rejected altogether (Miles, 1982). However, others have argued that, since people act *as if* 'race' was a reality, 'race' does have real effects on people's lives and it should be retained as a category of sociological analysis (Cashmore and Troyna, 1983). Current practice is to apostrophize the term to show that it is a construct of dubious validity, a practice which I have followed in this book.

The idea of 'race' is characteristically linked to the broader category of ethnicity. Ethnicity refers to belonging to a particular collectivity or community, sharing a culture, possibly with a distinct language. The bi-polar approach which saw Britain as divided into black and white groupings has given way to the appreciation that there is a multiplicity of ethnic groups in Britain, each with its distinctive set of cultural practices and many with their own languages.

The interest in the idea of ethnicity has also been encouraged by the events in Europe and Asia which followed the collapse of Russian communism and the break up of the Soviet Union and its empire. The emergence of long-suppressed ethnic loyalties and conflicts and the formation of new nations have drawn our attention to the force of national and ethnic identities as a base of social conflict and have contributed greatly to the notion that social fragmentation is on the increase. The overlapping categories of 'race', ethnicity and nationality will be fully discussed in chapter 5; it is evident that the growing importance of relations between all these groups greatly complicates patterns of stratification and challenges the traditional predominance of class analysis.

Age

It is only recently that age has been considered as an aspect of inequality and it has received scant attention within the sociology of stratification (Fennell et al., 1988). This is partly due to the fact that age has been seen in the past as a natural phenomenon, which affects every individual; all of us must go through each phase of the life cycle and suffer its characteristic effects (Rapoport and Rapoport, 1975). However, there is now much more awareness of how the fates of particular age-groups are socially determined and altered by social and historical contexts. Moreover, we appreciate that all within a particular age-group will *not* in fact share a common position, because the experience of inequalities of age is affected by the individual's class, gender and ethnic position.

The social standing of elderly people, for example, has changed considerably over the past two centuries. The changes brought to work and family relationships by industrial production meant that older people could no longer contribute until they became unfit to do so to the household enterprise (farm, craft or business). It became harder for those whose strength was on the wane to hold a job as a wage labourer, while at the same time traditional support networks within the family and community were loosening. Increasing numbers of old people ended up in workhouses and mental asylums. In Britain during the Edwardian period something like one tenth of elderly women ended up in the workhouse (Fennell et al., 1988). But as the twentieth century developed, older people were rescued from this fate by the old-age pension scheme and the further provisions of the Welfare State and the National Health Service.

However, it can be argued that in the last decades the position of the elderly has again deteriorated, owing to the erosion of the NHS and the Social Security system. The state, alarmed by the phenomenon of the ageing population and the growing burden of the cost of caring for the infirm elderly, has tried to thrust the burden of care back on to the community and the family. The result has been growing poverty and insecurity for many old people, especially women. In 1987, 35 per cent of older women were living on or below the poverty line (Walker, 1992).

Recent research has drawn our attention to ageism as a prevalent feature of our society (Hearn and Parkin, 1993; Bodily, 1994). In a society of rapid social and technological change, older people are increasingly seen as a burden and an irrelevance. However, they are not the only victims of ageism, as will be argued in chapter 6. All of us are affected by ageist attitudes which lay down rules of behaviour seen as appropriate for people of different ages and encourage different expectations of the capacities of each group.

This book will concentrate, however, on two particular groups who bear the brunt of age-related inequality: older people, whose declining situation has just been briefly outlined, and young people, who have been particularly vulnerable to the effects of recession and long-term unemployment in recent decades. It has been suggested by many that youth unemployment is leading to widespread disaffection among young adults in many Western societies. Drug-taking, criminal behaviour, involvement in extreme right-wing political movements, experimentation with alternative lifestyles such as that of the 'New Age' travellers can all be seen as manifestations of this latest variant of the 'generation gap'.

Interacting dynamics

The discussion so far has suggested that each dimension of inequality should be studied in its own right. The implication is that each one can be analysed as a distinct set of relationships with a logic of its own. However, it is obvious enough that in real life this is not exactly the case. It has become almost a commonplace to say that classes are gendered and that gender relations are class-specific. Similarly the other dimensions of 'race'/ethnicity and age impinge on individual class and gender experience and in any particular concrete example it is hard to separate out the different elements.

Take, for an example, the position of a twenty-year-old Afro-Caribbean woman, whose parents were manual workers, bringing up two children on her own in inner-city Birmingham, and having to choose between low-paid work as a hospital domestic and dependency on benefits. How do we start to explain her fate? Is it because of gender that she is faced with responsibilities for childcare with no help from a man and that she faces a limited range of labour market options? Or is it racism which means the only job she can find is the stereotypical 'servant' role which has historically been assigned to black women? Or is it class which has led her to leave school early with limited qualifications? Of course, it is all of these things. And age plays a part too, as many employers have a prejudice against young workers, and prefer to employ older married women whom they see as steadier, having 'settled down'.

In the past, a great deal of effort has been expended on arguing whether 'race', class or gender should be seen as primary in cases such as this. Such effort is fruitless because it is impossible to separate these factors from one another and assign each a weight. Nonetheless, though these dimensions cannot be separated in their effects within concrete social relationships, it is possible to separate them analytically. Indeed this is a necessary strategy if we are to develop a coherent sociological account of stratification and inequality. It is argued here that each dimension can be seen as based within a different aspect of social relationships, as having a different 'existential location' (Anthias and Yuval-Davis, 1992, p. 17). These locations are sketched out here and elaborated in chapters 3–6.

Class is a social category which refers to lived relationships surrounding social arrangements of production, exchange, distribution and consumption. While these may narrowly be conceived as *economic* relationships, to do with money, wealth and property, in this book it is suggested that class should be seen as referring to a much broader web of *social* relationships, including, for example, lifestyle, educational experiences and patterns of residence. Class, therefore, affects many aspects of our material lives.

Gender is a social category which refers to lived relationships between women and men; gender relations are those by means of which sexual divisions and definitions of masculinity and femininity are constructed, organized and maintained. It can be argued that relationships to do with the organization of sexuality and reproductive processes (pregnancy, childbirth and maternity) are particularly central here, and these have been the focus of radical forms of feminism. However, every aspect of social life is gendered; sexual divisions are constructed, organized and maintained not only within the family and private life but also in work and employment, in education, in politics, in leisure activities and cultural production. In every aspect of experience whether we are male or female has implications.

'Race' and ethnicity are social categories used to explain a highly complex set of territorial relationships; these involve conquests of some territorial groups by others, the historical development of nation states, and associated migrations of people around the globe. Particularly influential on racial and ethnic relations has been the colonial process whereby the nations of Western Europe carved up other parts of the globe between them. The institution of slavery has also played an important part in the construction of racial and ethnic categories, especially those between 'black' peoples of African descent and the 'white' populations of European descent. Through colonialism and slavery particular hierarchies of 'races' were consolidated, backed by ideologies of the innate superiority of whites. However, the development of racial and ethnic hierarchies did not end with colonialism and slavery. Complex patterns of racial and ethnic stratification have continued to evolve, linked to changing configurations of international relations and processes of migration. It is argued by some that we are now in a 'post-colonial' phase in which new hybrid patterns of ethnic identity are becoming characteristic (Bhabha, 1990a), an idea that will be explored in chapter 5.

Age as a dimension of inequality relates to social categories derived from the organization of the life course and lived relationships between people socially located as being in differing age-groups. People at different stages in the life course are subjected to different social rules and expectations, which we call ageism. Most Western societies display marked segregation between the various socially defined age-groups along with disparities of economic resources and power between the groupings, which are shored up by stereotypes of differential age capacities. Although ageist assumptions affect all of us, particular age-groups suffer more from social marginalization and economic exclusion.

Class, gender, 'race', ethnicity and age therefore refer to different aspects of lived social relationships, although they interweave together to produce an integrated structure of inequality. Age, gender and 'race' have all been popularly conceived as having some kind of biological referent, although sociologists would deny that they derive directly from biological differences. Here class appears as the odd one out. The lack of any visible physical manifestation in which people can *see* class relationships as being grounded may be one reason why class identity is rather contentious. More than the other three dimensions of inequality, class belongs purely to the social realm.

These sets of social categories and lived relationships together form what I have called the dynamics of inequality. I have used this term rather than the more conventional sociological term of structure to convey the fact that these categories and relationships are constantly changing. Yet, as was argued in the Introduction, they also demonstrate considerable stability and constancy over time so that they constitute an enduring framework of social inequalities in our society. So, for example, the *extent* and *precise nature* of ageist practices will vary over time, but the *general fact* of age discrimination remains a constant. Part of the reason for the fluidity of social relations is that these four dynamics, along with others such as those of religion and dis/ability which are not discussed in this book, are in constant interplay with each other. The realization of how complex are the intertwinings of the dimensions of inequality is in part responsible for the recent preoccupation with the idea of 'fragmentation'.

Polarization and fragmentation

It is commonly stated that in the later decades of the twentieth century society is becoming more fragmented. This is often linked to the argument that Western societies are now entering a distinct 'post-industrial' or 'postmodern' phase of development in which old-established social relationships are breaking down and being transformed into a more complex web of interlocking social groups:

> Postmodernity is marked by a view of the human world as irreducibly and irrevocably pluralistic, split into a multitude of sovereign units and sites of authority, with no horizontal or vertical order. (Bauman, 1992, p. 35)

Subsequent reworkings of the older theoretical framework of capitalism, such as Lash's and Urry's account of 'disorganized capitalism', also feature themes of fragmentation and social disintegration: 'All that is solid about organized capitalism, class, industry, cities, collectivity, nation-state, even the word, melts into air' (1987, p. 313).

The idea of social fragmentation is not new. It derives in part from the writings of Max Weber on stratification, and has long been used as a riposte to Marx's theory of class polarization. As stated earlier, Marx argued that society would become ever more divided into two polar camps as capitalism developed. The logic of competition would force smaller companies and self-employed people out of business, so they must either expand and join the ranks of major capitalists or be forced down into the proletariat; a similar fate would befall members of other groupings, such as the aristocracy or the peasantry, left over from earlier modes of production. Moreover Marx believed that tendencies inherent to capitalism would increase the economic gap between the bourgeoisie and the wage-earning class, as deepening crises of over-production and under-consumption left working people ever more vulnerable to poverty and unemployment.

By contrast Weber's theory of class pointed to cleavages within each class, with the propertyless wage-earners, for example, being split into different segments on the basis of different assets which they could offer in the labour market. Weber also introduced the notion of another form of fragmentation, when he argued that class groupings were cross-cut by two other types of social grouping deriving from the unequal distribution of power in society: status groups and political parties. Ralf Dahrendorf used these ideas to mount a powerful critique of Marx in his classic book *Class and Class Conflict in Industrial Society* (1959) in which he argued that the capitalist class, the working class and the middle class had all fragmented or 'decomposed', a process leading to a much more complex pattern of class relationships and antagonisms than the simple polarization envisaged by Marx. The working class was split on the base of skill divisions; the capitalist class itself had broken up into an owning group (shareholders and investors) and a managing group; while Dahrendorf saw the middle class as a heterogeneous grouping, with high-paid professionals and technicians being linked in interests to management, while low-paid clerical workers, foremen and other service workers had much in common with the manual working class.

In *The Fragmentary Class Structure* (1977), Roberts and colleagues advanced the argument by showing how people's self-perceptions of class contributed to the fragmentation effect; their research showed that some people working in manual jobs described themselves as 'middle class', while others in apparently middle-class white-collar positions nonetheless identified with the working class. Objective class situations, defined on the basis of occupational groupings, and subjective class identifications jointly produced a plurality of class positionings.

Neo-Marxists responded to these criticisms by incorporating the idea of fragmentation into their own class theories. They used the notion of a class 'fraction' to describe a group within a class whose economic situation differed in some significant way from the rest. For example, the skilled, unskilled and semi-skilled groupings in the working class which Dahrendorf had discerned could be described as class fractions although they still shared together the common characteristics of wage labour: they were dependent on selling their labour to make a living, they were powerless, exploited and alienated in Marxian terms.

The current wave of stratification theories have taken the idea of fragmentation a stage further. Classes are seen as subject to new processes of decomposition; and class is seen to mesh with all the other aspects of inequality mentioned in this chapter to produce a society made up of a multiplicity of overlapping groupings. Moreover, it is suggested that individuals move about more easily between these different groups. Society is not only more fragmented but more fluid. Indeed, some envisage a further development which involves the breaking up of all social groupings and a loss of all sense of social belonging. This idea is held by some postmodernists and is taken to an extreme by Beck, who speaks of Western societies undergoing 'a surge of individuation': a process of transformation is under way 'in the course of which people will be set free from the social forms of industrial society – class, stratification, family, gender status' (1992, p. 87).

Identities and fragmentation

Such ideas about the disintegration of classes and the increasing fluidity of social relationships have triggered increased interest in the notion of identity. Social fragmentation is linked to fragmentation of identity:

> It is no longer so easy to talk of the individual or the self as an autonomous and coherent unity but instead we have come to understand that we are made up from and live our lives as a mass of contradictory fragments. (Moore, 1988, p. 170)

As a result of social change, people are said to be losing their sense of social belonging, of being rooted in traditional collectivities, such as class, community or the kinship network. In Robert Bocock's phrase 'a state of flux has replaced earlier forms of stable group membership' (1993, p. 31). Now people draw their sense of identity from a much broader range of sources, including gender, age, marital status, sexual preference, consumption patterns; as Bocock puts it, in the late twentieth century there is a greater 'proliferation of identities – of the number of yous on offer' (1992, p. 160). Postmodernists argue that identity has become relatively free-floating, detached from the bases of social structure which in the past were seen to constrain it; we are now more able to pick and choose which of the various 'yous on offer' we want to be 'me':

> Each of us lives with a variety of potentially contradictory identities which battle within us for allegiance: as men or women, black or white, straight or gay, able-bodied or disabled, 'British' or 'European'. The list is potentially infinite. (Weeks, 1990, p. 88)

If we pursue our example of the young Afro-Caribbean woman, we can illustrate what the postmodernists are trying to convey. Does she identify herself primarily as a woman? Or perhaps as a single parent, in view of the state's preoccupation with the 'problem' of single parenthood? Does she consider herself working class because of her parents' manual occupations, or because she herself has experienced low-paid unskilled work options? If she grew up on a council estate she may take that as a sign of being part of the working class. But if she now lives in a more mixed area of inner-city housing, surrounded by students, perhaps she has developed loyalties to a more complex sort of community? Her ethnic origin will be very important to her. But does she think of herself as Afro-Caribbean? As Jamaican? Would she categorize herself as 'black'? As British? Or will she perhaps trace her origins further back to her African ancestry? Already we see that she has a wealth of sources of identification open to her and there are plenty of other possibilities we have not begun to explore, such as religion, sexuality, membership of clubs, cultural interests. Which of all these possible 'selves' is the primary one? Or are they all? Which of them will constitute her identity?

This interest in identity which is shown by postmodern sociologists is a relatively new one, which seems to have replaced an earlier theoretical interest in 'consciousness'. For Marxists, consciousness was a vital link between structure and action; but the concept was always seen as problematic (see chapter 3). Postmodernists who reject the Marxian framework have taken up the notion of identity to serve in a similar fashion to explore the ways in which people move to forms of political action. In the past, though, identity has been the preserve of social psychologists and its analysis has been relatively underdeveloped in sociology (Hall, 1992b). It is worth trying to define clearly what is meant by the term. Jeffrey Weeks defines identity in the following way:

> Identity is about belonging, about what you have in common with some people and what differentiates you from others. At its most basic it gives you a sense of personal location, the stable core to your individuality. But it is also about your social relationships, your complex involvement with others. (1990, p. 88)

Developing Weeks's ideas, we might first of all make a distinction between 'personal identity', which is primarily studied by psychologists, and 'social identity', which concerns sociologists. Personal identity refers to the construction of the self: our sense of ourselves as unique individuals, how we perceive ourselves and how we think others see us. Personal identity evolves from the whole package of experiences that each individual has gone through, and is highly complex and individualized. Social identity is also a complex issue, but is somewhat more limited. It refers to the way that we as individuals locate ourselves within the society in which we live and the way in which we perceive others as locating us. Social identities derive from the various sets of lived relationships in which individuals are engaged, such as the dynamics of inequality outlined in this chapter. An alternative and related term, used widely by postmodernists, is 'cultural identity', which has seemed of particular relevance to ethnic minorities affected by the 'diaspora': the spreading of people across the globe from their original homelands such as Africa. Cultural identity refers to the sense of belonging to a particular culture, past or present. Talking of the complex processes which go to construct a Caribbean identity, Stuart Hall emphasizes the way that cultural identities are not fixed but always evolving:

> Cultural identity . . . is a matter of 'becoming' as well as 'being'. It belongs to the future as much as to the past . . . Cultural identities come from somewhere, have histories. But like everything which is historical they undergo constant transformation. Far from being eternally fixed in some essentialized past they are subject to the continuous play of history, culture and power. (1990, p. 225)

As the example of our fictional young woman shows, a multitude of factors influence the development of personal and even social and cultural identity. It is probably beyond the scope of sociologists to predict in any individual case which potential aspects of identity will predominate. This depends largely on 'contingent' factors: specific personal circumstances, individual biographies, particular historical and political events. All that sociologists can do is to suggest what in any given time and place are likely to be the most powerful influences on the formation of social identities. For example, it is suggested that changes in work and the break-up of old urban communities are currently acting to weaken class identities. Or again, for Afro-Caribbeans in Britain 'race' is arguably a more potent source of identification than class because it is so highly visible (Gilroy, 1987). But despite these general statements, it is perfectly possible for one Afro-Caribbean to have a strong ethnic identification while another person may view herself in class terms. A third may reject both class and racial identification!

I suggest that it is helpful to identify three *levels* of social identity: passive, active and politicized. 'Passive identities' are potential identities in the sense that they derive from the sets of lived relationships (class, gender, ethnicity and so forth) in which the individuals are engaged, but they are not acted on. Individuals are not particularly conscious of passive identities and do not normally define themselves by them unless events occur which bring those particular relationships to the fore. Class in the late twentieth century is a passive identity for many people. The majority of the British population do not appear to think of themselves in class terms, although they recognize the existence of class inequalities (Scase, 1992; Bradley, 1994).

'Active identities' are those which individuals are conscious of and which provide a base for their actions. They are positive elements in an individual's self identification although we do not necessarily think of ourselves continually in terms of any single identity. For example, as Riley argues, there are times in most women's lives when they clearly perceive themselves as 'a woman'; when being whistled at or pestered in the street, for example, or when menstruation starts unexpectedly (Riley, 1988). In such circumstances the individual is likely to respond as 'a woman' to the circumstances, in one way or another. At other times that identification will lapse and she will think of herself simply as a person, not in gender terms. As this example suggests, active identification often occurs as a defence against the actions of others or when an individual is conscious of being defined in a negative way. Active identities are promoted by the experience of discrimination. Thus 'race' and ethnicity are currently likely to be sources of active identities. Ethnic identities are asserted where cultures and territorial rights are seen to be under attack, as in the former Yugoslavia. Racial identities are often forced on people because of prejudice relating to skin colour or cultural practices, as in the case of British Afro-Caribbeans or Muslims.

Where identities provide a more constant base for action and where individuals constantly think of themselves in terms of an identity, we can describe it as a 'politicized identity'. Politicized identities are formed through political action and provide the base for collective organization of either a defensive or an affirmative nature. As our current use of the term 'identity politics' suggests, politicized identities are common in late twentieth-century society. A proliferation of political bodies has sprung up to fight for the rights of particular groups. For example, the militant gay and lesbian movement in Britain and America has promoted positive and politicized homosexual identities linked to the process of 'coming out'. The feminist movement has also encouraged many women to adopt a politicized female identity; and, ironically, politicized male identities appear to be evolving as a result of the backlash against feminism in America, where a movement for 'Men's Rights' is growing to protect threatened male interests.

Such examples illustrate the complexity of social identification and give support to the theories of fragmentation. These ideas will be explored in subsequent chapters. But since this book has presented itself as a 'both/and' story rather than an 'either/or' one, fragmentation will be explored alongside a contention that processes of polarization can also be discerned in society. This chapter started with some examples of the growing gulf between the rich and poor in Britain and America, which suggests that Marx's insights are not yet exhausted.

Summary and conclusions

This chapter has offered a brief overview of four dimensions of inequality in contemporary societies: class, gender, 'race'/ethnicity and age. It was argued that each should be seen as both a social construct (a way to categorize social relationships) and as a set of lived relationships. Together, these can be seen as 'dynamics of inequality'. Each of these dynamics of inequality can be related to a different aspect of social reality, a different 'existential location'. Recently, stratification theory has begun to explore the ways in which the dynamics interact.

One view is that in recent decades there has been a fragmentation of social relationships, associated with the decline of traditional class loyalties. A plurality of social groupings has emerged. Associated with this is a claim that social identities, too, have become more fragmented.

So far, the discussion has looked at the dynamics of inequality in isolation from the society in which they are embedded. Sociology, however, promotes an understanding of the complex ways in which the parts of a society are related to the whole. Most sociologists would claim that we cannot gain a full understanding of any aspect of social life without some kind of account of its context and the kind of society in which it is placed. Thus the pattern of inequality varies as societies change. In turn, changing dynamics of inequality will affect the way society as a whole develops. The two things cannot be separated but are locked in what sociologists call a dialectical relationship, in which they mutually act upon one another to produce change. It is time, then, to think about how we can categorize the type of society in which we live. If we want a full comprehension of how stratification is changing, we must also consider how societies are changing.

2

Capitalism, Modernity and Change

> Constant revolutionizing of production, uninterrupted disturbance of all social conditions, everlasting uncertainty and agitation distinguish the bourgeois epoch from all earlier ones. All fixed, fast-frozen relations, with their train of ancient and venerable prejudices and opinions, are swept away, all new-formed ones become antiquated before they can ossify. All that is solid melts into air, all that is holy is profaned. (Marx and Engels, 1934, pp. 12–13)

In these famous words Marx and Engels celebrated one of the most important features about the society that confronted them. As Krishan Kumar (1978) has argued, something that struck virtually all nineteenth-century observers of industrialization was the pace and power of change. For example, the railway train symbolized to the Victorians the force and compulsion of technological and industrial development (in much the same way as we might take the jet plane to be an image of our post-war world). Although what we now call the 'Industrial Revolution' was an extremely long-drawn-out process, covering nearly one hundred years, nobody around at the time could doubt that momentous changes were taking place.

It is significant that writers discussing the idea that we are now entering a new 'post-industrial' or 'postmodern' era of social development have so often been drawn to quote Marx and Engels: 'all that is solid melts into air' (Lash and Urry, 1987, p. 331; Turner, 1990, p. 11; Hall, 1992b. p. 277; Bauman, 1992, p. 97; Tester, 1993, p. 40; Lyon, 1994, p. 2). Social theorists have continually grappled with the sense of monumental changes in society. Describing the changes in technology that started to occur at the end of the nineteenth century, with the development of mass production processes and new consumer goods, Georges Friedmann (1955) spoke of a 'second industrial revolution'.

Ever since industrialization people living in industrial societies have been apt to feel that they are living through major social upheavals and to fear that those upheavals may swallow them up.

Industrial capitalist society is notably dynamic. Relationships, institutions, technologies, production processes constantly alter, often quite dramatically. In pre-industrial societies the pace of change is slower and changes tend to be gradual and incremental. In pre-industrial Europe people saw little difference between their lifestyle and that of their parents and grandparents, while we not only live in a world very different from that of our parents but expect to see major changes within our own lifetime.

Auguste Comte, considered to be a founder of the discipline of sociology, argued that the experience of the more violent changes at the end of the eighteenth century, the French Revolution and the onset of industrialization, allowed people to begin to think in sociological terms (K. Thompson, 1976). Before the eighteenth century, people tended to think of society as a natural and persisting order ordained by God. Since then the writings of the thinkers of the Enlightenment had fostered broader acceptance of the idea that societies could be changed, and by human agency. The French Revolution brought this message firmly home. If societies could change, then it followed that different types of societies could be distinguished and also that the way one type of society changed into another could be studied and analysed. Thus all the major contributors to what is now called classical sociological thinking, Comte, Marx, Weber and Durkheim, were concerned with the construction of social typologies (systems of classifying societies).

This chapter looks at the way sociologists have subsequently categorized industrial societies and their key attributes. As I argued at the end of the last chapter, it is a key feature of a sociological approach that changes in social institutions cannot be viewed in isolation from broader social changes. There are a number of arguments that suggest we are experiencing the evolution of a new sort of society and that link the fragmentation processes described in chapter 1 to this process of transition. Chapter 2 briefly reviews classical accounts of 'industrial' and 'capitalist' society, followed by some versions which suggest that capitalism has entered a new and distinct phase. Finally, approaches which reject the label 'capitalism' and suggest that more radical types of changes have occurred are discussed. It must be stressed that these are complex theories which have many variants. No comprehensive survey could be offered in such a short space. Rather, the purpose of this chapter is to consider these various perspectives in terms of their implication for the analysis of social divisions and inequality.

Industrialism and capitalism

One obvious way to categorize societies is in terms of the prevailing form of production and its characteristic techniques. Economic historians, economists and anthropologists, for example, have used the terms 'agrarian' and 'industrial' to describe the types of societies that prevailed before and after the Industrial Revolution. Industrial society has become a familiar term within popular usage, acting as a shorthand to describe societies where the core of the economy is manufacturing and the factory system.

However, within sociology the use of this term has been particularly associated with the theories of functionalists and other mainstream American sociologists in the post-war period. A classic text of this era, *Industrialism and Industrial Man*, presented a model of 'the inner logic of industrialism'. The authors argued that the organization of industrial production required the development of a particular set of social institutions, which were common to all industrial societies; these included the factory system; urban development; a highly specialized division of labour; a meritocratic class structure with high levels of social mobility; a mass education system; a bureaucratic model for organizations; a welfare system; and a political system based on parliamentary democracy (Kerr et al., 1962).

This approach was associated with the framework of modernization which suggested that the advanced industrial societies of the West set the model for the developing societies of the 'Third World'; all such societies must develop the same institutions if they wished to modernize successfully. Kerr et al. argued that a process of 'convergence' was under way by which all societies, however diverse their original social structures, were becoming more alike: America, the furthest down the path of development, was the mirror of the future. Something similar has recently been argued by Francis Fukuyama (1989), who believes that the late twentieth century has seen the triumph of capitalism and liberal democracy over all other possible economic and political forms of society (particularly socialism). Contemporary America represents the culmination of social development, the 'end of history', and is the goal to which all other societies must inevitably be drawn.

Although the idea of capitalism is often linked to industrialism, the term has a set of different associations. While theorists of industrial society such as Kerr have distinguished societies in terms of the *techniques of production*, theorists of capitalist societies see the *social relations of production* as central (Scott, 1979). Both groups see economic relations as the most sociologically important ones, but they conceptualize economic relationships differently.

The idea of capitalism is most famously associated with Marx and his massive study *Das Kapital*. Marx developed a social typology based on the concept of 'mode of production'. Each type of society has a distinct mode of production: that is, the set of relationships by which people come together to produce goods and services. Marx distinguished between two aspects of the mode of production, the technical aspect relating to the use of particular tools, resources and technologies, which he called the 'forces of production', and the social aspect, the way the different functions of production are allocated to different social groups, which Marx called 'the relations of production'. For Marx and his followers the social relationships were more important than the technical ones. Thus class, as a relation of production, became central to Marxist theory.

Marx distinguished a number of different modes of production, but gave most of his attention to a meticulously detailed account of the capitalist mode. The characteristic relations of production under capitalism were those of private ownership of capital and the exploitation by a class of property-owning capitalists of the mass of propertyless wage-earners, who must sell their labour in the market to survive.

Marx's idea of 'exploitation' referred to the way the social surplus was extracted by the most powerful class from the subordinate class. The form in which surplus was procured under capitalism was through the mechanism of the wage. Marx believed that in a given period of time workers produced goods or services which were greater in value than the wage they received. This 'surplus value' was taken by the capitalist in the form of profit, which could subsequently be reinvested to increase the capitalist's wealth.

Part of Marx's hope for a socialist revolution lay in his belief that when the proletariat comprehended the process of exploitation they would combine to fight for a fairer system based on common ownership. But this development was impeded by another distinctive feature of capitalism as Marx described it: alienation. Alienation refers to the divorce of workers from the goods they make and the processes by which they are made. Because workers are powerless they have no control over what is made, how it is made or what becomes of it; they have no identification with their work. As Marx believed that production was central to human existence, he stated that alienation extended to people's relations to one another and to their own social selves: they are alienated from their 'species-being'.

Marx was by no means the only person to develop theories of capitalism. Weber also used the term in his famous study *The Protestant Ethic and the Spirit of Capitalism* (1938). Although Weber does not mention Marx by name, this text is taken to be a criticism of what Weber saw as the 'one-sided materialism' of Marx's analysis of capitalist development. Weber wished to improve on this by including within it some account of the ideas and motivations which are influential in promoting processes of social change. For Weber, certain types of Protestantism had a special affinity with capitalist values and provided the impetus for individuals to invest their money and efforts in capitalist enterprise, rather than indulging in conspicuous consumption like the rich in the previous feudal epoch.

In another work, the *General Economic History* (1928), Weber set out another account of the development of capitalism which focused more on the economic aspects considered by Marx. While his account had much in common with that of Marx in the stress placed on property and ownership and the centrality of the market, he also emphasised the importance of bureaucracy, as the most appropriate and efficient way in which to pursue capitalist enterprise. Bureaucracy was seen by Weber as the institutional form of what he called rationalization, a process he presented as inextricably bound up with capitalist development. Rationalization, at the most general level, referred to calculating the most effective way to gain a given end. Weber believed that a variety of rationally based institutions, such as a legal system, a banking infrastructure and rational systems of accounting, were needed to promote capitalist development. Technology and science can also be seen as an embodiment of rationality. The development of these rational institutions promoted the growth of middle-class groupings which were highlighted in Weber's theory of class.

Between them, Marx and Weber pointed to a number of elements central to subsequent theories of capitalism: the dominance of profits over needs; the market; private ownership of capital; wage labour; alienation; the pressures of competition and capital accumulation; bureaucracy; the application of science and technology to production; economic rationalism as the key principle of decision-making. For both Marx and Weber capitalist societies were societies stratified by class (although they conceived class somewhat differently). It is this form of inequality that features centrally in all theories of capitalism.

Late, disorganized or global capitalism?

While many would argue that the key elements of capitalism, as listed above, are still the central characteristics of societies such as Britain and America, there can be no doubt that things have changed greatly since Marx published the first volume of *Das Kapital* in 1867 and even since Weber published *The Protestant Ethic* in 1904. It has been suggested in chapter 1 that the antagonism between capitalists and waged labourers is now less marked as the class structure has become more complex. Other important changes include the greater involvement of the state in controlling and co-ordinating the economy, and the provision of welfare systems to offset some of the hardships brought about by the operation of the market and the wage labour system. Moreover, since the latter part of the nineteenth century, capitalism has been becoming steadily more internationalized in its scope and operations. This has occurred first through the development of international product markets under colonialism, then by the expansion of capitalist firms' investment and production systems across the globe, and subsequently by the freeing up of trade and of systems of financial investment and speculation.

These changes, among others, have led many sociologists to argue that capitalism has now entered a new stage or phase, with important effects on social relationships. The development of joint-stock companies as the prevailing form of capitalist enterprise, followed by the emergence in America at the end of the last century of giant monopolistic corporations, is usually taken as the crucial element in the evolution of this new phase which has therefore been called 'monopoly capitalism' (Scott, 1979). Others have described it as 'advanced' (Giddens, 1973) or 'late' (Mandel, 1976) capitalism.

Advanced, late, or monopoly capitalism is contrasted with the 'classic', 'liberal' or 'entrepreneurial' capitalism of the early nineteenth century in which the typical capitalist enterprise was owned and managed by an individual entrepreneur or family. The competitive demands for expansion and investment inherent to the capitalist economy led to the concentration of capital and the formation of joint-stock companies. Such companies tended to expand both the size and the range of their productive activities and gradually the giant monopolies emerged to dominate national economies. They also started to expand internationally, taking advantage of the colonial and imperialistic relationships which were typical of the period up to the Second World War. Expansion was also promoted by state support and intervention, as governments realized the need to help companies compete in the international markets. The switch to joint ownership of companies also greatly helped the development of the stock market and associated financial institutions, such as merchant banks, insurance and investment companies. Another key feature of monopoly capitalism has been the steadily growing dominance of the finance sector over industrial companies. The 1980s and the great boom in the financial markets of the City of London epitomized the triumph of speculative capital over productive manufacturing capital. All these developments promoted a more complex set of class relations, with a proliferation of middle groupings.

In the 1980s it has been suggested that capitalism is entering a third stage, referred to as 'disorganized' capitalism (Offe, 1985; Lash and Urry, 1987). The monopoly stage is seen as 'organized' in that it produced high levels of state intervention and co-ordination of the economy, along with a complex system of state welfare provisions, and promoted bureaucratization and centralization. It was also marked in a number of countries by the emergence of corporatism. Corporatism is a kind of alliance or collaboration between the different parties in the economy (the state, employers, working people) through means of collective organizations which represent their interests. Thus government, employers' organizations and trade unions negotiate together over the running of the country. Trade unions, for example, will agree to encourage restraint over wage demands among their members and limit strike activity, in return for consultation over government economic policy-making. Germany and the Scandinavian countries can be seen as examples of corporatist states, and many have argued that post-war Britain had what Middlemas (1979) called 'a corporate' bias.

In their study *The End of Organized Capital* Lash and Urry describe the key features of disorganized capitalism as follows: the globalization of capitalist economic structures and the spread of capital into 'Third World' countries; the dominance of multinational or transnational companies, whose power is now so great that nationally based economic and political elites have diminishing control over their activities; the break-up of corporatism; the decline of collective organizations (such as trade unions and professional bodies) within societies; the shrinking of the working class and continued expansion of the middle classes; the dismantling and disintegration of welfare states; and the rise of a more pluralistic culture, promoting social fragmentation.

Scott Lash and John Urry highlight a number of important developments in contemporary capitalism. In particular, many nations have witnessed considerable state withdrawal from direct economic intervention and erosion of state-run welfare services. The 'free market' rather than state control has become the dominant organizing principle. Despite this, it is doubtful whether 'disorganization' is the best way to describe the current state of capitalist society. It can be argued that capitalist companies are more tightly organized and integrated than ever before, albeit on a global basis. Processes of decentralization in private and public organizations and in the state have been matched by new processes of centralization. For example, if we look at the education and health services in Britain we can see that while some financial responsibilities have passed from government bodies to hospital trusts and to headteachers (decentralization), the powers of management have been expanded and the power and autonomy of professionals lower down the hierarchy have diminished (centralization). Moreover, the organization of some aspects of these services (such as the ground rules for financial organization in the health service, the establishment of a national curriculum and augmentation of nationally based assessment systems in schools) is more tightly under central government control than before. Rather than a decline of organization, it appears that new forms of organization are being developed, ones that further the power of private enterprise. The development of highly efficient computerized systems are also contributing to a process which we might call the 'reorganization' of capital.

Perhaps the most significant feature of Lash's and Urry's arguments is the notion of the globalization of capitalism. Globalization has been made central to many other accounts of contemporary social development, such as those of Giddens (1990) and Harvey (1989). It should be emphasized that capitalism has always been international in its scope and its arrangements. Wallerstein (1974) has analysed the rise of capitalism in terms of a 'world economy' dominated by the colonial powers. Hobsbawm (1968) describes how Britain's precocious start as the originator of industrialism was based upon the economic benefits of the 'triangular trade' in slaves, raw materials and industrial products between Britain, Africa and the British colonies in the Americas. The development of the monopoly phase of capital in the late nineteenth century was linked to further expansion of international trade. However, what globalization theory points to is an intensification of these international links and in particular a shift in the ground of the power of leading capitalist enterprises from a national to a transnational base. This has been facilitated by the development of microtechnologies, which make capital more portable, and information technologies which permit the flow of communications around the globe. The recent break-up of the Soviet bloc has extended the scope of a global market culture, based around commercialism and consumerism, into Eastern Europe and Asia:

> Nowadays, goods, capital, people, knowledge, images, communications, crime, culture, pollutants, fashions and beliefs all readily flow across territorial boundaries. Transnational networks, social movements and relationships are extensive in virtually all areas of human activity from the academic to the sexual. Moreover, the existence of global systems of trade, finance and production binds together in very complicated ways the prosperity and fate of households, communities and nations across the globe. (McGrew, 1992, p. 66)

A common feature of the frameworks outlined above is the focus on economic arrangements as the basis for distinguishing between societal types: by implication, economic relationships become central. All such approaches, then, imply an emphasis on class as a primary form of social stratification. Traditional theories of industrialism and capitalism treated inequalities of other types (for example, gender and ethnicity) as secondary, being incidental not central to social development. However, the more recent theories of capitalism (disorganized capital, globalization) have taken on board the criticisms of feminists and others and incorporated other dimensions of stratification into their analysis.

Often they have done this through the concept of 'new social movements'. Original class structures of capitalism are said to be weakening and fragmenting as a social and political force; and new social movements based on a range of communal issues (feminism, 'race', ecology, gay and lesbian rights, consumption) are coming to the fore in the political arena. Nonetheless, the slant of all theories of capitalism is such that the changing relationship between capital and labour is likely to be foregrounded. An important feature of the remaining perspectives discussed in this chapter is that they push the capital–labour relationship from the centre, allowing for a more open-ended approach to stratification.

Modernity: an alternative perspective

During the 1980s there has been a trend within sociology to use the term 'modernity' rather than either industrialism or capitalism in talking about contemporary social development; the more recent work of Anthony Giddens, for example, has demonstrated this switch in terminology. At a common-sense level, we may employ 'modern' simply as a synonym for 'capitalist' or 'industrial' societies. But the term modernity has a more precise set of sociological resonances. In part the use of the term by Giddens (1990; 1991) is a response to the challenging position of *post*modernity; Giddens explicitly rejects the idea of postmodernity and opposes the idea of 'late modernity' to it.

However, the idea also links back to older sociological traditions. It can be connected to the work of Emile Durkheim and his functionalist follower, Talcott Parsons. Durkheim eschewed the idea of capitalism. Rather than focusing on economic relationships, in his account of social development Durkheim was concerned to categorize societies in terms of what to him was distinctively *social*: the nexus of relationships which binds society's members together. This focus on moral and social solidarity reappeared in the work of Parsons and in his view of what made the social relationships of modern societies specific (achieved rather than ascribed status, universalistic rather than particularistic orientations, and so forth). Another link is to the work of Georg Simmel who also focused on the non-economic aspects of society; Simmel provided an influential analysis of modernity in terms of the distinctive relationships of urban living in the 'metropolis'. Simmel's view of modern life is one that focuses on fluidity, impermanence, social isolation, lack of close emotional ties. This melancholy view was influenced by the cultural writings of the poet Baudelaire, who coined the image of the 'flaneur', the stroller on the streets of modern life. Contemporary life is seen in such approaches as 'transitory, fleeting and contingent' (Frisby, 1985). Such an emphasis is not incompatible with some of Marx's statements about the dynamism and fluidity of modern capitalism or his concept of alienation, and for this reason Marxian thinking, too, can be seen to contribute to the idea of modernity. Weber has also been a central influence: the less explicitly economistic elements of Weber's work provide key concepts for the idea of modernity; Weber described the cultures of the modern world as dominated by rationality, scientific thinking, secularization and what he called the 'disenchantment of the world': the loss of belief in magic and myth. Finally, running through all these approaches is the notion of 'the shock of the new', the sense that the dynamism of modern life persistently confronts us with novelty, with change (Frisby, 1985; Lash and Friedman, 1992).

From these varied sociological influences theorists employing the idea of modernity have put together an account of contemporary societies which moves out from economic characteristics to consider more general cultural and social relationships. Perhaps inevitably the term appears somewhat imprecise in contrast to the earlier theories we have discussed. Rather than providing an analysis of *why* contemporary societies take a particular form, as is offered by theories of capitalism and industrialism, theories of modernity tend to offer a descriptive account of key aspects of social life, a view of *how* societies are.

Giddens in *The Consequences of Modernity* (1990) makes an attempt to offer a more precise and grounded sociological account of modernity. He conceptualizes modernity in terms of four interlinked sets of institutions and relationships: capitalism, industrialism, administrative power and military power. Here a classic analysis of economic relationships is supplemented by an account of political structures. This allows Giddens to include the emergence of new social movements (such as CND and the Green parties) as a core feature of modern politics, and indicates how potentially the framework of modernity can provide the basis for a more flexible account of social divisions, which goes beyond seeing class as primary. However, this particular version of 'modernity' also exposes some of the problems of this perspective. In a multi-dimensional model such as this, what precisely is the relationship between the different elements? Which of them is most important and how do they influence each other? Finally, if a more descriptive approach is employed, what do you choose to include and what to leave out? A notable omission from Giddens's model is any account of private life and the family. As in theories of capitalism, gender and ethnicity appear as a marginal aspect of social stratification.

Perhaps this should not surprise us. However wide the influences on the concept of modernity, some (not all) of which are listed above, generally speaking we can say that the key ideas derive from classical social theory of the nineteenth and early twentieth centuries. As was discussed in chapter 1, sociologists writing in these epochs had little to say about gender, partly because they saw sexual divisions as part of the natural order. The same would be true of age differences. Bauman (1992) also draws our attention to the fact that the spatial framework for classical sociological thinking was the nation state. When discussing social divisions, those thinking in terms of nation states were drawn to consider *internal* divisions and inequalities (such as class and occupation) rather than *external* divisions and inequalities such as those of nation, ethnos and racial group. Any approach derived from classical sociology is thus likely to privilege class as the most significant form of social division. To overcome this problem, many have suggested that we need a totally new kind of framework for considering society.

A new type of society? Post-industrialism and postmodernity

Two currently influential approaches suggest that things have altered so radically that a new theoretical approach is needed to comprehend the nature of contemporary social reality: the theories of post-industrialism and postmodernity. Bauman, for example, speaks of 'a fully fledged viable social system which has come to replace the "classical" modern, capitalist society and thus needs to be theorized according to its own logic' (Bauman, 1988, p. 811).

Post-industrialism is, in fact, not a very new idea. It is associated particularly with Daniel Bell, who produced *The Coming of Post-Industrial Society* in 1973. In line with the theory of industrialism, Bell suggested that a new form of technology was bringing about a new type of society. Computer-based technologies meant the evolution of new forms of employment which would overturn the old class system as manual work was replaced by white-collar and professional jobs. While Bell identified this quantitative shift from manual to service work as already having occurred in the United States, he was more interested in the working out of the qualitative effects of this change. The new society would mean greater material prosperity for all, a rehumanization of work relations, an increase in the amount of leisure time, all as a result of the immense wealth-generating potential of new technology. The result would be greater harmony among social groups, an end to alienation and class conflict. Bell's work, indeed, was a deliberate challenge to Marxism. Class as Marx understood it was now irrelevant, and class conflict would no longer serve as the 'motor of history'. Bell argued that a new 'axial principle' (driving force) in society had replaced the profit imperative. As society moved beyond capitalism into post-industrialism, knowledge would become the axis: scientific knowledge would dictate how the new technology evolved and was applied.

When it first came out, Bell's thesis was savaged comprehensively by British sociologists. Critics such as Kumar (1978) and Giddens (1973) suggested that the tendencies Bell noted were not a movement beyond capitalism but simply a working-out of principles inherent to it; the rise in service work, for example, and the dominance of scientific knowledge were already in evidence in the nineteenth century. This did not mean an end to class or class conflict, which were merely evolving in new ways; while scientific knowledge was important it was still subordinated to the objectives of capital accumulation. Only inventions which led to increased profit were taken up and produced.

Most sociologists in Britain accepted these criticisms and post-industrial theory fell out of favour for a time. However, the idea resurfaced in the 1980s, ironically in a very different context. Bell's optimistic vision of the post-industrial society was a product of post-war affluence, the 'you've never had it so good' feeling which produced the kindred idea of embourgeoisement in Britain. By contrast, the post-industrial theories of the 1980s were formulated as a result of the rise of mass unemployment. Particularly well known is André Gorz's account *Farewell to the Working Class* (1982). Gorz suggests that the advent of information technology, far from bringing wealth to all, makes a steadily increasing proportion of the labour force redundant. So powerful is computerized production that a society no longer needs all its citizens to be employed to produce the goods and services it needs. Thus, Gorz argues, a new class is created, made up of the unemployed and casualized under-employed (part-time, temporary, seasonal) workers, which he calls the neo-proletariat. In these circumstances, the traditional proletariat, greatly reduced in size, and fearful of losing jobs or being replaced by neo-proletarians, abandons its opposition to capital and loses industrial militancy.

Gorz used these ideas to suggest that the accounts of capitalism offered by Marx and by Weber were now redundant. Weber's notion of the 'protestant ethic' no longer holds good in a society where a majority of people face a future without work. Equally, Marx's vision of the proletariat as a potentially revolutionary force posing a challenge to capitalist production methods must be abandoned. However, in a useful critique of the post-industrial thesis, Clarke and Critcher (1985) suggest that this account of the 'death of the proletariat' is overstated. Rather they suggest that, as capitalist economies are highly dynamic, class relations are always changing. They believe that a new working class consisting of lower-paid service workers, along with remaining manual workers, is currently being formed.

It will be seen that the versions of post-industrialism outlined above are concerned with the issue of class, implying that class relations are being transformed or even that class is vanishing. These theories are critical of existing analyses of capitalism and industrialism, and both Bell and Gorz deliberately set out to attack Marxism; but the focus is still firmly on economic relationships, and gender, ethnicity and so forth tend to enter as side-effects of economic change.

A much broader, culturally based critique of theories of capitalism comes from the package of approaches which have become known as 'postmodernism'. As its own adherents have acknowledged (Lash, 1990; Smart, 1990) the term is often used quite loosely to signify a number of different trends in social thought. Lyon refers to it as a 'multi-layered concept' (Lyon, 1994, p. vii). However, there can be no doubt that it poses a radical challenge to previous forms of sociological theory.

Postmodernism is not in origin a theory of society. There are two main strands, which have come rather uneasily together. The first is a theory about art and cultural change, the second a philosophical position which attacks foundationalist accounts of social reality (accounts which postulate an underlying base from which patterns of social relationships arise) and the notion of progress in social development. It also challenges the claims of a 'rational' science to a privileged form of knowledge, based on objective and verifiable processes of observation. In this view there are multiple viewpoints rather than a single reality. Both these strands have subsequently been taken up by sociologists but, as Bauman (1992) and Turner (1990) both argue, a dilemma arises as to whether sociologists should be seeking a 'sociology of postmodernity', that is the analysis of a new postmodern phase of society; or a 'postmodern sociology', that is an analytic approach which takes on board the ideas of philosophical and cultural postmodernism. Does postmodernism amount to a new ontology (a theory of what reality consists of) or a new form of epistemology (a theory of how we know social reality)? Put simply, has society changed, or is it our way of thinking about it that must change?

Postmodern theory is complex and can only be explored very sketchily here. First, the cultural strand of postmodernism deals with the challenge to the modernist movement in art, literature and particularly architecture. While modernism was elitist, abstract, based on a strict aesthetic controlled by intellectuals, postmodern culture is popular, based on the experience of everyday life, and is led by commercialism and the market. Postmodern art forms often mix styles from different periods or schools (fusing opera and rock music, for example, or incorporating features typical of Roman or Greek architecture into a modern housing project or public building). Postmodern art is seen as playful, irreverent, often involving pastiche and parody, rather than presenting itself as a representation or distillation of 'real' life. It rejects Shakespeare's famous definition of the purpose of art: 'to hold, as 'twere, the mirror up to nature'. The postmodern artwork plays about with the notion of reality; the writer or artist may insert herself into the text, make ironic comments on it. No firm distinction is made between author, text or reality; the text is as real as what it portrays. All in all, postmodern culture encourages an 'anything goes' approach, which allows for a multitude of diverse cultural forms and a challenge to traditional 'canons' of art and taste (see, for example, Jencks, 1986; Harvey, 1989, for fuller accounts of postmodernism in art).

While this may seem remote from the analysis of social divisions, there are two senses in which this cultural theory is of sociological significance. First, it challenges the traditional hierarchies within society and promotes the idea of cultural diversity and social pluralism. The idea of 'difference' and diversity has become a central feature of theories of postmodernity. Second, in its challenge to the traditional distinction between art and reality it throws its weight behind the anti-foundationalist stance of postmodern epistemology.

This has been most clearly expressed in the seminal account of Jean-François Lyotard, *The Postmodern Condition* (1984). Lyotard offers an account of 'the condition of knowledge in the most highly developed societies' (p. xxiii) which involves an attack on what he calls 'metanarratives': historical accounts of social and intellectual development which promote the idea of orderly human progress towards a goal, often that of human 'enlightenment' or emancipation. While such metanarratives present themselves as scientifically validated forms of knowledge, Lyotard considers them to be no more than stories or myths used to justify particular views of how societies ought to be. Many classic social theories can be seen as metanarratives of this type, such as the liberal or 'Whig' view of history as the triumph of civilization over barbarianism or functionalist theories of modernization, but above all Lyotard's critique is aimed at Marx's theory of capitalism and its Utopian vision of socialist revolution. Lyotard believes that such theories are now discredited; he defines what he sees as the current 'postmodern condition' as 'incredulity towards metanarratives' (p. xxiii).

While it might be argued that it is possible to produce reworked versions of classic theories that eschew the notion of progress or of Utopian end states, the implication of Lyotard's argument is that we should abandon all attempts to construct grand theories of history and society, especially those which involve the idea of distinct stages of development. Rather than try to understand societies in their totality, which he sees as an impossible project, we should concentrate on 'local narratives': accounts of events in very specific and limited contexts. In particular Lyotard advises a focus on language and the 'language games' which people use to promote their own definitions of what knowledge consists of.

This last point indicates that Lyotard's interest is more in terms of 'how we know' than 'what we know', and this indicates a difficulty in applying these premises to the analysis of society. The types of sociology which would logically appear compatible with Lyotard's position are the various micro-sociologies of action (ethnomethodology, interactionism, phenomenology) which focus on interaction in specific contexts and on the accounts that actors offer to make sense of the interaction. Yet such procedures, while important and perceptive in themselves, have limitations in explaining aspects of social life, such as inequalities of class and gender, which are diffused across the whole of society. How do we move the analysis beyond what happens in any particular school, street, office or factory?

It can be claimed that postmodern thinking has not as yet provided definitive formulations about the nature of the 'social' as opposed to the cultural: the guidelines are unclear as to how changing social relations are to be analysed. David Lyon suggests that many accounts of postmodernity make assumptions about technological change (computerization, information flows, the spread of mass media) but devote little space to linking these to processes of 'social transformation' (1994, p. 50). Curiously, those who espouse postmodernism are often drawn to utilize the sociological theories of others to combine with their accounts of knowledge and culture. Lyon points to the frequent implicit use of 'a variety of post-industrial theory' which has 'survived its earlier critical battering to be recycled as postmodernity' (1994, p. 46). For example, Lyotard himself draws substantially on Bell's work, although Bell's version of post-industrialism is clearly a liberal form of a metanarrative of progress.

Others ascribing to aspects of postmodernism who are sympathetic to Marxism have drawn on theories of capitalism to supplement their accounts of postmodern culture (Harvey, 1989; Jameson, 1991). Jameson describes postmodernism as the 'cultural logic of late capitalism' which he sees as entering its 'third (or multinational) stage' (1991, p. 319). Hall and Jacques have fused aspects of postmodern cultural theory with the idea of post-Fordism as a new paradigm of capitalist work organization to produce their account of what they call 'New Times' (1989); while Bauman, although not a Marxist, suggests that a postmodern sociology would involve an account of consumer capitalism and its characteristic social relations (Bauman, 1992). It is interesting that none of these influential figures employs a micro-sociological approach such as ethnomethodology. Moreover, these very different postmodernists all draw on existing economically based typologies, meaning that once again class, however conceptualized, reappears as a central feature; paradoxically, the stress on diversity and social pluralism, so central to the idea of postmodern culture, seems to slip away at this point.

We may question whether the strategy used by these theorists, (even by

Lyotard himself) is a legitimate one, if we follow the logic of Lyotard's theoretical position. Indeed, it is not clear whether, within its own parameters, the postmodern epistemological position would permit any kind of *general* account of society (such as an account of 'postmodernity'). The alternative would be to study aspects of social divisions within specific local contexts. As we shall see in subsequent chapters, feminists and theorists of 'race' are beginning to explore this option, although such analysis is still under-developed in the major postmodernist texts.

One aspect of social relations which has received attention in postmodern texts is the idea of multiple identities. This is used, sometimes in combination with the notion of new social movements, to move towards a pluralistic account of social relationships (Rutherford, 1990; Crook et al., 1992). Consumption and exposure to the mass media are seen to have a crucial role in affecting people's social identification. This is a useful approach and the chapters which follow frequently draw upon work of this kind. However, a problem is that it is overly voluntaristic (i.e. people are seen as choosing from a package of identities on offer according to personal inclination). As O'Neill argues, there is a tendency to present identities as detached and free-floating: 'postmodern atomism dislocates individuals from their institutional contexts' (1995, p. 7). For an account of how these identities might be grounded in 'institutional contexts' – that is, how they are linked to sets of lived relationships and *constrained by them* – postmodernists again tend to fall back on traditional accounts of capitalism, although these may be supplemented with ideas drawn from feminism and from theories of colonialism.

Critics of postmodernism reject the view that we have moved 'post' the 'institutional contexts' of modernity. Our production system is still a capitalist one, and all the features of modern capitalist industrial societies which have featured in the discussion above (for example bureaucracy, the social dominance of scientific knowledge, rationality), are still central to our society. While many changes are occurring, defenders of modernism suggest they are insufficient to justify an 'ontological break', a complete rupture with the past (Pollert, 1988; Thompson, 1993). All this may throw doubt on the idea of 'postmodernity' as a distinct social phase and explain why postmodernists have found it hard to offer substantive accounts of the social implications of cultural change.

However, the 'epistemological' version of postmodernism and its critique of modernist forms of knowledge cannot lightly be dismissed. At the least, it provides a useful and stringent corrective to conventional sociological theorizing; it warns us to be wary of the idea of progress and to be cynical of claims about scientific objectivity in social analysis; it alerts us to be cautious in how we apply the social typologies we develop and to avoid totalizing approaches which distort the complex nature of social reality. As Weber (1949) long ago suggested, the knowledge generated by sociological analysis can only be seen as partial knowledge, at best. A stronger reading of postmodern epistemology renders problematic the whole sociological endeavour of explaining 'how society works' at least in terms of conventional causally based concepts of structure. This may have led sociologists sympathetic to postmodernism to evade the issue of how to approach social divisions. One way or another, postmodernist approaches have not yet provided us with a way to analyse societal relationships (such as the dynamics of inequality discussed in this book) which definitively replaces existing approaches.

Summary and conclusions

This chapter has reviewed a number of theoretical approaches which can be employed in seeking to understand the nature of contemporary societies. I have outlined the main features of each position and indicated the implications of each for the analysis of social divisions.

I have argued that because these positions derive from classical sociological theories, or have been elaborated in opposition to them, within most of them economic relationships emerge as the most important source of social division, even where the conceptualization of class is explicitly challenged. Other forms of social division are sometimes addressed in terms of the concept of 'new social movements' which are seen to arise to fill the gap as class consciousness is weakened and collective action based on class becomes less significant. But even here, new social movements are generally seen as a substitute for class; they do not emerge from the 'logic of the system' as do class divisions; they are contingent rather than necessary.

Postmodern theory goes furthest in moving away from the old economic frameworks, but I have argued that the postmodern approach does not in itself lead to any clear account of social structures or social divisions. Theorists of postmodernity tend to draw upon other theoretical positions, such as post-industrialism (Lyotard), or capitalism (Jameson and Bauman) for their account of social relationships as opposed to cultural change. In these versions an economic orientation creeps back in by the side door. Accounts employing concepts such as multiple identities and focusing on consumption, mass media and information technologies move beyond economism, but remain at the level of speculation and assertion. Postmodernism offers the promise of a plural account of inequality which it has not yet fulfilled.

No single one of these frameworks, then, can on its own and within its own logic provide a totally convincing account of social divisions. This need not mean that we totally reject these perspectives, since each of them offers useful insights into processes of social change and inequality.

For example, I would argue that the labour/capital relationship is still a central feature of modern Western societies. Such societies are therefore still capitalist, although it is clear that class relations have changed dramatically since Marx wrote his account of capitalism. As will be discussed in the next chapter, economic and social development has produced a new set of class configurations which can be described as 'post-industrial capitalist'.

However, economic relationships, of whatever kind, do not constitute the totality of social relationships. There is a general problem in the use of terms such as capital*ism*, post-industrial*ism*, modern*ity* – even postmodern*ity* – which convey the idea of totality. Behind such terms lurks the recurrent sociological image of societies as self-sufficient social systems. Epistemological postmodernists are right to reject the idea of system, which inevitably involves exclusions. The feminist term patriarchy raises exactly the same problems. To describe Britain as 'a patriarchy' inverts Marxism and elevates gender divisions above class and ethnicity. Any system theory will marginalize many important aspects of social reality.

This is why in this book I have used the idea of 'sets of relationships' as a way to conceptualize social order and structuration. While such an approach lacks the appealing clarity, the hard-edged quality, of the system concept, it avoids the closure and exclusions which systems theory involves. Social reality can be made up of an infinite number of interconnected sets of relations. Nor is there any implication, as with the concept of system, that relationships are fixed or that they need to replicate themselves in an identical form; the fuzzier concept of sets of relations is thus better able than the concept of system to cope with change. To put it in another way, it is compatible with the idea of reality as process rather than structure. This approach acknowledges the salience of some of the postmodern criticisms of traditional formulations of social structure, without abandoning the idea of societies as orderly.

The next four chapters look at social divisions in terms of four sets of social relationships: class, gender, 'race'/ethnicity and age. I start, perhaps controversially, with class. My reason is that economic relationships loom large in our lives. Governments are elected to manage the economy. The success of societies and the well-being of their citizens is linked *by us as social members* to the efficiency of the economy and the level of material prosperity. Economic considerations are viewed as predominant in managing processes of change in our social institutions; market principles, for example, have now been firmly introduced into all layers of the education system. Paradoxically, while at the individual level class seems to be of diminishing significance, at the societal level we see the economy as increasingly dominating every aspect of our lives.

3

Class: Beyond Marx?

'Class began and continued as a muddle' (Phillips, 1987, p. 33). Ann Phillips's remark pithily encapsulates both the complex and shifting nature of class as a set of lived relationships and the difficulty sociologists have had in defining class as a social category. Class is everywhere and it is nowhere. Because it has no very definite physical signs or markers it is hard to observe. These problems are reflected in the often virulent disputes about where class derives from, where the boundaries between classes lie and how class should be measured. Class has long been central to the sociological endeavour; indeed, Edgell refers to it as 'the most widely used concept in sociology' (Edgell, 1993, p. viii). Yet sociologists acknowledge that it is an 'essentially contested concept': that is, one about which there can never be ultimate agreement because different definitions of class rest upon totally different assumptions (Calvert, 1982).

The analysis of class as a sociological concept has historically taken the form of a set of debates, arising from the initial positions staked out by Marx and Weber. As well as continuing disagreements between neo-Marxists and neo-Weberians, Rosemary Crompton has pointed to another damaging set of 'pseudo-debates', within British class analysis. She suggests (1993) that a schism has developed between those who study class structure and patterns of social mobility using highly sophisticated statistical techniques, and those who focus on class formation and consciousness employing historical or ethnographic approaches. Conflicts between and within these two methodologically opposed camps have brought a stalemate which has caused other sociologists to lose interest in class analysis, perceived as becoming increasingly technical and arid. As Marshall comments, preoccupations with redefining occupational classification schemes have encouraged 'taxonomical exercises which tend to lose sight of the reasons that we should be interested in class analysis in the first place – to understand . . . processes and consequences of social inequality' (B. Marshall, 1994, p. 48).

Here I offer a broad definition of class; it is a label applied to a nexus of unequal lived relationships arising from the social organization of production, distribution, exchange and consumption. These include: the allocation of tasks in the division of labour (occupation, employment hierarchies); control and ownership relationships within production; the unequal distribution of surplus (wealth, income, state benefits); relationships linked to the circulation of money (markets, shareholding, investment); patterns of consumption (lifestyle, living arrangements); and distinctive cultures that arise from all these (behavioural practices, community relations). Class is a much broader concept, then, than occupational structure, though the latter is often taken as a measure of it.

Definitional problems are only one reason for the current decline in interest in class. Increased attention to other forms of inequality has combined with the postmodern critiques of classic theory to push class from the centre of the stage. Postmodernist thinking is explicitly critical of the narrowness of traditional Marxist class theory, which is seen to ignore other dynamics of inequality and reduce the multiplicity of social experience to its single 'metanarrative' theme of the anatagonism between capital and labour: 'the monologic concept of class struggle is inadequate to the plurality of conflicts at work in contemporary society' (Mercer, 1990, p. 48). As O'Neill (1995) points out, some postmodernists simply ignore class. Others suggest that as the postmodern phase develops traditional class structures will be eroded. Old class identities will be replaced by 'a mosaic of multiple status identities' (Crook et al., 1992, p. 133).

In response, class theorists point to the persistence of class inequalities. The Rowntree Report of 1995 revealed that inequalities in Britain were increasing, and at a rate faster than in any other industrial country. Unemployment, insecurity and deprivation remain the lot of many working-class people. A report for the Institute of Fiscal Studies found that one fifth of the British population were living below the Council of Europe's poverty line, over 11 million people. This compares with the century's lowest number of 3 million in 1977. Over the thirty-year period from 1961 to 1991 the share of national income of the poorest tenth of the population fell from 4.2 to 3.0 per cent, while the richest tenth increased their share from 22 to 25 per cent (Goodman and Webb, 1994). They also own nearly half the marketable wealth (Rowntree Report, 1995). The extent of poverty in Britain is brought home by a survey carried out by Nottingham Council in 1993 which found that almost half of Nottingham's citizens were dependent on benefits or income support. The 1980s and 1990s witnessed a series of scandals about the enormous increases in salaries of entrepreneurs and 'chief executives'. For example, a survey of top executives' pay in 1994 revealed an average rise of nearly 25 per cent; the top directors of Warburg (the merchant banking firm), Barclays and the Royal Bank of Scotland received rises of around 200 per cent in a year in which many employees in banking and finance had been made redundant (including many staff at

Barclays). Men at the top of such successful capitalist enterprises may be earning salaries of over one million pounds a year. Such evidence suggests that class inequalities are increasingly significant, rather than disappearing.

Moreover, class remains a key variable in sociological studies of many aspects of social life. Such studies continue to show the links between class, and ill health, early mortality, teenage pregnancy, low educational achievement, poor housing and crime (see Hudson and Williams, 1989, for a useful survey of these types of findings). Class remains crucial in determining the pattern of individual life chances. For example, a collection of studies of young people in education edited by Inge Bates and George Riseborough (1993) show that young people from different classes and class fractions go through very different patterns of educational experience. Young people from middle-class backgrounds go to elite schools, state-run or private, and are groomed for universities. Young working-class people go into further education or Youth Training schemes. Even the choice among YTS schemes is related to class; for example, girls from poorer working-class backgrounds are seen to be specially suited for care-based schemes such as working in homes for elderly people (Bates, 1993). Young people are subtly channelled through the various strands of the British education system into jobs which fit their class of origin.

This chapter surveys the debates on class, particularly in the light of contemporary changes. It starts with a brief account of changing class relations in Britain and then reviews classic class theories, before considering the challenges from post-industrialism and postmodernism.

Classes old and new

Marx developed his account of capitalist class relationship in the context of industrialization and the upheavals that accompanied it. Many ordinary people feared and resented the break up of the old ways of living and the new forms of work organization. Loss of agricultural jobs and the decay of traditional craft-based systems of production would eventually force the bulk of male labourers into the factory system but at first this change was resisted. The period of industrialization in Britain was a time of social and industrial conflict, marked by strikes, demonstrations, machine-breaking, riots, petitions to parliament, political campaigns for votes for working men and for regulation of hours and conditions within the factories. Public attention was drawn to the bitter and conflictual relationship between the labouring classes and their masters. It is not surprising that Marx's theorization of the new class relations of industrial societies rested on these two groups. It also reflected a longstanding perception of the gap between 'the rich' and 'the poor', which persists in popular usage to this day: 'it's the rich that gets the pleasure and the poor that gets the blame!', as the song has it.

Weber and Durkheim were working at a later date, when industrial societies had matured into a more stable state (Giddens, 1973). Where relationships between the classes appeared more settled and harmonious, attention was diverted to the various gradations within classes and allied forms of status distinction (Briggs, 1974). In such a context Weber was able to develop his more sophisticated account of a plurality of classes and Durkheim to suggest that the social division of labour had a positive integrating function. As industrial production became more technically sophisticated and firms became larger, bureaucracy and the employment of specialized staff burgeoned. Such developments are reflected in Weber's interest in the expanding middle classes.

Marx and Weber between them laid the ground for an account of what we might call the 'traditional class structure' that developed with industrialization. Post-war sociologists of class tended to adopt a three-class model of upper (or capitalist) class, middle class (the heterogeneous white-collar groupings) and manual working class (for example, Giddens, 1973). Research was especially concerned with the 'traditional' working class, the core of which was manual workers from heavy industries. It was argued that around such occupations stable working-class communities in distinct residential areas had evolved with their own distinctive culture. A sense of solidarity and class membership was imputed to the traditional working class, manifested, for example, in union membership and voting for the Labour party. Their experience and culture cut them off sharply from the other social groupings; they led 'a life apart' (Meacham, 1977). Although it is suggested that this vision of a solidaristic united working class is romanticized (Marshall et al., 1988), studies testified to the existence of communities displaying some of these characteristics (Dennis et al., 1956; Blackwell and Seabrook, 1985). In the post-war period, however, better-off workers in newer industries developed new more materialistic life-styles and privatized values, and moved into new suburban housing areas, as described in the *Affluent Worker* studies (Goldthorpe et al., 1969).

Recently this class model has been cast in doubt with the expansion of service employment. The traditional working class and the affluent workers are both said to be in decline. Two new class groupings have drawn sociological attention: the self-employed and the 'underclass'.

Self-employment in Britain doubled between 1981 and 1991. In 1994, 3.3 million people were classified as self-employed, amounting to 12.9 per cent of the labour force (Social Trends, 1995). This was partly a response to unemployment: laid-off industrial workers used their redundancy money to start small businesses. Where employment chances were lacking this was often the only alternative to life on the dole (Macdonald and Coffield, 1991). The switch to self-employment was favoured by Conservative governments as a means to promote an 'enterprise' culture and numerous schemes were designed to help business start-ups especially for young people. Other recruits to the ranks of the self-employed were members of ethnic minorities who faced discrimination in the labour market (Jones and McEvoy, 1986). It is also an option for women who find their career chances blocked by the 'glass ceiling' or who wish to combine a career with domestic responsibilities (Scase and Goffee, 1989). Internationally, the combination of mass unemployment and support for entrepreneurial values means that the trend to self-employment is likely to persist. It is becoming widespread, for example, in the reorganizing economies of Eastern Europe.

There is a debate about the class position of the self-employed. While they appear to be part of a re-generated 'petite bourgeoisie' as described by Marx, Dale has argued that in some cases self-employment is no more than a disguised form of casualized wage-labour, often marked by dependency on capitalist employers through some kind of sub-contracting system (1986). Self-employment can be precarious, with the potential for self-exploitation or the exploitation of family members, and the economic rewards may be limited (Curran et al., 1986; Macdonald and Coffield, 1991). But whether they are seen as part of an expanding petite bourgeoisie, a special segment of the new middle classes, or a distinctive group within the working class, it is clear that this expanding group adds another element to the complexity of contemporary class relations.

So does the underclass. The use of this term, in the sense of a socially marginalized group outside of the traditional class structure, is relatively recent. It was coined to describe the position of black people in the ghettoes of America. However. the idea of some such outsider or outcast group is hardly new (Bagguley and Mann, 1992; Morris, 1994). The Victorians referred to such a group as the 'residuum' and Marx used the term 'lumpenproletariat' in reference to 'the social scum, that passively rotting mass thrown off by the lowest layers of the old society' (quoted Morris, 1994, p. 15). Such a group, often considered a threat to the order of a stable society, is seen as occupying a position that is structurally or culturally distinctive.

For example, Glasgow (1981) defines the underclass as a group at the bottom of the class hierarchy, permanently trapped and unable to move upwards because it faces multiple disadvantages. Glasgow was referring to the position of African Americans, but the term has also been used to explain the position of black minorities in Britain (Rex and Tomlinson, 1979), women (Giddens, 1973), the long-term unemployed (Dahrendorf, 1987). Most recently it has been applied by Charles Murray to those who are dependent on benefit for their income. Murray argues that such an underclass already exists in the USA and is rapidly emerging in Britain. He sees three crucial interlinked factors as manifestations of the underclass: young single mothers who choose to bring up children on state benefits and reject the young fathers as husbands; young unemployed working-class men who do not want to work; and the development of a culture of crime among such young men in neighbourhoods where a high proportion of people depend on benefits (Murray, 1984; 1990). He believes that the underclass develops its own distinct set of cultural values which are sharply different from those of the rest of society:

> Britain has a growing population of working-aged, healthy people, who live in a different world from other Britons, who are raising their children to live in it, and whose values are now contaminating the life of entire neighbourhoods. (1990, p. 4)

Murray's culturally-defined version of the underclass has been widely criticized by British sociologists. Some, such as Field (1989) and Dahrendorf (1987), accept the notion of an underclass, but argue that its genesis is structural, the result of government policies leading to long-term unemployment along with poverty for marginalized groups, such as elderly pensioners and sick and disabled people. Others, such as Pilkington (1992) and Dean (1991) reject the notion altogether, arguing that it is merely a rhetorical device used to blame the disadvantaged for their own plight and distract attention from those really responsible, the government and the capitalist class. Marxists also dismiss the concept, arguing that the unemployed are part of the working class. They constitute a 'surplus population' or 'reserve army', a pool of spare labour available to capital.

Whichever view is held, the underclass has become the focus of considerable attention. It can be linked to many changes which are affecting patterns of stratification: the growth of long-term unemployment; the decay of industrial employment; women's changing labour market position; the collapse of established working-class communities; attempts to dismantle the welfare state. Can traditional class theory cope with these changes in the 'lived relationships' of class or must the old categories be abandoned?

The classic inheritance

Three recent texts on class, in different ways, assert the continuing viability of the concepts derived from classic class theories. Richard Scase's study of class (1992) is a defence of Marxism. Scase operates with the traditional Marxian distinction between 'class in itself' (the existence of objective class relations which individuals may or may not be aware of) and 'class for itself' (the development of a common sense of class awareness among class members). For Scase, basic antagonistic capitalist class relations as described by Marx still generate patterns of inequality, although he accepts that the majority of people demonstrate little awareness of class. Stephen Edgell advocates an approach which combines elements from Marx and Weber (property ownership and market divisions). He states that taken together the two 'provide the essential conceptual tools for analysing contemporary class structures' (Edgell, 1993, p. 15). Finally, Peter Saunders calls for a re-examination of the 'long-neglected' functionalist theory, suggesting that it shows us that class divisions are not necessarily a 'bad thing' (1990, p. 130). The fact that all these writers emphasize the continuing relevance of classic theories more than a hundred years after Marx wrote *Das Kapital* shows how powerful the original insights were. It is still impossible to review theories of class without considering the influential classic legacy.

Marx's theory of class has already been referred to in chapter 2. He believed that each 'mode of production' produced characteristic class relationships, involving a dominating and a subordinate class. These two classes were linked together in a relationship of exploitation, in which the subordinate class provided the labour that generated a social surplus and the dominant class then appropriated the surplus. Under the feudal system, which preceded capitalism, surplus was secured by the legal power of the feudal lords over the serfs and peasants who worked on their lands. Legal power could be reinforced by violence and repression if the peasantry resisted handing over the surplus. Under capitalism, the extraction of surplus is managed more subtly, through the mechanism of the wage. The wage is only equivalent to some of the value of the work performed by the labourer; the remaining 'surplus value' is taken by the capitalist in the form of profits. What is going on is concealed from the labourers under the idea of 'a fair wage for a fair day's work'. Thus, in a capitalist society, the power and wealth of the dominant class is seen as legitimate, rather than simply backed by coercion as it was in feudal societies.

The typical class relations of a capitalist society involve the private ownership of the 'means of production' (factories, land, machines, tools) by the capitalist class. The labourers own nothing but their labour power (capacity to labour) which they sell in the 'free' market for a wage. Wage labourers are peculiarly powerless and vulnerable, dependent on their employers for subsistence, and with minimum autonomy over their work in the labour process. Capitalism produces a relationship of mutual dependence between the bourgeoisie and the proletariat (without labourers the capitalist cannot make a profit), which is also inherently antagonistic: the interests of the two main classes are opposed. Marx believed that various tendencies in capitalism would promote class conflict. The progressive development of technology would bring deskilling of jobs, creating a more homogenized and potentially united labour force; the relative gap in wealth between the dominant and subordinate classes would steadily increase; and processes of capital accumulation and competition would generate periods of recession and unemployment Such factors would combine to produce ever more extreme 'crises' of capitalism, propelling processes of class conflict towards an ultimate social revolution.

This idea of class polarization, which Marx set out in the *Communist Manifesto*. contributes to the perception that Marx's theory of class is essentially a dichotomous one. However, in his more historical and descriptive writings Marx referred to many other classes in capitalist society, such as peasants and aristocracy (remnants of feudalism), the petite bourgeoisie (small owners and the self-employed) and the lumpenproletariat.

In the *Communist Manifesto* Marx and Engels suggested that these middle groupings would be absorbed into the two major classes. However, the *Manifesto* was an early and highly polemical piece. In a later work, *Theories of Surplus Value*, Marx wrote of the growth of what we now call the new middle classes, managers, technicians, professionals and bureaucrats. Marx called them the 'surplus class' as they worked for capitalists but unlike the working class they did not produce surplus value. Instead, their salaries were paid out of the surplus. Capitalists were prepared to yield some of their profits for this as the surplus class performed very useful services for them, helping to keep the proletariat in order. Marx labelled them the 'flunkeys, bootlickers and retainers of capitalism' (Nicolaus, 1967).

However, Marx can be criticized for his failure to perceive the growing social and economic significance of this new middle class. The major focus of Marx's interest was in the overarching relationship between capital and labour; it was this relationship which, for Marx, determined the shape of the class structure as a whole and provided the axis for conflict. This remains a defining feature of Marxist class theory and is rejected by Weberian opponents.

The other most controversial feature of Marx's class theory is the notion of class struggle and the socialist revolution, both of which are rejected by Weberians. Weber believed a socialist revolution was an unlikely outcome, and, if it did occur, would not improve the lot of ordinary citizens but would lead to heightened bureaucracy and tyranny. He also believed that economic conflicts did not occur around a single axis but were complex and as likely to occur within classes as between them. History has vindicated Weber, in the sense that most working-class people have not espoused the socialist ideal or acted as the 'revolutionary actor' envisaged by Marx. Even Scase, a contemporary supporter of Marx, accepts that this part of Marx's theory is untenable; the course of historical events in the twentieth century has been to discredit attempts to construct socialist alternatives:

> To share with Marx his ideas for abolishing class must, towards the end of the twentieth century, be seen as Utopian . . . It is the rise and fall of state socialism which the twentieth century has witnessed rather than the demise of capitalism. The question is no longer whether or not capitalism but of what variety or type. (Scase, 1992, p. 89)

The power and continuing appeal of Marxian theory lies in the fact that Marx provided such a systematic account of the origins and basis of class divisions. However, those parts of his theory which deal with class consciousness, class action and socialism are seen to be flawed. 'the weakest link in the chain' (Lockwood, 1988). Moreover, as discussed in chapter 2, Marx's framework cannot deal adequately with other dimensions of inequality. To conceptualize a society as a 'mode of production' is inevitably to privilege economic relations over other aspects of inequality. This is what Mercer means by the 'monologic' of the class struggle concept (Mercer, 1990).

Weber set out a more potentially open-ended framework for studying inequality. His class theory used to be presented as in opposition to Marx; nowadays we tend to view it more as an extension (Edgell, 1993). Weber accepted some aspects of Marxian theory, especially the notions of the broad cleavage in society between the owners of the means of production and the 'propertyless classes'. But he also emphasized the divisions within both propertied and propertyless groupings. The propertied were split according to what kind of property they possessed (for example landowners, major entrepreneurs, small family businesses, financial speculators). The propertyless were divided in terms of what they had to offer in the market. Some had credentials and qualifications, others had apprenticeships and craft experience, others nothing but sheer physical labour power. Followed through this could lead to an almost infinite plurality of propertyless groupings, each with its distinct market offering. But most neo-Weberians accept a fundamental distinction between mental labourers (offering credentials like university degrees and professional training) and manual workers. Weber, with his interest in bureaucracy, focused strongly on white-collar groupings, and rather than seeing them as servants of capitalism in the Marxian fashion emphasized that they too were deprived of ownership, in their case of the means of mental (or bureaucratic) production.

Weber's concepts are the base for theories of class fragmentation. This is reflected in Weberian thinking about class action, which focuses on a plurality of competitive struggles between and within class groupings. There is no single logical dynamic of class struggle and so no thrust towards the demise of the capitalist system. Instead, different interest groups will continue to compete indefinitely for a better deal within the system. Often such conflicts take the form of exclusionary practices, by which groups fight to keep lesser qualified or skilled groups from their section of the market (Parkin, 1979). Like Marx, Weber saw economic relations as inherently conflictual, but believed such conflicts could be accommodated within a democratic pluralist system.

The other great advance of Weber's class analysis was that it allows for the interaction of class with other dimensions of stratification. Weber described stratification in general terms as related to 'the distribution of power within a community' (Gerth and Mills, 1970, p. 181). As well as economic power (class), Weber drew attention to 'status' (social prestige) and 'party' as two other aspects of power. Party, which refers to political dimensions of power, is the least developed of Weber's three categories. It seems to refer to a variety of groupings, including, but not confined to, those we now refer to as political parties, which mobilize for political power and influence. This notion challenges the Marxian view of political power as ultimately derived from economic power. It is possible for members of the economically subordinate classes to mobilize successfully and procure political resources, either through their own distinct organizations (trade unions and labour parties) or by participating in political movements of other groupings. In this scenario it is perfectly possible for working-class people to join a party associated with the dominant political class (for example the Conservative party) and use it to gain resources for themselves.

Weber argued that in any given society class, status and party relationships could be found cross-cutting each other. It was a matter of historical contingency which form of stratification would be dominant, although he suggested that in stable times status considerations came to the fore, while class interests would predominate at times of social upheaval. Thus Weber is moving away from a position that privileges economic relationships. However, his account of gender and ethnicity as aspects of status did not carry this insight far enough. Gender, ethnic and age divisions reflect more than differential social evaluation, also encompassing divisions of labour and differential material resources. Status does not seem a robust enough concept to encompass all of these.

The appeal of Weberian class analysis and his understanding of the politics of capitalism rests in its pluralism and its acknowledgement of the complexity of lived social relationships. In the intellectual and political climate of the late twentieth century, with its stress on diversity and fragmentation, neo-Weberian class analysis is in the ascendant. However, this is a recent development. Post-war sociology has witnessed a prolonged debate between proponents of Marx and of Weber.

The legacy of Marx: the struggle continues

The broad objective of neo-Marxian class theorists is to adapt the principles of Marxian analysis to produce a model or 'map' of the class structure which is more appropriate to contemporary societies. While recognizing the limitations of Marx's original account, neo-Marxists retain some of its key features: the assumption that class is based in relations of production; the concept of exploitation; the concentration on capital and labour as the two most significant classes; the notion of class conflict and class struggle.

Neo-Marxist class analysis is often quite abstract and has been marked by complex theoretical disagreements, which are well summarized in a number of studies (for example, Parkin, 1979; Abercrombie and Urry, 1983; Crompton, 1993) and are not considered here. Instead I discuss some strands of neo-Marxist theory which appear currently relevant: the idea of a 'ruling' class; the proletarianization thesis; and the notion of 'contradictory class locations'.

The ruling class?

An important distinguishing feature of Marxist class theory is a continuing interest in the capitalist class. By contrast, much Weberian class analysis has been based on survey data, in which the numbers of capitalist owners are too small to merit much discussion. As a result Weberian theory focuses very much on the next group in the hierarchy, the service class. Most Weberians acknowledge that a capitalist elite exists; but it tends to slip out of sight in their writings. For Marxists, however, the continued existence and indeed increasing power of the capitalist class is still perhaps the most crucial feature of the contemporary class dynamic.

John Scott has conducted a series of important studies of the dominant economic and social groupings in Britain, defined by ownership and control of corporate wealth (1979; 1982; 1991). This 'inner circle' (Useem, 1984) of individuals and families is tightly linked together by common social background, shared educational experience (attendance at public schools and 'Oxbridge' colleges) and intermarriage. It is also linked through complex arrangements of shareholding and through the institution of 'interlocking directorates' by which powerful entrepreneurs have seats on the boards of a number of companies. Such links maintain the economic and social dominance of the class and help it to secure disproportionate political power. This has been particularly true during the long period of Conservative power from 1979, when there were extensive connections between Tory MPs and ministers, many of whom were from the elite and held directorships, and the capitalist group. Scott concludes:

> Britain is ruled by a capitalist class whose economic dominance is sustained by the operations of the state and whose members are disproportionately represented in the power elite which rules the state apparatus. That is to say, Britain does have a ruling class. (1991, p. 151)

Scott concedes that the ruling class may be divided into fractions (finance capital versus industrial capital, big business versus small and medium-sized firms) and has distinguished three key groups within it: entrepreneurial capitalists, with stakes of ownership and control in particular companies; internal capitalists, managers who have risen to be top executives; and finance capitalists. Despite these internal divisions, the power of the capitalist class is seen as increasing not waning. Coates (1989) describes the British ruling class as being of 'immense political sophistication' (p. 43) and as 'one with truly hegemonic power' (p. 20), able to persuade the majority of the people that its interests are legitimate and represent those of the nation as a whole. He concludes that 'in the battle between the classes it has so far taken all the honours' (p. 43).

A changing proletariat?

Bottomore and Brym (1989) link this increased capitalist power to the contrasting weakness of the working class. In every advanced capitalist society the growth of service employment has brought a decrease in jobs in manufacturing, diminishing the numbers of the factory-based proletariat. As Esping-Andersen puts it: 'the older cornerstone of class theory, the industrial working class, is in rapid decline' (1993, p. 7). This is the kernel of post-industrial theory.

However, neo-Marxists reject the notion of post-industrialism and argue that the working-class is not vanishing but changing in constitution. Because capitalist development is so dynamic, we can expect that the main classes will be in a process of constant transformation. It is suggested that we are currently witnessing the 'remaking' of the working class (Clarke and Critcher, 1985; Blackwell and Seabrook, 1985). Low-paid unskilled service employment may be the basis for this emergent new proletariat. Seabrook (1988) refers to a 'new servant class' which is developing to cater for the needs of the capitalists and the 'yuppie' section of the middle classes: an army of nannies, cleaners, caterers, beauticians, leisure specialists and so forth.

These latest developments can be placed in the context of the much older idea of 'proletarianization', derived originally from Marx's discussion of polarization. In the early twentieth century Klingender applied it to clerical workers. He argued (1935) that the traditional status and skills associated with office work in the nineteenth century were disappearing; the job conditions and pay of clerks were now little different from those of factory workers. Klingender's ideas were criticized by Weberians, notably by David Lockwood in his well-known study *The Black-Coated Worker* (1958). Lockwood showed that there were still many differences in the market situation and job conditions of clerks and factory workers: clerks had better chances of promotion, more fringe benefits, more autonomy at work and were more closely associated with managers. Above all, Lockwood suggested that the status gap between office work and 'dirty' factory jobs was noticeable: clerks considered themselves 'a cut above' manual labourers and factory workers despised clerks as effete and parasitic 'pen-pushers'.

Despite the Weberian critique, the proletarianization thesis has been constantly revived and applied to other groups of workers, such as public-sector employees, whose autonomy and pay was subject to curbs during the Thatcher years. The most famous recent proponent of proletarianization was Harry Braverman (1974) who argued that new technology was being used to degrade the labour process. In his view, computerized office systems had reduced this mental labour to little better than automatic manual work. Braverman anticipated that other white-collar groups would eventually be subject to this downward pull, seeing proletarianization and degradation as inherent tendencies in a capitalist production system. While Weberians have continued to resist this position, many Marxists view lower white-collar groupings as part of the working class.

Many of these disputed jobs are filled by women or, in the case of North America, by young people. This illustrates the interaction of class with other dynamics of inequality. The original Marxist version of the proletariat was often used to refer only to male manual workers. We now accept that the working class has two sexes. But this raises questions about who the working class are which are not easily answered within the Marxian framework which links class to production and wage labour. How do we incorporate women working at home in domestic labour into this class 'map'? The retired? The unemployed? We shall return to this issue, but note that this need not invalidate the idea of a 'new working class'.

Between capital and labour: contradictory class locations

While lower-grade non-manual workers may be viewed as proletarians, there remains the broader problem of how to fit the heterogeneous groupings of the new middle classes into a model of the class structure. What can connect a lawyer, an airline pilot, a disco dancer, a nurse, an academic scientist, a business manager and all the other mix of occupations that fall under the umbrella of 'white-collar work'? At what point exactly does the cut-off point between them and the working class occur?

One solution offered by neo-Marxists is the idea of 'structurally ambiguous' or 'contradictory' class locations (Wright, 1976; Carchedi, 1977; Crompton and Gubbay, 1977). The middle classes are half-way between capitalists and proletariat, sharing some aspects of the class situation of each group. Like the proletariat they need to sell their wage labour, they are barred from ultimate procedures of decision making and they contribute to the process of realizing profits for capital. But they have more autonomy over the day-to-day features of their jobs; as Marx's notion of the surplus class implied, they also help capitalists to secure profits by keeping wage labourers in order. They are at the same time exploited wage-labourers and the allies of capital. The higher up the white-collar hierarchy the more they fall into the latter category.

One account of contradictory locations was provided by Eric Ohlin Wright (1976), currently the most noted neo-Marxist class analyst. Wright's original model involved the identification of three main class positions: the capitalists, the working class and the petite bourgeoisie. Between each pair of these lies a set of contradictory locations: small employers between capitalists and petite bourgeoisie, semi-autonomous employees, such as craftsmen or artists, between the working class and petite bourgeoisie and a range of white-collar employees (managers, technicians and supervisors) between capital and labour. Wright distinguished these groups in terms of how much control they exercised over the production process, with the working class lacking all control, the capitalists all powerful and other groups having varying degrees of control.

Wright's ingenious model has been criticized by some neo-Marxists because it neglects the key issue of exploitation and surplus value. However, in a revised version of his class map Wright faced up to this criticism. In this model class locations are distinguished on the basis of different forms of ownership: of property and, among the propertyless, of organizational assets (positions of power) or of skills and credentials. The 'polar classes' are the bourgeoisie (owning property) and the proletarians (owning nothing). The other groups have varying degrees of organizational assets and skills. For example 'uncredentialled managers' have powerful positions in companies but no qualifications and 'experts' have qualifications but no organizational assets (Wright, 1985). Wright claims that by returning to the concept of ownership he is restoring the notion of exploitation and producing a properly Marxian model. The revised map also has the advantage that public-sector employees can be slotted more easily into it: 'organizational assets' is a term broad enough to include the holding of power in a state bureaucracy. However, this stress on divisions among the propertyless groups and the importance placed on assets have led Savage et al. (1992) to label Wright 'a closet Weberian'.

In fact, as Edgell claims, 'there has always been an overlap between the Marxian and Weberian conceptualizations of class' (Edgell, 1993, p. 36). However, this discussion has attempted to highlight the distinctive features of the neo-Marxist approach. First, there is a much stronger stress on the centrality of the capitalist class; this, for example, distinguishes Wright's model from that of Goldthorpe. Secondly, the focus is still firmly on the two main classes as identified by Marx. The position of the middle classes is defined in relation to these 'polar' groups. Thirdly, the goal of neo-Marxist theorists is to provide an account of the structure of class locations, 'empty slots' in Esping-Andersen's phrase (1993, p. 226). They are not very concerned about how individuals are allocated to them, whereas such a concern is central to the neo-Weberian approach.

The legacy of Weber: flux and fragmentation

Weberian class theory is currently dominant, as its more complex, pluralistic vision appears to fit better with the late twentieth century context and our perceptions of change and fragmentation. Indeed, the title of Erikson's and Goldthorpe's book *A Constant Flux* (1992) seems nicely to encapsulate the paradoxical perceptions of neo-Weberianism: that class inequalities do persist but at the same time class relations are fluid and open. As in the case of Marxism, there are conceptual disagreements among Weberians, which are usefully reviewed by Abercrombie and Urry (1983), Crompton (1993) and Edgell (1993). But here I consider some characteristic focal concerns which unite Weberians: social mobility; fragmentation; and the crucial role of the middle groupings.

Social mobility: an open society?

The Weberian interest in social mobility – that is, the movement of individuals between different classes, might be linked back to Weber's own dictum that sociological explanation should be adequate at the level of meaning as well as causally adequate. Consequently, Weberians are interested in studying actors' perceptions as well as structures. What does class mean in people's lives? Weberian class theorists have produced many useful empirical studies, such as the *Affluent Worker* studies (Goldthorpe et al., 1969) or the Nuffield mobility surveys (Halsey et al., 1980), which deal with class consciousness and with mobility.

While Marxists have neglected the study of social mobility, Weberians argue that it has a strong effect on how people view class divisions. If a class structure is open, class will be invested with less hostile meanings and the pattern of stratification will be seen as legitimate. For example Blau and Duncan, who studied mobility in the United States and claimed to identify high levels of long-range mobility, suggested that 'the stability of American democracy is undoubtedly related to the superior chances of upward mobility in this country' (Blau and Duncan, 1967, p. 439). Moreover, John Goldthorpe (1980) has claimed that mobility has significant effects on class formation and development. For example, he has described the intermediate groupings as classes 'of low classness', because there is so much movement in and out of them; while the relative infrequency of downward mobility in Britain has fostered the development of a 'mature' working class.

There is debate about the extent of mobility in Britain. Glass's early study (1954) suggested that mobility in Britain was mainly short-range (such as from factory work to clerical work) and that the elite was more or less self-recruiting. Goldthorpe's later research found considerable evidence of long-term mobility. However, he argued this could be explained by changes in the occupational structure. Expansion of service-class jobs had necessitated the recruitment of people of lower class origin; in other words the whole occupational structure had taken a kind of upward heave. Goldthorpe (1980) referred to this as 'absolute mobility' but argued that the chances of a member of the working classes reaching high-level jobs had not increased relative to those of people from higher classes. This line of argument has been criticized by Saunders (1990) who imputes it to a reluctance among left-wing British sociologists to accept that class barriers are breaking down. To him absolute rates of mobility are the significant ones and indicate an opening-up of opportunities for people of working-class origin. Whichever argument is accepted, it is clear that many individuals in the post-war decades have experienced mobility and that this contributes to the general affect of class fragmentation.

Fragmentation: the break-up of traditional classes

As we have seen, the notion of fragmentation arises directly from Weber's pluralistic model (p. 53). Dahrendorf's account of class fragmentation was outlined in chapter 1 (p. 22). He suggested that as a result of these processes of class decomposition, the class struggle between the capitalists and the working class had been defused.

Divisions among the working class were also explored by Lockwood (1975), who identified three different groups, each arising from a distinct social 'milieu'. Traditional proletarians were the classic working class described earlier in the chapter. Close working relationships were the basis of a strong sense of class solidarity and a 'them and us' mentality. Traditional deferential workers were associated with agricultural work, retail and small businesses. They had personal links with their employers and they accepted social inequalities as legitimated by the superior talents of those at the top of the hierarchy. Finally Lockwood identified a growing group of privatized or affluent workers, found in the newer consumer industries. Affluent workers were family-orientated, materialistic and individualistic in their attitudes to work. They measured social success in terms of money and access to consumer goods.

Savage et al. have explored fragmentation among the middle class, distinguishing groups on the basis of the different types of groups assets they possessed (property, cultural and organizational). Managerial groups have organizational assets derived from their place in the employment hierarchy. Professional groups have cultural capital (especially credentials) and some property in the form of housing; the self-employed possess capital. Savage et al. suggest that a new political schism is appearing among the middle classes, 'between a public sector, professional, increasingly female middle class . . . opposed to an entrepreneurial, private sector, propertied middle class' (1992, p. 218).

Two influential accounts have been sketched out here, but there are many different ways in which class groupings can be seen as fragmented. Classes are split by region, public or private sector membership, gender or ethnic origin, among other things. But Weberians have been most concerned with occupational differences, as is reflected in their interest in the middle classes.

The middle classes: service and intermediate

Unlike the neo-Marxists, Weberians see the divide between manual and non-manual work as being still significant, while conceding the heterogeneity of white-collar occupations. A particularly influential account of the middle groupings is offered by John Goldthorpe, whose various classificatory systems have been the base for much empirical research. Goldthorpe's latest schema is an eleven-class model (Goldthorpe and Heath, 1992). He suggests, however, that the eleven classes can be aggregated into three: the service class, the intermediate groupings and the working class.

The service class includes managers, administrators and professionals (the wage-earning elite) and also 'large proprietors'. By combining these, Goldthorpe seems to be glossing over the original distinction between the propertied and the propertyless made by Weber. This move negates the importance and distinctiveness of capitalists as the socially dominant group.

However, if proprietors are left aside, most would accept the view that the service groups identified by Goldthorpe are in a position of economic privilege.

Below the service class is the less coherent group of intermediate workers, in which Goldthorpe includes small owners, farmers, foremen, routine non-manual workers or service workers. Many of these groups are seen by Marxists as proletarianized. While Goldthorpe and other neo-Weberians maintain that the intermediate groupings have distinct work and market positions, they acknowledge the amorphous nature of this group and the fact that individuals frequently are moving in and out of these occupational sectors. Evidence from the USA and Canada shows that lower-grade service jobs are characteristically filled by young people and students at the start of their careers who may eventually end up in the service class (Myles et al., 1993; Jacobs, 1993), while in some European societies it is older workers who take these jobs (Esping-Andersen, 1993). The intermediate occupations and the individuals who fill them are a kind of social mish-mash; this can be seen as an important source of fragmentation.

The focus on fragmentation enables the neo-Weberian approach to grapple more successfully than Marxism with the complexities of current employment change. However, Weberians share with Marxism a concentration on employment. Both base their analyses of the class structure on an analysis of occupations, whether these are defined in terms of relations of production or the market. This is an important limitation of traditional class theory, which is also a feature of the functionalist approach.

The functionalist alternative: a meritocratic structure of inequality?

Functionalist class theory has been more influential in America than Britain. Its vision of an inherently orderly and harmonious society is out of line with the British perception of marked social inequalities.

The best-known functionalist account of stratification is that of Kingsley Davis and Wilbert Moore (1945). They viewed classes as inevitable and important for society. Espousing the functionalist premise that if social institutions exist they must have some useful function, they argued that economic inequalities serve to make sure that the best-qualified people get the most important jobs. Pay is related to talent and the amount of investment that individuals devote to gaining qualifications and skills. Davis and Moore posited a basic consensus as to which jobs are the most socially valuable which means that inequalities are accepted as legitimate. The class system, then, helps societies function efficiently and does not promote antagonism.

The Davis and Moore thesis was much criticized by British sociologists, who argued that it under-played the importance of class conflict. Class relations were still antagonistic, often leading to industrial and political unrest, so that class could not simply be viewed as functional for society. They also attacked the idea of a social consensus about the ranking of jobs and rewards. During the 1970s and 1980s the functionalist position was virtually ignored in Britain. However, Saunders (1990) has more recently called for its re-evaluation. He endorses the view that some kind of inequality is inevitable and may be useful to society; for Saunders, the completely egalitarian society is something which 'could only be realized at the price of individual liberty' (p. 67) and, like political conservatives, he comes down on the side of liberty.

Saunders also maintains that British society is essentially meritocratic. Attacking Goldthorpe and others for their interpretation of mobility, he argues (1994) that the existence of long-range upward mobility from the working class and of downward mobility from the service class indicates that people get the jobs they deserve. He suggests that patterns of inequality are not caused by class privilege but by differential distribution of talents to individuals as measured by IQ testing: 'not everybody is born equal . . . In a society which is probably much more meritocratic than is generally believed by sociologists, unequal talents do get reflected in unequal rewards' (1994, p. 109).

Saunders's position is close to that described by Edgell as 'multi-class classlessness' which involves 'the equal opportunity to be unequal' (1993, p. 120). This is the kind of 'classlessness' which John Major aspired to for Britain and which justifies the claim of many Americans that class is not a marked feature of their society. But do contemporary societies really offer equal opportunity? Most British sociologists would argue that the road to equal opportunity is blocked by inequalities of condition. Many individuals are handicapped from the start and not just by 'natural' deficiencies such as those which IQ is claimed to measure.

Education is vital to the arguments of both Davis and Moore and Saunders, as they believe that the education system sorts out which people are equipped for particular jobs. Yet research into education has consistently revealed that members of the privileged classes are able to pass on to their children both material advantages and cultural advantages which give them a headstart in life. Middle-class parents can buy into the expensive private education system which offers smaller classes, better resources and a more firmly academic atmosphere, while working-class children are often handicapped from the start by their parents' lack of resources for educationally useful expenditure and lack of knowledge of the system. Indeed, Durkheim, whose theoretical ideas provided the basis for the functionalist perspective, argued that a meritocratic division of labour could never be achieved while inequalities of inheritance existed: inequalities in 'the external conditions of competition' compromise meritocracy (1964, p. 379).

Table 3.1 summarizes some of the key differences between the three classic positions which have been discussed in this chapter.

All three theoretical camps have one thing in common: the link of class to occupation. While for the purposes of empirical surveys it may be useful to

Table 3.1 Classic Perspectives on Class

	Neo-Marxist	Neo-Weberian	Functionalist
Class divisions arise from:	Relations of production	The operation of the market	Meritocratic processes of job allocation based on shared values
Major classes	Bourgeoisie Working class Other classes, especially the new middle classes and the petite bourgeoisie, acknowledged but seen as less significant	Propertied class Working class (divided by skill levels) Middle class (divided into service class and intermediate class)	Socially ranked occupational strata
View of class conflict	Conflict between classes arises from exploitation	Competition between and within classes	Class relations are harmonistic
Trends in class development	Polarization Proletarianization	Fragmentation	Diminishing inequalities Meritocracy
Key concerns	Class struggle Exploitation	Fragmentation Mobility	Mobility Education and meritocracy

take occupation as an indicator of class, there are dangers in reducing class to employment. For one thing, the problems of assigning particular occupations to different classes mean that many findings about 'class' are no more than artefacts of the particular occupational class schema employed; for example, if clerical workers are assigned to the working class instead of the intermediate class it will drastically alter findings about the extent of mobility (which will be much lower) and the proportion of the populace in the working class (which will be much higher). But more fundamentally, although employment is clearly an important aspect of class experience, it is not co-terminous with it; and making class synonymous with occupation presents great problems in classifying individuals who are marginal to production but are still affected by class dynamics. For example, a young school-leaver from a council estate who has never found employment, a widowed pensioner living in a run-down inner-city area and our previously mentioned young single-parent on benefits are all suffering class fates just as much as a male factory worker. This suggests that class is linked to families and communities as well as individual employment; and that broader processes of economic differentiation, involving the creation, exchange and distribution of wealth, must be considered as well as occupation.

Such an approach would be better able to cope with those groups marginalized by the classic models of class (women, especially housewives, the unemployed, retired people, children, the sick and disabled). Are newer approaches to class more able to handle these deficiencies of classic theory?

New directions: post-industrial classes

Newer approaches to class are inspired by the post-industrial and postmodern frameworks. Post-industrial theory was developed as an explicit criticism of Marxist class theory. Daniel Bell (1973) suggested that technological change would lead to the upgrading of the occupational structure and a shift to professional work and white-collar work. A new technical and professional elite would emerge, replacing the propertied capitalist class, while the majority of the population would be in the middle groupings. In addition, the general prosperity which Bell believed would be brought by post-industrial change would mean that remaining manual workers would experience better working conditions, an increased standard of living and enhanced leisure time. In this way Bell countered Marx's theory of proletarianization and revolution.

Bell's position seemed invalidated by the spread of mass unemployment in the late 1970s. But, as we have seen, a version of Bell's scenario is incorporated into some postmodern visions which assume the growth of highly skilled and professional forms of work as a consequence of the spread of information technology (p. 41). The post-Fordist approach also reflects Bell's optimism in its discussion of an end to routine assembly-line forms of production and their replacement with flexible systems more akin to craft work.

André Gorz is less sanguine about the post-industrial future. In *Farewell to the Working Class* (1982) he suggested that, because of the power of new technologies, there was no longer need for all of a society's population to be employed in order to produce the requisite amount of services and goods, a development which is often referred to as 'jobless growth'. Gorz linked this to the evolution of a new social grouping, the neo-proletariat, made up of unemployed or partly employed people (see p. 38), while the traditional proletariat would dwindle to a small privileged group of full-time workers. Gorz believed these changes had deprived the working class of its traditional role as 'historic actor' in opposition to capital. The changes would also lead to a decentring of work in people's lives. The neo-proletariat could not develop work-related interests, while remaining jobs would be degraded by technological development, a process that would destroy any sense of pride or meaning in work. Personal identification would hinge on new community-based non-work issues such as the environment or gender inequality. Gorz, like others, predicted that the 'new social movements' would replace class-based politics.

What is novel in Gorz's position is the idea of the neo-proletariat. This is an attempt to bring non-employed people into a class model and move beyond the occupational framework of stratification. Confusingly, Gorz calls the 'neo-proletariat' a 'non-class'; this is because he is using class in the orthodox Marxian sense of relationship to production and the neo-proletariat has only a minimal one. We could take the logic one step further and suggest that it could be seen as a class if class is defined in terms of distribution and exchange as well as production.

The concept of the neo-proletariat bears some obvious resemblance to that of the underclass. There are crucial differences, though. Rather than being an additional grouping to the working class, it is seen as gradually replacing it. It is defined structurally (by its exclusion from full-time employment) rather than culturally. There is no association with deviant patterns of behaviour such as scrounging or crime; neo-proletarians are just like everybody else except they are out of a job. Indeed, Gorz at times envisages a potentially positive social role for the neo-proletariat in challenging the materialistic values of a work-based society and promoting new forms of social critique, though he also acknowledges their lack of power and of an organizational base.

Farewell to the Working Class had little to say about the middle class, but in a later account Gorz took up the issue of the service class and offered a conception of a society polarized between a privileged professional elite of 'overworked decision-makers and technicians' (1989, p. 7) and a new 'servile' class of personal servants and others catering to the elite. The servile class, in low-paid and casualized jobs, are contracted out by private service organizations to do the things the busy professionals have no time for. This bleak vision resembles that offered by Seabrook (1988) in his account of a leisure-based capitalist society.

A recent account which steers between extremes of optimism and pessimism is offered by Gøsta Esping-Andersen and colleagues (1993). They studied patterns of employment and mobility in six countries, looking for common trends. They state that dynamics of stratification are currently in flux so that it is difficult to predict outcomes, but conclude that 'a distinctive post-industrial class structure may be emerging' (p. 239).

Esping-Andersen's approach is clearly derived from neo-Weberianism, for

Table 3.2 Esping-Andersen's Post-industrial Classes

The Fordist hierarchy	The post-industrial hierarchy
a) Managers and proprietors	a) Professionals and scientists
b) Non-manual workers (the middle class)	b) Technicians and semi-professionals
c) Skilled working class	c) Skilled service workers
d) Unskilled/semi-skilled workers	d) Service proletariat
	e) Outsider surplus population

Based on G. Esping-Andersen, *Changing Classes*, 1993, pp. 24–5

example in its stress on the service class and on mobility. But he suggests that neither Wright nor Goldthorpe go far enough in 'breaking with theoretical orthodoxy' (p. 226). While both Marxists and Weberians see classes as deriving directly from market or production relations, he argues that the dynamic of class is also determined by a set of crucial social institutions, notably the welfare state, mass education and institutions of collective bargaining. In particular the state has a key role in shaping class development. In this way, Esping-Andersen acknowledges that economic differences are structured by forces other than production. Another advance is the stress given to gender relations. Esping-Andersen suggests that the traditional sexual division of labour is breaking down and that the post-industrial economy has a 'female bias'. Service jobs are being feminized and women have an important role in the new occupational hierarchy, although they are over-represented in its lower ranks.

Esping-Andersen offers a tentative model of a post-industrial class structure which he argues derives directly from post-Fordist as opposed to Fordist work principles. The new post-industrial hierarchy consists of five tiers as shown in table 3.2.

At the top is a professional elite similar to the service class. At the base of the occupational hierarchy a new service proletariat is emerging, such as that identified by Gorz and Seabrook. The case studies indicate that at present there is considerable mobility in and out of unskilled service jobs. But Esping-Andersen suggests that a future polarization may develop based on education, with the elite becoming more closed and self-recruiting and the service proletariat becoming trapped in low-paid work. Outide the four occupational classes, he identifies an unemployed grouping which he calls an 'outsider' or surplus population group (his version of the underclass or neo-proletariat), and which he sees as an important new factor in post-industrial societies. It emerges as a result both of labour market change and of welfare policies which jointly encourage, for example, the formation of groups of long-term unemployed or early-retired people.

Esping-Andersen's theoretical position promises an appr
beyond the reduction of class to occupation and pays much
to gender, race and age. However, the model set out in table
much an occupationally based one, derived from an account
employment structures. Since post-industrial theory is descende
trial theory it replicates many of its assumptions and preoccupa
all, post-industrial theory is still concerned with the logic of produ ... Thus, Bell and Gorz offer accounts which could be criticized for technological determinism, and Esping-Andersen seems to veer in that direction in utilizing the notion of post-Fordism.

Gorz and Esping-Andersen move class analysis on by incorporating an unemployed group into their models. In doing this they acknowledge the crucial social significance of unemployment in contemporary capitalist economies. Pahl has suggested that the cleavage between the work-rich and the work-poor is now the most important form of social division (Pahl, 1984; Wallace and Pahl, 1986). In this way post-industrial theorists have acknowledged some important aspects of change, but it could be argued that their rethinking of class is still insufficient. Can post-modernism offer more radical reformulations?

New directions: postmodern possibilities

As suggested in chapter 2, class was not a central concern within original postmodern theory, with its interest in cultural change. However, sociologists concerned to develop a 'sociology of postmodernism' have started to explore the issue of social divisions. As we have seen, postmodernism is a broad church with divergent strands. We can distinguish three tendencies, however:

1. Some theorists attempt to combine a postmodern account of culture with traditional Marxist class theory.
2. Others suggest that postmodern culture is bringing an end to class inequalities.
3. A third group argue that class is still relevant but that it should be conceptualized in terms of consumption more than production.

Jameson (1991) is one of the former, as is Harvey (1989). Both combine an account of postmodern cultural development with analysis of a globalizing capitalism. For Jameson the significant features of the new phase of capitalist development are the power of transnational corporations and the development of a co-ordinated world market. Harvey and Jameson display the Marxist concern with the changing nature of the capitalist ruling class and lend support to the arguments of Bottomore and Brym (1989) that capitalist power has been greatly strengthened in recent decades. However, neither has much to say about other class groupings. Harvey seems to assume 'business as usual';

Jameson justifies his vagueness by the idea that we are still in the 'trough' between two capitalist epochs and cannot predict class outcomes:

> The postmodern may well . . . be little more than a transitional period between two stages of capitalism, in which the earlier forms of the economic are in the process of being restructured on a global scale . . . That a new international proletariat (taking forms we cannot yet imagine) will re-emerge from this convulsive upheaval it needs no prophet to predict. (1991, p. 417)

While this may be true, it as of little help in developing an account of the contemporary class dynamic.

At the opposite extreme Beck (1992) and Crook et al. (1992) both suggest that postmodern change is inexorably bringing an end to class and other sorts of inequality. Beck believes that old class communities are breaking down and class ties weakening as a result of what he calls 'a social surge of individualization' (p. 87). He envisages the future as an 'individualized society of employees' (p. 99). It should be noted that Beck's account was derived from his study of European societies, primarily West Germany, a society in which working-class affluence was a well-established fact up to the period of German reunification. Beck actually makes an exception of Britain, of which he says:

> Class membership is very apparent in everyday life and remains the object of consciousness and identification. It is evident in speech . . . in the sharp class divisions between residential areas . . . in types of education, in clothing and in everything that can be included under the concept of 'lifestyle'. (1992, p. 102)

Crook et al. (1992) offer a similar account, drawing on the Australasian context; they predict a decline in the social significance of class, gender and ethnicity as society becomes more individualized and the media play more part in influencing people to identify with particular 'symbolically simulated communities' (p. 111) such as various consumer groups. In stark contrast to Jameson, they suggest that the service class has now replaced the capitalist class as the elite; but they see membership of the service class as so fluid 'that the very existence of a class system will have to be called in question' (p. 118). The future for all forms of stratification they see as 'fluid and apparently chaotic' (p. 124).

While Beck and Crook et al. present these arguments as a general theory of change (a position at odds with some postmodernists' insistence on local narratives), we could alternatively read these as accounts of particular societies where fragmentation and individualization have progressed further than is the case in Britain. But their claims are subject to the criticism that can be aimed at all versions of classlessness: that is, the continuing evidence, both quantitative and qualitative, of substantial economic inequalities within most capitalist societies (Edgell, 1993) and the lack of substantial proof that collective identification is waning. At this stage, the postmodern version of classlessness cannot be seen as more than a vision of a possible future.

These forms of postmodernism offer two scenarios: one in which nothing very much has changed and one in which everything is changing. An intermediate position affirms the reality of capitalist inequality but offers a new reading of its nature. In this view consumption rather than production becomes the key aspect of class formation. Lyon states 'if postmodernity means anything, it means the consumer society' (1994, p. 68), and speaks of the new world of 'rock videos, theme parks and shopping malls' (p. 50). Some postmodernists see class communities dissolving in the face of consumerized lifestyles. Others suggest that consumption-based cleavages, based for example on housing tenure, are replacing classes (Saunders, 1984). The most sophisticated approach links consumption to other aspects of class formation and reproduction.

Zygmunt Bauman, in one of most powerful accounts of a 'postmodern society', argues that its key feature is that capital has emancipated itself to a considerable extent from labour, an idea also put forward by some Marxists, such as Sivanandan (1990). The core relation between capital and the other social classes has changed; capital now engages labour in the role of consumers rather than producers. (Bauman, 1992, p. 111). As a result of these developments, a key new social group has come into being which Bauman here calls the 'new poor' (another version of the underclass etc.). This group, characterized by unemployment, dependency and poverty, is not to be seen as part of the labour reserve but as *permanently displaced*. However, because of people's increasing dependency on the market, the social unrest which one might expect to develop in such circumstances does not manifest itself; seduced by the glamour of the new consumerism, most people conform. Capital, Bauman believes, has made use of the 'pleasure principle' to win the battle for control of production, thereby greatly reinforcing its position of social dominance. He argues, as has Dahrendorf (1987), that the state may be forced to take repressive measures to keep the losers, 'the new poor', in order: increasing policing and surveillance, the loss of citizen rights. Seduction and repression become the twin axes of class domination.

Bauman's account clearly owes much to Marxism in its stress on an all-powerful capitalist class and a manipulated working class. Others have used the consumption scenario in a less pessimistic way. Turner (1988) suggests that the expansion of mass culture and consumerism, accompanied by the interweaving of 'high' and 'popular' cultural styles that typifies postmodern culture, may erode traditional status hierarchies, bringing a cultural democratization even if economic inequalities endure. Others draw on the influential work of Bourdieu (1986) on taste and status distinctions to explore the role of consumption as an aspect of class. They discern groups sharing a common 'habitus' or life-world with a distinctive set of practices, attitudes and tastes which individuals use to shape their perception of social space. For example, Savage et al. (1992) use this framework to distinguish a number of different consumer groupings within the 'new middle classes'. Managers and bureaucrats share an old-fashioned, middle-of-the road pattern of consumption, which can be distinguished from that of public-sector professionals, who favour more intellectual pursuits, and a high-minded health-conscious lifestyle, such as that often satirized by reference to the *Guardian* reader. (The former group, we can assume, would choose *The Times* or *Telegraph*). The trend-setting group, however, are the upwardly mobile 'yuppie' young private-sector professionals who exemplify the postmodern spirit with its mix of high and low culture (opera *and* rap music, visits to the theatre *and* to theme parks) and its pursuit of expensive pleasures of all kinds.

Consumption patterns, then, can be seen either as equalizing or divisive; but whichever view is held, it is suggested that consumption is becoming more important in people's self-identification. Such consumption groups can be seen as recent manifestations of status, as described by Weber. Turner (1988) argues that in contemporary capitalist societies status is more politically and socially crucial than class (a view quite in line with Weber's discussion of status groups). while stressing that it is necessary to analyse contemporary societies in terms of both status *and* class.

The stress on consumption as an aspect of class is to be welcomed in line with my argument that versions of class limited to occupation are too narrow. But there is a danger of going too far in the other direction and ignoring production altogether. There is as yet little empirical *proof* of the assertion that consumption and consumption identities are more important to people than employment and work identities. This remains to be explored.

Postmodern thinking about class raises some interesting questions, but so far the answers are sketchy. There is a need for careful empirical exploration to justify the claims that are being made. Such research might centre on the issue of identity, since this is crucial to the ideas of the non-Marxist postmodernists.

Class, identity and action

Traditional class theory raised this issue in terms of class consciousness, which has long been a contentious concept. Marx argued that consciousness rises directly from social being: that is, that material experiences, such as that of exploitation, are the basis of class identification. But Marx also claimed that those who control the means of production also control the production of ideas in society. From this derives the notion of the dominant ideology by which the capitalists legitimate their own social domination and which produces a 'false consciousness' in the proletariat that blocks an awareness of their true class situation. The idea of false consciousness has been considered crude by later Marxists, who have employed the alternative notion of a 'contradictory' consciousness, where elements from people's direct experience combine with ideas drawn from media and other vehicles of dominant thinking, to produce an often inconsistent package of ideas about society (Mann, 1970).

Weberians reject these ideas, arguing that there is no necessary one-way causal link between material experience, consciousness and action. Consciousness can be influenced by a whole range of factors, not just material conditions. For Weberians, class consciousness has to be approached through empirical research into people's ideas and images of class. However, such research is difficult to conduct and its findings are often hard to interpret. For example, twenty years after Goldthorpe et al. (1969) had surveyed Luton workers and concluded that their attitudes to work were instrumental, individualistic and economistic, Devine revisited the affluent workers' community and found that a more ethnographic approach revealed a more complex mix of attitudes (1992).

Marshall et al. (1988) also argue that working-class culture displays both collectivist and individualistic, instrumental and solidaristic values, and has always done so. Their national survey of class in Britain in the 1980s suggests that people show a clear awareness of class inequalities and of their own class positions. The British Social Attitude surveys of recent years have also demonstrated a consistent sense of class among respondents. However, sometimes these findings are influenced by the questions that are asked, for example if people are presented with a list of fixed choices of class positions to select from. Scase argues that sociologists often have to work very hard to get their informants to formulate a class identification and offer them 'considerable assistance' (Scase, 1992, p. 79). Where a more open-ended approach is employed, the results are likely to be more ambiguous and complex. Lash (1984) interviewed working people in America and found that they came up with a bewildering variety of images of class. A small survey of working people carried out in the early 1990s in the north-east of England, a region where traditional class loyalties and ties are believed still to be stronger than in southern England, found that a majority of respondents did not identify themselves as belonging to any particular class (Bradley, 1994).

Postmodernists approach this question using the concept of identity rather than consciousness, the latter term being associated with discredited 'grand narratives'. They suggest that class as traditionally defined is no longer a potent source of identity. As the old stable communities based around class and occupation break up, 'collective sources of membership' which promoted social identification are displaced (Mercer, 1990, p. 50). Complexities surrounding changing patterns of work, the changing gender composition of employment and the rise in unemployment add to the confusion around class. It is suggested that consumer identities may be replacing class identities, especially in view of the importance of media and fashion in most people's lives (Featherstone, 1991).

As Parmar puts it, 'identities are not fixed but always in a state of flux' (1990, p. 101). Postmodernists stress that identities are not determined by a single aspect of 'social being' such as class but are made up of a multitude of elements. In such a view, individuals are perpetually adapting their identities in line with personal choice. Crook et al. (1992) explore this possibility through their idea of 'symbolic communities': numerous foci for belonging and identification are provided by the experience of modern living, especially through the media. Some of these may provide an enduring source of social identification (lesbianism or gayness, for example). Others are relatively transient. They suggest that some such 'simulated symbolic communities' might develop around worthy causes such as peace or the environment: 'they also form on such diverse unifying themes as soccer, feminism, *Neighbours*, retirement, sociology, Placido Domingo, being gay, socialism, monarchism, *Star Trek* and astrology' (Crook et al., 1992, p. 133).

These arguments are persuasive in stressing the complexity of processes of social identification. However, the accounts may go too far in dismissing class as a source of identification. It was suggested in chapter 1 that class is now a passive rather than an active identity. We could go further and say that at the moment class identities are submerged identities, pushed out of sight by others which jostle more urgently for public attention. Moreover, people are often reluctant to talk in class terms in a society in which classlessness, though not attained, is seen as the desired ideal. Class becomes a stigmatized or spoiled identity, rather than one which people acknowledge with pride (Bradley, 1994).

While I was writing this book in 1994 the campaign for the Labour leadership was being conducted and the class background of the two main contenders became an issue. Tony Blair, with a middle-class public-school Oxbridge background, was seen as lacking in personality but more likely to appeal to electors who were not convinced Labour supporters. John Prescott, openly working-class in background and style, had support from rank-and-file union members. But his trade union links and working-class self-presentation were considered a potential handicap in winning over the nation as a whole. The class background of the third candidate, Margaret Beckett, was, strangely, never referred to; her class identity was completely submerged by the fact that she was a woman!

This small example shows how class still enters into people's calculations and informs the judgements they make of people. But these class attributions are largely negative. For a passive stigmatized identity to be transformed into an active positive one, some form of political activity is usually needed. Class has been the loser in the identity politics of the post-war decades. While labour movement institutions such as the Labour party or the unions were originally formed to promote working-class interests, they have been under attack for the narrowness of their constituencies (white, working-class, skilled male workers); subsequently they have attempted to broaden their appeal by shedding their class associations. Class, thus, has lost its voice. No movements have evolved to promote 'class pride' analogous to Black Power, Gay Pride or the Women's Liberation Movement.

Yet elements of working-class identification still emerge within communities or through industrial struggles. One example is the Miners' Wives Support Groups which evolved during the coal dispute of 1984–5. Suspicious of feminism which they saw as a middle-class movement, the miners' wives nevertheless built a campaign on a specific identification of class and gender interests, reflected in their campaign anthem:

> United by the struggle, united by the past,
> Here we go, here we go, we're the women of the working class!

Class meanings are not yet extinct; and they are more easily judged to be so by people in comfortable positions. Mark Hudson describes tellingly the shock of a middle-class encounter with a traditional working-class community:

> If you had wondered if terms like 'middle class' and working class' still had any meaning, or if such a thing as 'working-class culture' could still be said to exist, you were immediately disabused of your illusions. The moment you arrived in East Durham, you were *in it* – up to your neck. In East Durham, it often seemed that there *was* nothing else. And . . . if it made you feel uneasy, if you couldn't wait to get away from it, that meant you were middle class. (Hudson, 1994, p. 73)

Interacting dynamics: class, gender, ethnicity and age

The miners' wives referred to above were fighting in support of their menfolk against pit closures in order to maintain traditional sources of employment for their husbands and sons; but they also realized that as women in the mining communities they had in the past been excluded from politics and confined to domestic roles. The women experienced 'divided loyalties' in Anne Phillips's phrase (1987), demonstrating how class must be viewed as in interaction with other dynamics of inequality.

Gender

Gender has historically served to divide the working class. In the nineteenth century, capitalist employers set women and men in competition for jobs, whether as a conscious strategy or as a by-product of the process of surplus accumulation. Trade unions attempted to keep women out of jobs seen as 'men's work'. The drive to push women from work was backed by the campaign for a 'family wage' which would enable a man to maintain a non-employed wife and children at home. Although the family wage remained an ideal rather than a reality, the result was the stereotyping of women as housewives and their marginalization in class-based politics.

Classes are not only divided by gender: they are 'gendered' in the sense that gender is integral to processes of class formation, action and identification. While the stereotypical image of the working class is of male workers, women have had a crucial role to play in the reproduction of working-class cultures through their position in the family and community. They have born the brunt of working-class poverty, constituting the bulk of workhouse inhabitants and of welfare claimants. In times of long-term unemployment women have to prop up their unemployed menfolk and keep the family going through tight household management along with their own subsistence activities. If the working class exists as a set of distinct communities, rather than as an aggregate of wage-earning individuals, it is largely through women's efforts. In *Goliath* Beatrix Campbell (1993) suggests that depressed unemployed communities in Britain are maintained largely through the struggles of women, as men give way to despair, apathy, crime or violence. While so many male working-class jobs in Europe and America have disappeared in the last decades, on a worldwide basis the globalization of capital has depended crucially on manipulation of low-paid women as new sources of labour. Mitter (1986) argues that a new international division of labour has created a 'third world proletariat' of female assembly workers, garment-makers and others. Such women work in sweated conditions, not only in the 'Third World' countries of Latin America, South East Asia and the Indian subcontinent but also in the inner cities of the 'First World'.

At the top of the class hierarchy women appear more marginalized: there are conspicuously few women in company boardrooms. But women have a crucial social role in the 'inner circle' in cementing social networks and maintaining elite cohesion through intermarriage with other members of the entrepreneurial class, as well as passing on dominant values to their families. Middleton (1988) has argued that women's earnings and other financial contributions (such as marriage payments) were very important in the original processes of capital accumulation as capitalist industrialism developed. Women still provide backing for the economic and social reproduction of capital.

It is, however, in the new middle classes that gender is most clearly an issue, witnessed in the numerical dominance of women in lower-grade non-manual work. In their study of clerical workers, Crompton and Jones (1984) argued that if a 'white-collar proletariat' did exist it consisted of women; men had profited from the marked gender segregation in offices to escape the effects of degradation and were able to monopolize the career jobs. Braverman

(1974) pointed out that the typical American working-class couple consisted of a male factory worker and a female clerk. This gendering of white-collar work adds to the general confusion surrounding the middle-class groupings and contributes to the weakness of their sense of class identification. This analysis is taken a stage further in Esping-Andersen's account of the feminized nature of the emerging post-industrial service classes.

Women also are an important element in the outsider or labour surplus class. Although it would not be correct to talk of a 'female underclass', women are vulnerable to dependency on benefits as single mothers, as impoverished pensioners, as low-paid workers and as wives of unemployed men (Morris, 1994). We can see that gender is significantly involved in the way the new post-industrial capitalist economies are developing, both at national and global level, and thus in processes of class recomposition.

'Race' and ethnicity

'Race' and ethnicity also act as a source of division within classes, where, for example, black and white workers are in competition for jobs. A prime example is America. The relative political and industrial weakness of the American working class can be linked to the presence of a large minority population. Black African Americans are at the bottom of the employment hierarchy, therefore allowing white working people to see themselves as in a position of relative privilege. Race struggles and antagonisms have persistently preoccupied Americans and diverted working people from issues of class injustice (see chapter 7).

But like gender, race contributes to processes of class formation in a more integral way. The exploitation of colonial plunder and the labour of colonial slave populations made a central contribution to the emergence of capitalist industrial production. Since then, there has been extensive movement of both labour and production around the globe to help capitalists increase their profits, develop new markets and appease indigenous working classes. Processes of international migration have been crucial to the development of capitalist economies.

Migrants often find themselves in a very weak position when they arrive in a new country. Thus minority groups, especially those of colour, are generally over-represented in the working class in European societies. For example, Asian refugees to Britain from Kenya and Uganda, who were highly educated and held good professional or entrepreneurial jobs in Africa, had difficulty finding employment commensurate with their qualifications and former status: some were forced to accept unskilled jobs. In the 1990s refugees from trouble spots in Africa and the Middle East, if they manage to gain entry to European countries, are likely to find themselves moving straight into the outsider class; people with a background of middle-class affluence may join displaced peasants as recruits to the 'new poor' struggling to build a new life on welfare payments.

Although in time of recession ethnic minority members experience a greater threat of unemployment, they are often used to supplement the indigenous working class when labour is short. Characteristically they fill the worst, low-status 'dirty' jobs rejected by the native populace. The successful post-war West German economy depended greatly on the employment of 'guest-workers' from Turkey, southern Italy and elsewhere, while Britain and France have employed immigrants from their former colonies in the West Indies, Asia and North Africa. Such employment practices shape the future development of the working class and its modes of action. For example, the extensive recruitment of Afro-Caribbean workers into public-sector jobs in transport and the health service has probably contributed both to low pay in those areas and to the growth of public-sector militancy. Better-paid jobs remain the preserve of white workers and influence the values of the core working-class communities. Labour, therefore, is not an ethnically neutral category. The working class is characteristically composed of ethnically distinct layers, shaped by the particular patterns of migration in each country.

It is very hard for minority members, especially those of colour, to join the capitalist elite (see chapter 5). However, self-employment is an option for those who face racism in the labour market and is a way out of the working class for Asian men in Britain. By contrast, Afro-Caribbeans are more prone to join the ranks of the labour surplus class. Indeed, in America the 'underclass' is specifically associated with the African American populace along with increasing numbers of young males of Latin American origin (see chapter 7).

While no minority group in Britain appears as yet to have become marginalized to such an extent as in America, post-industrial change is likely to affect European minorities adversely. They may well continue their slide into the outsider group, especially young males. Minority women may find a place in the emerging service proletariat. Increasing experience of racism and violence may impel minority members to look for sheltered employment within their own communities. The working class and the self-employed class are likely to be fragmented further on ethnic lines.

Age

Age has also been fundamental to capitalist development. Young people are particularly vulnerable to the worst forms of capitalist exploitation. Many of the workers in the first factories in Britain were children, especially unprotected pauper apprentices. In industrializing America and Japan, young girls from rural areas were a favoured source of labour for the cotton mills. Some were literally kidnapped by labour contractors or sold by their parents into near-slavery, locked into sleeping quarters at night. As capitalism matured and children gained some protection through state legislation and compulsory education, the cheapness of young people's labour continued to be exploited through the apprenticeship system. In periods of recession, cheap young workers often found themselves laid off as soon as they had 'served their time' and become eligible for the adult wage. Globalizing capital continues to make use of child labour and the labour of young rural women in many developing countries; such young people can be seen as a core component of the 'Third World Proletariat'. Nor are First World employers adverse to using child labour if the occasion arises. Capitalist agriculture has been notorious for its use of 'gangs' often including young people illegally employed in very poor conditions, while increasing numbers of children work in British factories and shops.

The best and most secure jobs at all levels of the class structure are occupied by middle-aged people; while old people whose skills are considered redundant are pushed out to join young people in the labour surplus class and risk dependency on the state. Both face ageist prejudices on the part of employers and the vested interests of the middle-aged who have worked themselves into stable and power-holding positions. This trend looks set to continue as post-industrial change proceeds.

Young people are currently at the sharp end of the changing class dynamic. The cultural changes discerned by postmodernists manifest themselves among young people rather than the older age groups. Young people are especially responsive to media and fashion changes. They have often formed distinctive subcultures which signify their distance both from wider society and their own parents. For this reason, their awareness of class is often less developed. Lash (1990) argues that the traditional working class, as it became affluent, provided its young people with the means to become consumers; the adolescent youth cultures that developed subsequently undermined traditional working-class values. The growth of youth unemployment contributed to this process of class dissolution. Willis et al. (1990) argue that unemployment meant that young working-class people were no longer socialized by their workmates and through trade union membership into working-class values and practices. According to Hollands (1990) YTS schemes often train young people to accept individualistic and aspirational values that further undermine potential class collectivism. For all these reasons the decline of class awareness is likely to affect young people most fully. Cultural and consumer identities may well fill the void. Studies show that young people are especially likely to be members of the new social movements (Crook et al., 1992); for example, young 'New Age' travellers in Britain have spearheaded the environmental direct action movement.

Yet, ironically, young people are far from free of class constraints. Many are doomed to poverty and unemployment. Tahlin argues that in Sweden 'age is the most important determinant of overall class transitions' (Tahlin, 1993, p. 95). Despite their involvement with postmodern cultural change, many young people in post-industrial societies are losing out.

Summary and conclusions

This chapter has surveyed the long and chequered history of class theory. There is still considerable support for classic class theories. The Marxist tradition remains useful for its insistence on the need to study the evolving capitalist class and its relationship with working people, especially in terms of the globalization of capitalist production. Marxists, however, pay insufficient attention to other social groupings. The insights of the Weberian tradition, with its stress on social mobility and social fragmentation within broad class groupings, are needed here. This leads to an appreciation of the fluidity of the class dynamic, although the functionalist view of capitalist industrial societies as open and meritocratic must be questioned.

However, classic approaches have two important limitations. First, their view of class in terms of production or occupation is too narrow. Groups who are not in employment are thus marginalized, although they are still subject to the forces of economic differentiation. Secondly, despite recent acknowledgement that class coexists with other forms of inequality such as gender, classic theory still tends to marginalize them.

Post-industrial and postmodern theory go some way to confronting these deficits. Post-industrial theories highlight the existence of the non-employed group and make moves to identifying it as a separate class. with its own unique economic situation, rather than as a segment within the working class. While the term 'underclass' is most popularly used for this group, the moral stigmatization associated with it makes its usage problematic; alternatives such as Esping-Andersen's 'outsider population' might be preferred. Here I use the term labour surplus class.

Post-industrialism, however, bears the traces of the frameworks of industrialism and capitalism from which it evolved. It remains economistic and inclined to slip into an occupational definition of class. Postmodernism promises a more flexible approach, which could move the analysis of class to a broader framework and deal with its relation to other aspects of inequality. I have argued here that the promise has not yet been fulfilled. Some postmodern accounts of class reinvent older ideas of embourgeoisement and classlessness or alternatively reassert the centrality of the changing labour/capital relationship in a global context. Others have focused on consumption as increasingly central to economic relationships. This promising new direction as yet lacks sufficient empirical backing. There is a tendency simply to *assume* that class awareness is vanishing. Research needs to be done to ascertain exactly how class meanings and identities relate to other aspects of social identification.

It has proved very difficult to conduct credible sociological research into class without using some kind of occupational-based schema to categorize individuals in the study. Such schemes enable sociologists to study factors such as mobility using sophisticated statistical techniques. It is unlikely that such impressive research tools will be abandoned, but there is need for redefinition of categories to include the excluded sections of the population. It is worth endorsing Marshall's proposal (1988), that study of class should take a more qualitative turn, which could better uncover class meanings.

The final message of this chapter is that neither class, as a set of lived economic relationships, nor class analysis, as a set of social categories, is dead. But there must be recognition of how class relations are shaped by other forms of inequality. As Jonathan Rutherford argues:

> Class is still a conceptual necessity for understanding the dynamics of society, but the restructuring of its processes and the decline of old class identities and cultures has coincided with a proliferation and dispersal of other political and social antagonisms. (1990, p. 12)

Further Reading

The best and most comprehensive introductory text on class at the time of writing is Rosemary Crompton, *Class and Stratification* (Polity, 1993). Also useful are Richard Scase, *Class* (Open University, 1992) and Stephen Edgell, *Class* (Routledge, 1993). Lydia Morris, *Dangerous Classes* (Routledge, 1994) provides an excellent survey of the underclass debate, and John Scott, *Who Rules Britain?* (Polity, 1991) admirably covers debates on the 'ruling class'. Two more difficult texts which are worth looking at on class and change are André Gorz, *Farewell to the Working Class* (Pluto, 1982) and Gøsta Esping-Andersen (ed.), *Changing Classes* (Sage, 1993, opening chapter).

4

Gender: Rethinking Patriarchy

Among the Hamar people of Ethiopia, a girl child is referred to as a 'guest' while a boy child is considered to be a 'person'. This is because the girl will eventually leave the parental home and become the property of her husband, while the male may establish his own household; the girl is considered on loan to her parents until she goes to the home of the man to whom she really belongs. This conceptualization inverts the English folk-saying:

> A daughter's a daughter for all of her life,
> A son's a son till he gets him a wife.

But both show the strength of ideas of gender difference and demonstrate that historically women have been seen as other people's property.

If class as a topic has recently become 'non grata' (Barrett, 1992, p. 216), the opposite is true of gender. Throughout the 1980s and 1990s gender has been a topic of burning interest both popular and sociological. The rise of second-wave feminism in the late 1970s forced the issue of inequalities between women and men into the arenas of world politics. Feminism was warmly embraced by women within the academic world who felt that gender issues were ignored or marginalized within their own disciplines. The study of gender has since become an important part of the curriculum in most disciplines within the arts and social sciences. During the 1980s, particularly in North America, the study of gender has also become the basis of the new disciplinary frameworks of women's studies and gender studies. A flood of publications on every aspect of gendered experience has subsequently poured from the academy, along with more popularly targeted texts from within the activist strand of the feminist movement. Books such as Betty Friedan's *The*

Feminine Mystique and Germaine Greer's *The Female Eunuch* became best-sellers and led many non-academic women to begin questioning their own lives and relationships.

Along with this explosion of feminist ideas and texts and the assertion of gender as a crucial category for social analysis (J. W. Scott, 1988), the lived relationships of gender have been in a state of flux during the equivalent period. Changes which have been under way since the Second World War seemed to take off in a vertiginous fashion in the 1980s. Transformations in the economy hastened the advance of women into the labour market, to such an extent that many have spoken of the 'feminization of the labour force' (Jenson et al., 1988; Esping-Andersen, 1993), while the decline of manufacturing led to widespread male unemployment. Divorce rates steadily increased and the number of single-headed families grew, along with the numbers of people living alone; in Britain between 1971 and 1991 the proportion of families headed by a lone parent rose from 8 to 19 per cent and 11 per cent of people now live in single-person households. Continued innovations in the field of contraception, the freer availability of abortion and new reproductive technologies made it easier for women (and men) both to plan their reproductive life more securely and to explore more liberated patterns of sexuality. The vigorous gay and lesbian movement asserted the rights of people to develop different forms of sexuality and sexual practices and to display their sexuality openly without fear of retribution (although such rights have not yet been fully achieved). Such changes challenged the conventional arrangements between women and men.

The advances made by women during these decades led in the mid 1980s to the assertion in some quarters (notably popular journalism) that sexual equality had been gained and that the industrial world was now in a 'post-feminist' state. Young women, in particular, were purported to hold this view. The singer Madonna was taken as an emblem of the new generation, offering a public representation of female power and wealth alongside untramelled and polymorphous sexuality. At the same time a male 'backlash' (Faludi, 1992; Walby, 1993) developed, asserting that 'it had all gone too far'; disgruntled men started banding together in groups to call for 'men's lib' or 'father's rights' or to explore ways of 'getting back in touch' with masculine identity, some through following the back-to-nature prescriptions of Robert Bly. The backlash was supported by conservatives, both male and female, calling for a reassertion of 'traditional' family values and the return of women to maternal responsibility. There were attacks on liberal policies on contraception and abortion, strengthened by strands of fundamentalism in world religious movements.

Despite the post-feminist claims, the 1990s have demonstrated that gender issues and conflicts remain firmly on the agenda. The moral panic over young women and single motherhood; the worries about parenting and teenage delinquency; the spate of cases involving sexual harrassment; the legal wrangles over rape, especially the controversial idea of 'date rape'; the concerns about older and post-menopausal women using new fertilization techniques: these very different issues show that the battle over gender is as fierce as ever. We can feel reasonably confident that in the early twenty-first century, gender, both as a category of social enquiry and as sets of lived relationships, will still occupy centre stage.

I speak of gender in this chapter in reference to lived relationships between men and women through which sexual differences and ideas about sexual differences are constructed. Some of these differences, which relate to the sexual division of labour both in and outside the home, are economic: women have lesser access to and control of shares of social wealth. But gender differences are not only rooted in the economy; in this they differ from the class relations discussed in the previous chapter. Gender relations are pervasive and operate at every level of social life. For example, girls and boys have different patterns of play and women's and men's leisure activities are differentiated; women are under-represented, or relegated to specific roles defined as suitable for them, within most areas of the public sphere; sexual practices and orientations take different meanings for women and for men; and women and men figure differently in cultural representations of various kinds, from classical paintings to advertisements, from television dramas to the lyrics of rap songs. Every aspect of our individual histories is subtly affected by the fact of being male or female.

There is a longstanding dilemma relating to the non-economic aspects of gender differentiation, as to whether such differences actually constitute inequalities. Are women and men, perhaps, different but equal? Do not women *choose* different leisure activities, different ways of constructing themselves as sexual beings? Against this position, feminists argue that such differences *do* constitute inequalities, because they occur in the context of discrepancies in power between the sexes. Male social dominance means that men are able to impose their definitions and evaluations upon the social world. Thus, men tell women how they should be; and, as Ortner (1974) has argued, what men do is more highly valued than what women do. Male power is also manifested in the social division of labour, with men assuming positions of authority and using them to control women's labour. Differences in economic power also affect the more cultural aspects of gender difference. For example, women's lower earning-power helps to explain differences in leisure activities; women are less able to afford expensive leisure activities and are less likely to have a car for transport to leisure venues.

It was conventional in 1970s versions of feminism to make a distinction between *gender*, as relating to the socially constructed aspects of sexual difference outlined above, and *sex*, relating to the biological identity as male or female with which (most) individuals are born. Biological reproductive differences constituted a kind of fixed substratum on which variable social constructs of gender developed. Nowadays, however, this clear distinction is considered less tenable (Butler, 1990). Bodily differences are bound up with social identities of gender to such an extent that we can hardly separate them; and biological physical differences are themselves regarded as partly socially constructed and historically variable. Reproductive experiences, for example, are quite different for women in Britain today from those of women in pre-industrial societies. Moreover, the new developments in embryo technology and fertilization throw all our longstanding assumptions about 'natural' biological phenomena such as kinship and parenthood into question (Strathern, 1993). Sex is not fixed. I use gender broadly, then, to cover both these aspects of male/female relationships.

This chapter explores ways in which differences of gender have been conceptualized, beginning with the classic contributions which derived from the feminist movements of the nineteenth and twentieth centuries, before moving on to newer approaches influenced by postmodernist and post-structuralist ideas.

Classic feminist standpoints

While I am linking the theorization of gender to the feminist movement which formed in the mid-nineteenth century, that does not mean that people ignored gender differences up to that time. People have written about differences between women and men throughout recorded history. In literature relations between the sexes were often portrayed as conflictual, from Chaucer's wife of Bath seeing off her five husbands, to the playful sparring of the heroes and heroines of Shakespeare's comedies, to the stylized sexual predation portrayed in Jacobean tragedy or, very differently, in Restoration comedy. A prevailing attitude, however, within the history of Western culture was that gender differences were god-given ('male and female created he them') and thus 'natural'. As societies secularized and religious backing for this view waned, science took over; nineteenth-century biological, medical and psychological sciences again proclaimed that gender differences were innate. The sexual division of labour was said to reflect differences in aptitudes and personality derived ultimately from reproductive function. Michel Foucault describes the processes of 'hysterization' of Victorian women, a 'thorough medicalization of their bodies and their sex' (Foucault, 1979, p. 146), whereby the womb was symbolically extended to encompass the whole female being which was subsequently pathologized. Women were seen as vulnerable, neurotic and inherently frail because of their subjection to the reproductive phases of puberty, menstruation, pregnancy, childbirth and menopause. These weaknesses were believed to make them unfit for non-domestic work and for public life; where they stepped out of their prescribed social roles their biological functions might be jeopardized. Some American doctors seriously believed that the education of young women would cause their breasts to shrink and wombs to atrophy (Ehrenreich and English, 1979). These feminine weaknesses were also thought to make women more vulnerable than men to insanity (Showalter, 1987).

Religion and science provided backing for the 'traditional' conservative view, that gender differences are natural and innate and consequently inequality is justifiable. But throughout history individual women and men have contested that view and argued for justice for women. For example, there were impassioned pamphlets written by women in the seventeenth century protesting against their treatment by men and pointing out the contributions made by women to the social good (Kimmel, 1987). However, it was the Enlightenment which, as in the case of class analysis, provided the spur to sustained exploration of gender relations.

It is now common for postmodern feminists to criticize the grand narratives of Enlightenment liberalism for their gender-blindness (J. W. Scott, 1988; Phillips, 1992). Yet, as Randall (1982) points out, the liberal framework was crucial to the evolution of the feminist critique in its assertion of individual freedom and civic rights. Feminists utilized the claims abut the 'rights of man' to call for the rights of women, as did Mary Wollstonecraft in *A Vindication of the Rights of Woman* published in 1792. The classic liberal feminists, Wollstonecraft, John Stuart Mill and Harriet Taylor, were able to use the idea of the rational human agent to attack the view that differentiated gender behaviour was natural. Wollstonecraft, for example, argued that the seemingly 'natural' frivolous, emotional and childish personalities, which she considered typical among women of her class, were a product of the characteristic forms of upbringing of young women. If girls' education was reformed they could be brought up to be rational and useful citizens like their brothers. Liberalism, then, allowed feminists to develop ideas about the social construction of gender with which to counter the biological essentialist position.

Barbara Taylor's study *Eve and the New Jerusalem* (1983) has shown how influential feminist ideas were in the early socialist movements of the nineteenth century. But it was not until the 1850s that feminism really took off as an autonomous movement, first in America, then in Britain and other European countries. Victorian feminism was primarily a campaigning movement, but like its twentieth-century successor it also stimulated research into many aspects of women's lives. Although the movement lost part of its impetus with the gaining of the vote and the general social upheaval surrounding the First World War, individual women continued to study gender issues and some influential work was produced, such as Alice Clark's *Working Life of Women in the Seventeenth Century* (1919), Olive Schreiner's *Women and Labour* (1911) or, more latterly, de Beauvoir's *The Second Sex* (1949). Apart from de Beauvoir's great text, the study of gender fell into a slump in the post-war period: in the epoch of the Welfare State and universal suffrage it was considered that sex equality had been achieved and that what residual gender differences remained were the result of 'natural' endowments; moreover, the 'master' sociological narratives of the 1950s and 1960s were largely gender-blind, as discussed in the previous chapter.

Parsons did give attention to gender differences, distinguishing between instrumental male social roles (based on rationality and competition in the capitalist marketplace) and expressive female ones (based on caring and domesticity). But he saw these as functional for society, linking them rather unquestioningly to a stereotypical nuclear family form seen to be 'normal' in society and rooting them ultimately in reproductive functions. It was left to the second-wave feminist movement, emerging on the heels of the student protest movement and the radical social critiques of the late 1960s and early 1970s, to reformulate those social roles in terms of gendered power and inequality.

It has become conventional to distinguish three main strands or 'perspectives' in feminist thinking which predominated in the 1970s (Charvet, 1982; Tong, 1989). These are liberal, or equal rights, feminism; socialist or Marxist feminism; and radical feminism. Sub-categories, such as materialist feminism, may be distinguished within them, and psychoanalytic feminism added as an additional strand. Recent texts, however, have been critical of this approach, and have suggested that it tends to 'essentialize' feminist thinking and pigeonhole thinkers into boxes where they may not exactly fit (Barrett and Phillips, 1992; Stacey, 1993). Nor are the positions so clearly distinguishable as the categorization suggests. Individual feminist writers draw on ideas from all three 'perspectives' and their position shifts as their thinking develops. Moreover, the triple categories hardly exhaust the range of feminist positions. Stanley and Wise (1983) offered an early challenge to structuralist thinking in feminism from an ethnomethodological stance which prefigured many subsequent postmodern critiques. The 1980s and 1990s have seen a proliferation of newer feminist positions, such as black feminism and deconstructionist feminism. Stacey, arguing that the old categorization tends to encourage stereotyping ('all radical feminists are lesbians and separatists') suggests that it 'obscures more than it reveals' (1993, p. 52).

While these criticisms are valid, I believe it is helpful to retain these terms as labels for earlier forms of feminist thinking, as long as it is realized that they do not refer to theoretical perspectives in the more formal sociological sense; that is, they never constituted themselves as self-contained and competing sets of explanatory premises (in the way that, for example, functionalism and classic Marxism did). The image used by Banks (1981), 'faces' of feminism, captures the way in which the strands were interlinked, three facets of a single movement. Alternatively we may view them as differing 'standpoints', in the sense that Hartsock (1987) has used that term. The notion of a 'feminist standpoint' has been elaborated as part of a critique of mainstream science. This attacks the view that science, or any form of knowledge, can be absolutely detached and objective; all knowledge is 'situated', derived from a specific context which affords a particular angle on reality. I suggest that liberal, Marxist and radical feminism constituted three differing standpoints from which to procure feminist knowledge.

Liberal feminism

Liberal feminism grew out of the broader liberal movement and shared many of its assumptions, notably the ideals of equality of opportunity, and individual rights. Liberal feminism asserted that women as well as men should attain these goals. Gender differences were linked to blockages to achieving equal rights, such as prejudice or legal and institutional arrangements set up in less enlightened times. The way forward was through education and legal reform. Liberal feminism, which was the bedrock of the nineteenth-century movement, focused particularly on gains for women in the public sphere: the vote, equal opportunities at work, legal rights equivalent to those of men (over property and within marriage for example) and proper representation within democratic institutions.

Liberal feminism has been criticized as insufficiently radical in its explanation of gender inequality. This relates to its acceptance of the broader liberal assumption that capitalist development will inexorably bring with it advantages of freedom and democracy and is part of a long-term movement towards 'the best of all possible worlds' which is signified in Fukuyama's neo-liberal vision of the 'end of history': the global triumph of benevolent capitalist democracy (Fukuyama, 1989). Like its (male) parent, liberal feminism has sought reform within the system rather than transformation of the system. Liberal feminist political objectives have been criticized as individualistic, as helping individual women (usually middle-class and white) to gain access to male preserves and achieve equality with male compeers. Indeed, it can be argued that the impetus of liberal feminism is to make women more like men. It does little to question the gendered cultural assumptions which underlie prevailing social arrangements (for example, that it is more socially valuable to go out to work than to stay at home and look after children, or that some types of work, like management and money-making should be more highly rewarded than others like cooking and cleaning). While liberal feminism has arguably been the most effective standpoint from which to develop successful political action, its social critique is limited.

Marxist feminism

The liberal standpoint has been highly developed in America and Australia, where feminists have been particularly involved in working for women's rights within state agencies (Gelb and Palley, 1982; Curthoys, 1993). In Britain, where feminists are more wary of the state, the predominant standpoint has been Marxist feminism, with its view of the state as an instrument of capitalist (and subsequently patriarchal) oppression. Many British second-wave feminists within academia had been involved in the radical student movement and were influenced by Marxism. Barrett's influential text *Women's Oppression Today: Problems in Marxist Feminist Analysis* (1980) epitomizes British feminist thinking of the period, with its focus on labour exploitation, ideology and the state.

Socialist standpoints within European feminism had developed in the nineteenth century (see Banks, 1981; Lovenduski, 1986). Politically, socialist or Marxist feminism locates the fight for gender equality alongside the class struggle within the movement to build socialism. Theoretically, Marxist feminists attempt to take the key concepts of Marxism, along with the techniques of the materialist method of analysis, and apply them to gender relations. While critical of traditional Marxism's neglect of gender issues, the Marxist feminist standpoint still viewed gender within the framework of capitalist production relationships. Characteristically, the focus was on economic aspects of gender: women as wage labour, the exploitation of women as a labour reserve, the contribution of domestic labour to capitalist accumulation, the role of the state in promoting the traditional family: all these were central concerns.

A feature of the Marxist feminist standpoint which is now seen as problematic was its view of society as an integrated and unified system. At first, Marxist feminist sociologists tried simply to subsume an analysis of gender within the broad idea of a mode of production. Women's subjection was explained in terms of the needs of capitalism as a system. The political corollary of this was that the struggle for women's rights was only an aspect of the broader class struggle and that gender inequality would disappear once socialism was achieved. Indeed, many socialist activists, both male and female, have been critical of feminism, viewing it as a distraction from the class struggle, and sometimes stigmatizing it as a movement of privileged middle-class women (Phillips, 1987).

This highlights the problem of the relationship between class and gender as forms of inequality. The Marxist analysis tended to handle the issue of gender inequality either by seeing women as members of the exploited working class (which they are clearly all not) or as housewives contributing either directly or indirectly to capitalist profits (which again they are all not). Moreover, gender divisions were shown by comparative and historical study to be characteristic of all societies, not just capitalist or even class-divided societies, and to be marked in the Soviet bloc where capitalism had been rejected. It became apparent that it was impossible to conceptualize gender adequately within the single framework of the capitalist mode of production.

The solution taken by Marxist feminists was to combine an account of capitalism with an analysis of a parallel system of patriarchy. Sometimes this took the form of what was known as unified systems theory, discerning a single complex structure of capitalist patriarchy or patriarchal capitalism (Young, 1981). Miriam Glucksmann (1990) has recently produced an ingenious version which extends the notion of relations of production to include reproduction and the complexities of the social division of labour in the household as well as at work. However, there was a tendency in these accounts for gender issues to slide out of sight and imperatives of class to come to the fore. For this reason most feminists preferred the 'dual systems' option, which conceives patriarchy and capitalism as two equivalent and analytically separable systems which, however, are always found in interaction in any concrete social context. Feminists such as Hartmann (1981) and Walby (1986) developed an account of patriarchy as a system and explored its historical interaction with capitalism.

Radical feminism

Dual systems theory could be seen as a way of fusing radical and Marxist standpoints within feminism, for the concept of patriarchy was associated with the radical stance. The term patriarchy, literally meaning 'rule of the father', was not a new one; it had previously been used to denote specific types of family or household structure and forms of inheritance based on the authority of a male head of household over younger male and all female family members. Weber used the term 'patriarchalism' (1964, p. 346) to describe types of society or social institutions where forms of power were analogous to this family model. However, radical feminists broadened the use of the term to refer to a general structure of male domination in society, as defined by Kate Millett in *Sexual Politics*:

> Our society, like all other historical civilizations, is a patriarchy . . . The military, industry, technology, universities, science, political office, finances – in short, every avenue of power within the society, including the coercive force of the police, is entirely in male hands. (1971, p. 25)

Radical feminism is the newest strand in feminism. It was stronger in America than Britain, and acted as a counterpart to the more moderate liberal mainstream. It achieved notoriety for its political strategies, including direct action tactics such as disruptions of beauty queen contests. Especially controversial was the separatist tendency within the radical wing, which ranged from supporting women-only meetings (designed to prevent men dominating the agenda and to allow women to build confidence in a less combative environment) to the espousal of lesbianism as a political strategy. This arose from the key theoretical premise of radical feminism that gender inequality was the primary source of social division from which all others evolved. The implication, that all men as a category oppress all women as a category, was explored for example in Shulamith Firestone's *The Dialectic of Sex* (1971), which inverted Marxist thinking through the idea of 'sex classes'.

Firestone's concern with sexuality and reproduction reflected the radical slogan 'the personal is political'. Where the Marxist feminist standpoint focused primarily on labour, radical feminists explored intimate personal relationships of love, marriage and desire. They were interested in the link between sexuality and male violence, seeing issues such as rape and pornography as crucial aspects of male social domination which is ultimately backed up by the threat of force (Brownmiller, 1976; Dworkin, 1981; Griffin, 1981). These analyses moved the feminist critique firmly beyond the public sphere, the focus of the liberal standpoint, and into the private. Indeed, Firestone claimed that 'love, perhaps even more than childbearing, is the pivot of women's oppression today' (1971, p. 142). She believed that gender inequalities fundamentally expressed themselves around men's control of reproduction. Her provocative solution was that women should free themselves from male domination through new reproductive technologies which might remove the need to bear children within their bodies.

Radical feminist politics and theory were considered by many, men and women, to be disturbing. They were meant to be! This was the form of feminist practice which was caricatured and demonized in the popular press. Theoretically, radical feminism can be criticized for its essentialist tendencies. In highlighting reproductive and sexual differences and citing them as the basis of women's oppression it veered towards replicating the conservative view that biology was destiny (although unlike conservatives it saw reproduction as the base of a socially constructed hierarchy of power and inequality). It tended to marginalize differences among women which rise from class, ethnicity, age and so forth, and to assume a commonality of interests among women. Men were angered by the way it presented the whole male sex as an oppressing group; they called for an appreciation of the complex subtleties of power between the sexes.

While these criticisms point to serious weaknesses in the radical standpoint, its contribution to feminist thinking should not be underestimated. Its great achievement was to highlight the different view of the world that rose from a specifically female way of seeing. While liberal feminism was based on an assertion of asexual *personhood*, portraying the subject of feminism as an androgynous individual fighting for equality, and while Marxism subsumed gender as one position among many in the general struggle against social hierarchies of all types, radical feminism insisted on the distinct nature of female experience and the feminine subject. However crude and essentialist some aspects of the theorizing may have been, radical feminism laid the ground for the 1990s feminist interest in culture, sexuality and subjectivity. The idea of a specific woman's culture inspired the development of a wealth of autonomous women's organizations, from rape crisis centres and homes for battered women to women's bookshops and theatre groups. These political achievements can be considered as crucial as the liberal feminist campaigns in opening up new horizons for women in the latter part of the twentieth century.

Psychoanalysis and feminism

In comparison to radical feminism, Marxism was weak on the more personal aspects of gendered experience. This led Juliet Mitchell (1975) to combine a Marxist account of the economic aspects of gender inequality with a Freudian analysis that could be used to theorize psychic structures of oppression. She suggested that a theory of the unconscious would explain why, despite the campaigns of feminists, female subordination was so hard to eradicate. Through the interrelations of psychosexual development within the family as described by Freud, acceptance of male superiority and female inferiority became embedded in the individual's unconscious mental processes.

There has been a longstanding, if wary, flirtation between feminism and various forms of psychoanalytic theory. The wariness arises from the fact that psychoanalysis presents accounts of universal patterns of psychic development, based in relations between parents and children, while a key principle of feminism has always been that gender relationships are socially constructed and culturally variable. An appreciation of the wide variety of forms of relations between men and women in families and kinship groups, or of constructs of the ideal male or female personality, was fostered by study of anthropological evidence (for example, Rosaldo and Lamphere, 1974; Rohrlich-Leavitt, 1975). Nevertheless, the desire to understand the place of sexuality within gendered inequalities has often induced feminists to turn to psychoanalysis.

Many feminists have found Freud's version of psychoanalysis hard to take, despite Mitchell's attempt to show that his theories might be appropriated and revised for feminist analysis. The prominence given by Freud to the phallus and genital difference lays his work open to charges of biological determinism and sexism. The theories of the Oedipus complex (including the male child's terror of castration) and of female penis envy portray women as inferior versions of men, with adult femininity evolving as an incomplete form of masculinity. Lacking the phallus, could women ever hope to achieve equality with men? Freud's presentation of his findings as a set of universal dilemmas that must be solved by all individuals if they are to achieve psychic health and stability as adult sexual beings overlooks the historical specificity of family relations and sexual practices; his theories, based on the experiences of repressive white bourgeois families in late nineteenth-century Vienna, need severe modification to fit with today's world of single parents and flexible family forms.

For this reason, many feminists have found a more acceptable version of psychoanalysis in Nancy Chodorow's account (1978) of childhood and gender development derived from the 'object relations' school of Winnicott. This improves on Freud in focusing on the social rather than biological aspects of parent/child relationships. Chodorow bases her analysis on the strong identification babies and young children have with their mother. To achieve male identity boys have to rupture that identification and establish themselves as separate entities. The pain and isolation inherent in this process means that adolescence is more problematic for boys than girls and that masculine identity is more fragile than femininity. To achieve secure masculinity the boy may react by vehemently rejecting all aspects of his own experience and personality which could be seen as female; from this follows the depreciation of women by adult men. By contrast, the girl's childhood is more secure as she is able to retain the identification with her mother to a much later date. However, her individuality is less marked and she has trouble in achieving the self-confidence and autonomy of the male. Through these childhood processes the psychic structures of typical masculinity and femininity continue to reproduce themselves and will only be changed, Chodorow suggests, if parenting is transformed with fathers becoming equally involved.

Chodorow's theory indicates why prevailing definitions of femininity and masculinity are so enduring. As Jackson (1988) suggests, without its psychoanalytic trappings the account makes sociological sense; it is highly compatible with the work done by sociologists on gender socialization on the family, which also suggests that young children internalize gender norms transmitted from generation to generation (Sharpe, 1976; Oakley, 1981). But like theories of socialization, Chodorow's approach can be seen as too deterministic. Feminine and masculine identities and sexualities are not fixed; they *do* change.

All versions of psychoanalysis tend towards determinism. They imply that the relations of early childhood are crucial for the development of adult identities, whereas current approaches to gender assert that feminine and masculine identities are perpetually being created and recreated through processes of social interaction. This is a lifelong process. All this poses problems in reconciling psychoanalytic thinking with a sociological approach to gender.

The contribution of classic feminist thinking

Since the mid-1980s classic feminist thinking has been subjected to a series of intensive critiques commencing with the attack by black feminists for its ethnocentric bias. The black feminist critique opened up the subsequent debate on the diversity of women's experience. Criticisms of a more theoretical nature came from feminists influenced by post-structural and postmodernist ideas. They argued that the classic theories were 'essentialist': that is, based on the assumption that a particular social category is marked by unchanging qualities, a common 'essence' shared by all members of the category. An essentialist approach to gender implies that all women (or all men) are united by common characteristics, experiences or interests.

Postmodern thinking also challenged notions of structure and system inherent in Marxist and radical feminist theories. It was argued that these theories were tainted by the rationalist and teleological tendencies of the modernist grand narratives from which they had emerged. In the early 1990s the volume of criticism appeared to reach a kind of critical mass, to the extent that Barrett and Phillips in their survey of recent developments in feminism speak of 'a "paradigm shift", in which assumptions rather than conclusions are radically overturned' (1992, p. 2). They discern a gulf, which may or not be bridgeable between 1970s and 1990s feminism.

I suggest that there is a danger of writing off the classic legacy and undervaluing its achievements. Whatever the theoretical limitations of 1970s feminism, its standpoints acted as stimuli for indispensable research into all aspects of gender relations. The liberal feminist standpoint promoted research into education and the state; socialist feminists explored the inequalities of gender in waged and domestic work; and radical thinking opened up the way to explore sexuality, and varying aspects of male violence. Without this rich basis of empirical evidence, contemporary feminism would not have been able to develop its understanding of the complexities of gendered power and its interrelation with other forms of oppression that are current preoccupations.

I want to highlight three of the key concepts of classic feminism: patriarchy, the sexual division of labour and compulsory heterosexuality. Insights gained from debates over these concepts have been vital to the development of a sociological account of gender.

Theorizing patriarchy

As has been implied, the analysis of patriarchy was in many ways the core contribution of 1970s feminism, although the concept has always been the target of critical attack. It was developed to indicate systemic arrangements which maintained male social dominance. The project of many feminist theorists, both Marxist and radical, was to develop a model of patriarchy analogous to the Marxian analysis of mode of production. Thus there were various attempts to distinguish the 'base' of patriarchy. For example, Hartmann (1981) argued that it lay in male control of female labour power, while Firestone (1971) considered that patriarchy arose from men's control of reproductive arrangements. Delphy (1977), taking domestic labour as central, suggested the alternative conception of two coexisting modes of production: the capitalist mode in which capital exploits the labour of the working class and the domestic mode of production in which men exploit the unpaid labour of women. The influence of Marxism is clear in all these versions. Sylvia Walby (1990) moved further away from the strict attempt to replicate the base/superstructure model of Marxism with her conceptualization of patriarchy which she defined as 'a system of social structures and practices in which men dominate, oppress and exploit women' (1990, p. 20). She isolates six types of structure: paid work, domestic labour, sexuality, the state, violence and culture.

However, many feminists were unhappy with the concept, arguing that it tended to imply that *all* societies in *all* historical periods were characterized by male domination. Rowbotham's well-known critique (1981) is typical.

She argued that the concept was too universalistic and ahistorical; it could not encompass variations in the balance of power between the sexes in different societies nor the different ways that power was exercised. The framework of patriarchy rules out the possibility of types of society where women and men are equal, or even where women are dominant.

One response was to explore historically exactly how and to what extent male power was exercised in various social contexts. Barrett suggested that the adjective 'patriarchal' should only be used to describe concrete historical instances in which 'male domination is expressed through the power of the father over women and over younger men' (Barrett, 1980, p. 250). Walby, in a series of publications (1990; 1992; 1993), has developed an account of a move from 'private patriarchy' (that is, the control of women by individual men within the household) to 'public patriarchy', where women are subordinated in the public sphere (especially at work and within the state) by structures of segregation:

> In public patriarchy, women are not confined to the household and the mode of expropriation is more collective than individual, for instance, by most women being paid less than men. In private patriarchy the main patriarchal strategy is exclusionary, and women are not allowed into certain social arenas, such as Parliament, while in public patriarchy women are allowed in, but segregated and subordinated there. (Walby, 1993, pp. 87–8)

While such accounts emphasize the variability of power relations, other problems with the concept are less easily solved, and have been highlighted by postmodernist critiques of classic feminism. Postmodernists see patriarchy as an inadequate way to conceptualize gendered power. It is a zero-sum concept: that is, it suggests that all the power rests with men, none with women. Contemporary feminists reject the portrayal of women as passive victims of male power. Recent conceptualizations emphasize the complexity of power relations between women and men, pointing out that some women are in positions of power over other women, and indeed, over men (for example, women of the aristocratic and bourgeois classes who employ servants of both sexes, or female employers and managers).

Despite these criticisms, feminists have been reluctant to abandon the term altogether. In part this is due to its important place in the history of second-wave feminist political campaigning: it has come to be a symbolic marker of a feminist position. It is a theoretical tool which feminist theorists have claimed and developed themselves, by contrast to, for example, the ideas of postmodern feminism, which has borrowed extensively from male writers such as Foucault and Derrida who have little specific interest in gender analysis. For these reasons many feminists continue to use the term. One strategy is to use it adjectivally ('patriarchal ideologies', 'patriarchal practices'), rather than as a noun with the implications of adherence to a system approach. The use of system theories has already been criticized in this book (chapter 2) for the way it inevitably carries exclusions. But I see it as legitimate to speak of 'patriarchal relations' in reference to the gender differences which are the topic of this chapter.

The sexual division of labour

Those chary of the term patriarchy have preferred to use the alternative term 'sexual division of labour'. This term has proved acceptable to all feminist standpoints and is also the object of much current research within the social sciences under the influence of feminist analysis.

Initial explorations of the sexual division of labour in paid work drew on ideas from existing sociological theories. For example, Marxists took up the idea that women were part of the reserve army of labour drawn in and out of the labour force according to capitalist needs, although study of trends in unemployment suggested that, while possibly true in some historical periods, this did not fit women's labour market experience in the post-war decades: men have lost jobs rather than women in recent recession. Alternatively Humphries (1983) suggested that women, because they are used as cheap labour, constituted an 'ideal proletariat', a position that was criticized because of the history of collusions between employers and organized male workers to keep women out of 'men's jobs' (Hartmann, 1976; Bradley, 1989). Humphries's arguments about 'female proletarianization', however, merit reconsideration in the 1990s with the advance of women into the work-force. Beechey (1977) drew on the Marxian theory of value to suggest *why* female labour was cheaper, arguing that because women were habitually dependent on fathers and husbands the cost of the reproduction of their labour power was literally less; they could be paid a wage below what was considered necessary for male subsistence. An alternative to these and other Marxist formulations was to employ the Weberian framework of dual or segmented labour markets; this posits that the labour market is split into segments, between which it is difficult for workers to move, because of employers' requirements for different types of labour. Women can be seen to occupy secondary segments in the market, characterized by low pay, tight control, poor conditions and lack of opportunities. Workers in the secondary sector who can easily be hired and fired serve employers' need for flexibility, while they also rely on the stable commitment of a core of privileged primary workers, usually male and white.

While these approaches offer insights on employers' deployment of women, all slot women into pre-existing analyses of class, ignoring the gender dynamics which make such discriminatory practices possible. None of the theories is adequately able to explain why and how the sexes were segregated at work or account for the persistence of segregated structures (although dual labour market theory comes closest to doing so). The notion of gender segregation, both horizontal (the clustering of women and men in different sex-typed jobs and occupations) and vertical (the concentration of men in top grades in each occupation), became the central concern. Various factors were seen to contribute to the formation and maintenance of segregated structures: employers' motivations and attitudes; patriarchal and paternalist controls which treated women employees differently from men; the exclusionary policies and practices of trade unions and professional associations; ideologies or discourses of masculinity and femininity; work cultures which promoted preferences for same-sex workmates; sexual harassment which served to police the boundaries between men's and women's jobs (see, for example, Spencer and Podmore, 1987; Bradley, 1989; Witz, 1992). Cynthia Cockburn's studies (1983; 1985; 1991) have demonstrated the subtle processes through which jobs and workplaces become gendered. She highlights the role of technology and the way in which the association of men with technical competence serves to maintain gender hierarchies. Her research documents the resistance of men to the breakdown of segregation.

The domestic division of labour has also received much attention, starting with the pioneering studies of 'housework' by Oakley and others (Oakley, 1974; Hunt, 1980). Despite claims that marriages are becoming more symmetrical and domestic tasks being shared more equally, surveys persistently reveal that women still take the major share of housework and childcare even where both partners work (Martin and Roberts, 1984; Morris, 1990; Jowell et al., 1992). Where the labour is displaced on to paid helpers, such cleaners, childminders and nannies are inevitably female. In this way the idea of women's responsibility for domestic labour persists and with it the view of women as 'naturally' orientated towards domestic life and motherhood (Crowley, 1992). More recent research indicates that, especially with the rise in male unemployment, many couples are beginning to renegotiate the domestic division of labour, with men taking more part (Wheelock, 1990; Morris, 1990; Brannen and Moss, 1991). But men remain selective in the tasks they undertake, and the ultimate responsibility remains with mothers. Child-rearing responsibilities are still a major reason for women's restricted labour market opportunities.

The many studies of the sexual division of labour reveal the extent and strength of gender segregation in contemporary societies. While feminist research has recently shifted towards the exploration of cultural aspects of gender, these studies remain the basis of our understanding of gender as a form of inequality.

Compulsory heterosexuality

While *all* classic feminist thinking encouraged a critical approach to long-standing notions of the public and the private spheres and sought to bridge the analytical gap between them, the radical standpoint in particular was the base for delving into personal relationships. The traditional view of the family, marriage and romance was that these were areas of freedom and individual fulfilment, set apart from the constraints of economic and public life (Zaretsky, 1976; Lasch, 1977). Feminists challenged this view, suggesting that marriage was an unequal contract in which women were trapped (Comer, 1974). Bernard (1976) suggested that men rather than women benefited from marriage, while wives suffered from the frustrations and isolation associated with the housewife role. The espousal of romantic ideals by young unmarried women was shown to draw them into same trap as their mothers (McRobbie, 1978; Westwood, 1984). In this way marriage and love were portrayed as social, not natural, institutions which served to further patriarchal dominance.

From this standpoint feminists were able to attack the view of emotions and sexual orientations as natural and given. In a famous essay 'Compulsory heterosexuality and lesbian existence' Adrienne Rich (1980) argued against the view that individuals were endowed with a fixed sexual identity. Rather, she claimed, heterosexual and homosexual desires and practices should be seen as points on a continuum of sexual behaviours.

Feminism divorces sexual behaviour from biological dimorphism, and suggests that individuals are potentially bisexual and androgynous; heterosexuality is so prevalent merely because it is socially constructed and learned as the norm of sexual behaviour. Those who reject the rules of 'compulsory sexuality' are liable to be stigmatized as abnormal, 'queer' and sick. However, those who accept the conventional version of sexuality also suffer, since their potential for exploring and expressing their individual sexuality in a variety of ways is suppressed. Rich laments the loss of the rich possibilities of warmer, more intimate bonds between women through such processes. Also, since the prevailing or 'hegemonic' version of male heterosexuality (Connell, 1987) encourages predatory, aggressive and sometimes violent sexual behaviour, the ideal of the male stud 'putting it about', compulsory heterosexuality contributes to the maintenance of male dominance.

Recent approaches to sexuality have emphasized the variety of straight, gay, lesbian and transexual identities on offer, speaking in terms of 'heterosexualities' and 'homosexualities' rather than one prevailing sexual code. Moreover postmodern feminism is concerned to emphasize the pleasures and desires that can be enjoyed within sexuality even by women who accept the heterosexual norm unquestioningly. Nonetheless, the work of Rich and others speaking from the radical standpoint opened up the exploration of the way sexualities are socially constructed. The notion of 'compulsory heterosexuality' is still a very important insight into how we view sexual behaviour and the way some forms of sexual behaviour are accepted and others condemned. In such ways, classic feminist analysis laid the foundations for an understanding of gendered subjectivity.

Newer moves: 1990s feminism

Since the mid-1980s, the feminist approach to gender has taken a 'cultural turn' and a 'linguistic turn'. As Barrett and Phillips suggest (1992), literary and cultural studies and philosophy are replacing sociology as the core contributors to contemporary feminist debates. Study of gendered representations and discourses has taken centre stage in the 1990s, pushing the old concerns about inequalities of gender somewhat to the margins. Above all, there is an overriding interest in the differing ways in which women experience gender.

The black critique

The initial impetus for rethinking the assumptions of classic feminism can be said to have come from minority ethnic women who were developing their own standpoint, that of 'black feminist thought' (Collins, 1990). Black feminists argued that the feminist analysis of gender was biased and ethnocentric, taking the experience of white middle-class women as the norm and then claiming to speak on behalf of 'all' women. By contrast, black critics highlighted the specificity of minority women's experience and how gender relationships impacted on them in quite divergent ways (see for example, Carby, 1982; hooks, 1982; Anthias and Yuval-Davis, 1983; Brah, 1992). For instance, while white feminists tended to view the family as an agent of patriarchal domination, black women argued that for them the family was a source of solidarity and support against the racism and subordination they experienced in white-dominated society. Moreover, black family forms often differed from white ones, yet the middle-class nuclear family was discussed as if it was common to all social groups. Or again, reproductive controls acted differently on black women: while white women campaigned for the rights to contraception and abortion as a way to assert their control over their own bodies, black women were often subjected to pressure to employ contraceptive techniques (sometimes of damaging kinds) or to undergo abortions because of white fears about black fertility and their desire to limit it (Amos and Parmar, 1984; Mama, 1984; Collins, 1990; Knowles and Mercer, 1992).

The notion of 'sisterhood' among women was thus exposed as a myth. Indeed, some claimed that in its assumption of common experience, white feminism could itself be seen as racist. Amos and Parmar (1984) argued that the gains of feminist politics were often at the expense of black and working-class women. The freedom gained by white middle-class women to pursue careers or achieve economic equality with men depended on the exploitation of low-paid black or working-class women acting as servants or childminders. The feminist movement minimized the contributions of black women and failed to study or prioritize their needs. Moreover the very theories developed to analyse gender were contributing to making black women invisible. 'Dual systems' theory, for example, looked at the intersection of class and gender inequalities but overlooked racial hierarchies. The theory of patriarchy elevated gendered power over forms of racial oppression which black women saw as central to their lives.

While these criticisms were warranted and opened up new areas of research and debate, it can be argued that they were also divisive, at a moment when feminism as a coherent political movement was in some disarray. Looking back on these debates, Parmar (1990) regrets the tendency to construct a 'hierarchy of oppression', with various groups of women seeking to portray their own situation as that most demanding of attention. Such arguments could be exclusionary and lead to suppression of genuine debate as people feared to speak from a position of privilege. A recent concern has been to establish unity across divisions, emphasizing that the diversity of women's experiences could promote a more democratic movement based on coalition, or at the least could provide opportunity for dialogue and exchange of experiences (Tang Nain, 1991; Yuval-Davis, 1993).

Theoretically, the black critique had a crucial effect on the analysis of gender. It was evident that it was no longer possible to employ the category 'women' and assume a common oppression. The category of 'women' needed to be deconstructed (Riley, 1988) and the history of different groups of women explored. The recognition of the diversity of women's experience heightened the need to consider the interaction of gender with other dimensions of inequality, age and class as well as ethnicity.

In this way the black critique not only highlighted the issues of difference and diversity, but led to an interest in studying identities and subjectivities. Moreover, the criticism of patriarchy as a unidimensional theory added to the growing interest in reconceptualizing power. In these ways the concerns of black feminism were similar to those of feminists influenced by postmodern theory and deconstructionism.

Postmodern, post-structural and deconstructionist feminism

As Barrett and Phillips (1992) imply, postmodernism and post-structuralism are becoming the new orthodoxies among feminist theorists of the 1990s. In some ways this is strange, as key postmodern and post-structuralist thinkers, such as Lyotard, Jameson and Foucault, have paid little attention to gender. There is also unease with the pluralistic and individualistic vision of society which often emerges from such approaches, and which can be seen as potentially undermining the feminist contention that women as a category are oppressed. Is it possible to have a version of feminism without some notion of gender inequalities as structured or built into societal organization? However, what has particularly drawn feminists to postmodernism is its critical stance towards science, with its claims to objectivity and neutrality, and towards mainstream social theories developed in the stance of rationalist enlightenment. This accords with feminism's own longstanding critique of science and of 'malestream' social theories for their gender-blindness, their assumption that male experience is the norm (the 'universal male subject'), along with their rejection of radical work which is considered to arise from subjective and therefore 'biased' political attachments. Such approaches, it is argued, present a partial male vision of the world as absolute and universal truth. The postmodern position allows feminists to pursue their claims that all knowledge is partial and relative to the standpoint of the knower; that rather than a single objective truth there are multiple voices and multiple truths; and that emotions and intuitions are as valid a base for the pursuit of knowledge as 'reason' and 'objectivity', so long seen as attributes possessed by men and counterposed to feminine 'irrationality' and 'subjectivity' (Harding, 1986; Fraser and Nicholson, 1988; Nicholson, 1990).

Postmodernism has other attractions for feminists. The stress in postmodernist sociology on multiple sources of identity connects with the growing awareness of the differentiation among women promoted by the black critique. Postmodernism encourages discussion of sexuality, desires, popular cultural expressions, the fluidity of subjectivity. The postmodern stress on culture rather than structure allows feminists to develop an account of the ways in which women, as active agents, are involved in the construction of their own worlds, rather than presenting them as victims and puppets of structures beyond their determination. The pleasures women derive from femininity and feminine pursuits can be explored within this framework.

More controversial is the critique offered by postmodernism of the modernist metanarratives of social development, since, as Phillips (1992) and Marshall (1994) point out, feminism itself evolved as part of the modernist quest for equality and emancipation. In an early postmodernist account Jean Bethke Elshtain (1987) criticized liberal, Marxist and radical feminist approaches as teleological: that is, assuming a progressive development towards a given, possibly Utopian, end-state. Liberal and Marxist accounts she considered predicated on a 'sex neutrality' narrative (in Marxism linked to the equivalent idea of a classless society), while the radical narrative of 'sex polarity' suggested that intrinsic differences in male and female experiences would inevitably lead to separation of the sexes, but that in the future such a separation could be based on women's assertion of the value of their own culture.

Whether or not one accepts Elshtain's contention that the feminist narratives rested inevitably on essentialist concepts of gender and on an acceptance of linear progress in society (which could certainly be challenged), it is true that classic feminism was based on views of society as systematic and structured. The analysis of structured inequalities of society was used as evidence for the need for social reform. If the idea of social structures leading to a common oppression of women is abandoned, it can be questioned whether feminism can mount a case for the need to transform gender relations. If all truths are partial and relative, and all versions of the world have equal validity (Fraser and Nicholson, 1988) there is no logical reason why patriarchal and conservative accounts of gender should not be as 'valid' as those of their feminist critics. As McNay expresses it:

> It is not desirable, or ultimately even possible, for feminism to take on the postmodern rejection of metanarratives. Whilst feminism has to guard against the dangers of generalization, it nevertheless rests on the fundamental assumption that the inequality between the sexes is indefensible and unjust. Such an assumption informs feminist analyses of the position of women in society, it underlies their call for a global abolition of gender-related inequalities. (1992, pp. 196–7)

Despite these political difficulties, many feminist theorists have been drawn to the post-structural approach elaborated by critics of Marxism and of structural theories of language, such as Derrida, Foucault and Lacan. Derrida's work inspires an investigation of the categories used to understand social reality and the way they themselves become constitutive of it. Foucault develops this into the idea of 'discursive' frameworks, sets of interlinked statements and practices through which we make sense of the world and which are implicated in the reproduction of relationships of power (Foucault, 1972; McNay, 1992). Lacan offers a linguistic version of psychoanalytic theory, transposing Freud's theory of the phallus to a symbolic level. Individuals develop gendered subjectivity and sexual identity only through entry into language, but language itself is phallocentric, transmitting the patriarchal law of the father. Thus both sexes will come to speak (and think) of masculinity as superior; indeed the phallocentric nature of language means that women lack a voice of their own and can only speak in masculine terms (Tong, 1989). Although the problems of psychoanalysis discussed earlier in this chapter reappear in the Lacanian framework, it has been strongly influential within feminism. Cixous and Irigaray call on women to create their own versions of femininity based on new linguistic forms which reflect the specific female experience of the gendered body and female sexuality (Duchen, 1987; Tong, 1989).

Post-structuralist influences have led feminists to explore dominant discursive frameworks which are used to marginalize women and to promote certain constructs of femininity at the expense of others (for example, Steedman et al., 1985; J. W. Scott, 1988; Pringle, 1989). Pringle and Watson argue that this idea of 'discursive marginality' can be the base for a new unity among women to replace the old (essentialist) vision of common interests arising from common experience (1992, p. 68).

New themes

Such new moves in feminism have foregrounded new themes. Four connected issues are briefly considered here: the deconstruction of the category of women; difference and diversity; discursive frameworks; and power.

Deconstructing women

The structural view of language sees it as a system of signs which is linked in some intrinsic way to the reality (the material world) it represents. The post-structuralist view treats language as a set of arbitrary and floating signs. Thus rather than reflecting reality, language can be seen as constitutive of it. Put crudely, what we say determines what we see, rather than the other way round. These ideas lie behind the 'linguistic turn' in feminism and the interest in deconstruction and discourse.

Derrida's work has promoted a critique of the categories, especially those based on binary oppositions such as 'man/woman' or 'black/white', which are used to describe the world. Such categories do violence to the variety of potential experience by forcing it to cohere to one of the polar options. The 'submerged middle' of the range of positions in between is suppressed. As Donna Haraway (1990) argues, the very act of naming something or somebody (even oneself) brings exclusions. Categories also construct one (essentialized) set of people as 'the other' ('woman' or 'black'), whose experience is defined against that of the dominant group and often pathologized, seen as 'deviant' or inferior. These oppressive categories need deconstructing, if a different 'reality' is to be built allowing individuals to think in different and freer ways

Denise Riley's influential work (1988) set about deconstructing the notion of 'women'. She posed the question of what it means to 'be a woman' and pointed out how this has varied according to historical epoch: '"Women" is historically, discursively constructed and always relatively to other categories which themselves change' (pp. 2–3). Not only is the category of women as an identifiable collectivity with a common political interest unstable, but our individual self-consciousness of ourselves as 'women' (or 'men') is fluid. Most of the time we think of ourselves as 'a person'; moreover, to accept being 'a woman' is to accept being part of a category discursively presented as inferior. Discourses of gender induce us to act in certain ways because we are socially defined as being 'a man' or 'a woman'. Only by overthrowing such categories entirely (although this may be an impossible task) could we attain the freedom to act simply as persons. Preoccupation with the idea of women as a category, which was the analytic slant of radical feminism, conceals the fact that people could also be constructed as, or realign themselves as, members of other categories such as class or 'race':

> A chicana or a US black woman has not been able to speak as a woman or as a black person or as a chicano. The category 'woman' negated all nonwhite women; 'black' negated all nonblack people as well as all black women. (Haraway, 1990, p. 197)

Difference and diversity

The deconstruction of women as a category is linked to the need for more adequate understanding of how different women are placed within the dynamics of gender inequality. Feminists are now committed to exploring how gender relations are related to ethnic, class and other sources of variation in lived relationships (for example, Anthias and Yuval-Davis, 1993; Afshar and Maynard, 1994).

The initial black critique opened up an opposition between white and black women's experience. However, even at the time Anthias and Yuval-Davis (1984) pointed out that the use of the notion of 'black' women to represent racial difference might cover up the divergent experiences of other minority groups (Jewish, Cypriot or Muslim women, for example). Research has begun to deconstruct such package notions of race and discover the specific way in which the plurality of ethnic groups in our societies are located in the gender dynamic; and also to explore how differences *within* each ethnic group may be created, in terms of position in the life cycle (age, marital status), class and occupation, sexual orientation, dis/ability, religious affiliation and so forth.

Although the exploration of difference and diversity is perhaps *the* central task in contemporary gender analysis, the dangers of overstressing difference at the expense of unity have been pointed out (Maynard, 1994; Stacey, 1993). As the list above indicates, there is the risk of a remorseless fragmentation as each new specific group is distinguished, the more so as Yuval-Davis warns against the tendency towards 'essentializing' each group in turn (Anthias and Yuval-Davis, 1993). Moreover, persistent stress on difference may lead to marginalizing those who do not fit into any of these often dichotomized categories, for example, people of mixed 'race' (Allen, 1994). Stress on difference may entail the setting up of uncrossable boundaries between 'them' and 'us'. The other danger is of a spiral into individualism, an infinite process of fragmentation, in which we lose all sight of the commonality of gendered experience. A balance is needed between notions of unity and difference.

Walby (1992) suggests we can achieve this by retaining the broader modernist frameworks for explaining social structure, while remaining sensitive to the need to explore differences, and being careful not to allow slippage back into a unidimensional theorization such as the metanarrative of traditional Marxism (p. 33). Her approach entails showing how the various structures (gender, class, ethnicity, age etc) interrelate, a task which she suggests has not yet been adequately accomplished. Broadly, that is the approach advocated in this book.

An alternative more in line with postmodernist prescriptions is to explore the 'local narratives' of particular groups in particular contexts – for example, young black women in schools (Mirza, 1992), Muslim women in the labour market (Brah, 1994), lesbians within academia (Wilton, 1993) – and show how they are positioned within the various discourses of gender.

Discourse

Stuart Hall defines a discourse as 'a group of statements which provide a language for talking about – i.e. a way of representing – a particular type of knowledge about a topic' (1992b, p. 291). These interlinked sets of statements, working together to provide a 'discursive formation', construct the topic under consideration (such as gender) in a particular way, in line with particular objectives or institutional and political strategies. Michel Foucault (1972) used the notion of discourse as a challenge to the prevailing ideas about scientific knowledge and its privileged claim to reveal absolute, objective truth. Science (and of course social science) was to Foucault no more than one of many discursive formations which laid claim to particular versions of what truth consists of; powerful discourses may become part of what Foucault called a 'regime of truth' in any given society or context. Regimes of truth establish what may be known and how it is known.

The idea of discourse is now very influential in feminism. Although some of its uses are rather marginal to the concerns of this book, it can relate to study of gendered inequality through the notion that women occupy subject positions within discourses. Within prevailing discourses of gender women often appear as 'the Other'. Through their own engagement with such dominant discourses, particularly with popular versions of thinking on gender, women and men are actively engaged in reconstituting gender relations in ways that allow power disparities to be perpetuated.

For example, Davies (1989) has shown that the exposure of very young children to discourses on gender disposes them to accept prevailing views of appropriate male and female behaviour; this is an important way in which children begin to make sense of the world and locate themselves within it. It becomes very difficult to change people's expectations about gender. Pringle's research into secretaries (1989) revealed how their involvement with prevailing discourses on femininity and masculinity helped to reproduce power relations within the office; the secretaries associated certain types of behaviour (such as bitching about other women, or favouritism and bossiness displayed by women in positions of power) with being female, and so accepted the view that men were more fitted to hold superior positions. The research of Wetherell et al. (1987) into students' attitudes to gender and equality revealed how exposure to competing discourses about gender produces confused and contradictory attitudes. The young people believed in an equal division of labour within marriage yet still felt that women should be ultimately responsible for childcare. In such ways discourses act to constitute and recreate patterns of gender inequality.

A problem with the concept of discourse is that it may be used quite vaguely. Some people employ it merely to indicate linguistic practices, while others, such as Pringle and Watson (1992) claim that it also includes 'material practices'. Griffin (1993) uses it as if it were interchangeable with ideology. The relationship between linguistic practices and material aspects of inequality, between 'words' and 'things' as Barrett puts it, is ambiguously presented in these accounts. Barrett (1992, p. 201) points out that Foucault proclaimed his desire to 'dispense with things'. Others are not so sure. Moreover, since we are given to understand that people are active in constituting new meanings, it is not clear why some discourses stick and others do not. For example, Davies shows that young children reject alternative discourses on gender when presented in feminist rewritings of fairy-tales. To solve this problem some theory of power is needed.

Power

Foucault linked truth regimes and knowledge to power, and it is increasingly to Foucault that many feminists turn in an attempt to replace the much criticized notion of patriarchy with a more subtle account of gendered power (McNay, 1992). Rather than presenting power as something that is exercised hierarchically from the top down (men holding power over women, the bourgeoisie over the proletariat), Foucault sees power as embedded in everyday relationships at every level of society, and as commonly operating through various regimes of discipline and surveillance. Moreover for Foucault, power is not just linked to repression; it is also used 'to incite, exhort and create' (Still, 1994, p. 152). The experience of power can be pleasurable to its objects. For example, Foucault shows how regimes of control and surveillance designed to discipline and normalize the body (for example sport, exercise and health programmes) are experienced pleasurably by those who undergo them. Such regimes are connected to discursive frameworks, in this instance those concerning the body and sexuality

Foucault's framework allows for analysis of the subtleties of power in everyday interactions between women and men. A problem for feminists, however, is that this is a theory of power which lacks a subject or a firm sense of agency. Foucault, as a post-structuralist, refuses to link power to any account of structured inequalities. He shows us how power is exercised, but not why. Who gains from the disciplinary procedures he describes? This is at odds with the feminist assumption that women are subordinated to men. However, some feminists have combined a Foucaultian analysis with an account of patriarchy. Bartky, for example, considers women's preoccupation with their bodies, beauty and slimming as a case of a disciplinary regime. She suggests

(1990) that in a patriarchal society women have internalized men's definitions of ideal female bodies and continually subject themselves to an imaginary male gaze, a kind of psychic panopticon.

An alternative approach to power that has been explored by some feminists is offered by Anthony Giddens (Davis et al., 1991). Giddens conceptualizes power in terms of access to and control of various social resources. Such a framework offers a multi-dimensional view of power which can allow for complexities and variations, while also incorporating a view of agency. For example, men may control more resources than women and so be dominant, but women may control certain types of resources and use them as countervailing bases; social changes may open up greater access over certain resources to women, as is arguably happening now with shifting patterns of female and male employment.

Although Giddens himself does not apply his theory to gender, I suggest that his ideas hold potential for a more satisfactory theory of gendered power. It is possible to identify a number of dimensions of power in terms of access and control of different resources and investigate how these are deployed in specific empirical cases. For example, we might distinguish economic resources (property, wealth and money); positional resources (access to various positions of authority in both the public and private sphere); symbolic resources (including language, the various media of communication); domestic resources (control over the provision of subsistence needs in the household); sexual resources (the giving and withholding of sexual pleasures); and personal resources (use of individual character and qualities to exercise control). Although historically men have appropriated more of the first three of these, women's control of sexual, domestic and personal resources has often allowed them to exercise power especially in personal relationships or in the home.

The work of Foucault and Giddens points the way ahead. An urgent task for feminists, whether they espouse postmodernist thinking or not, is to develop a theory of power which can handle the complexities of post-industrial social relationships and avoid the crude view of women as victims.

Gendered identities

Barrett suggests that the appeal of post-structuralism to feminists arises partly from the fact that it deals with 'the issues of sexuality, subjectivity and textuality that feminists have put at the top of the agenda' (1992, p. 215). Such new concerns in gender analysis bring the issue of identity to the fore.

Unlike class, gender currently is viewed as an active and politicized aspect of identity. The feminist movement, with its stress on 'consciousness-raising', promoted the notion of being a woman as a crucial aspect of individual subjectivity. Involvement in feminist activities of various kinds made gender central to many women's identities. Even women who reject feminism may demonstrate an active gender identity because of the high level of awareness about gender issues raised by, among other things, equal opportunities programmes and media coverage of women's issues.

But there are many ways of being a woman. Gender may for feminists be a source of politicized identity which leads them to work for equality and women's causes. For other women, awareness of gender may involve traditional ways of displaying femininity, through domestic or caring roles, motherhood or assertion of sexuality. Given that gender experience is so differently felt by women of different ethnic groups, ages, religions, nationalities or sexual orientations, it is evident that there are multiple versions of womanhood. The experience of the gendered body is also important here. For a post-pubescent young woman exploring the pleasures (and problems) of her newly sexualized body in relation to young men, the experience of womanhood is quite different from that of an ageing post-menopausal woman, struggling to adjust to bodily changes in a culture that puts high valuation on youth and fertility. Gender identities, then, are multiple.

Early feminist research borrowed the concept of consciousness from stratification theory to explore this issue. Research was directed to the debate as to whether class or gender consciousness was more significant to working-class women (Pollert, 1981; Porter, 1983). These studies suggested that women did have a specific consciousness, a 'woman's consciousness' rather than a 'feminist consciousness'; this was linked more to home lives and concerns than their work experience (Cavendish, 1982; Westwood, 1984). By contrast work has commonly been linked to masculinity (Cockburn, 1983). After two decades of feminist campaigning, recent research has revealed a much sharper sense of conflicting gender interests at work (Crompton and Sanderson, 1990; Cockburn, 1991). But the long history of women's involvement in industrial struggles shows that class, too, can be a politicized identity for women in specific contexts, and is often seen to outweigh gender considerations (Phillips, 1987; Briskin and McDermott, 1993). These findings show us the error of conceiving the problem in terms of whether class or gender is the dominant source of identity. Rather, the interplay of gender and class dynamics (along with others) is displayed in shifting processes of identification. Under the influence of postmodernism, the concept of identity has displaced the analysis of consciousness and allows more easily for the understanding of the multiple elements constituting an individual identity. The assumption of postmodernists is that gender is more central to identity than class in contemporary societies; the burden of research certainly indicates that gender matters to women.

By contrast, masculinity, at least until recently, could be seen as a more passive element in identity. Kitzinger and Wilkinson use the term 'default identity' to describe those which 'constitute the "normal, natural way to be"', such as white, able-bodied or male. They argue (1993, p. 32) that default identities are always 'less articulated, less self-conscious, than are oppositional or oppressed identities: lack of reflectiveness is the privilege of power'. However, at certain historical moments when a 'crisis of masculinity' occurs

(Kimmel, 1987), men may become much more reflexive about their gender. Such a crisis has been identified in many contemporary societies, as men face the feminist challenge to conventional gender relations and experience the erosion of the breadwinner role. The emergence of men's consciousness-raising groups and the men's rights campaigns of the 'backlash' suggest that masculinity may be displayed in more active or politicized forms of identity.

Riley's work (1988) alerts us to the fact that our gender is not to the forefront of our awareness all the time. She suggests that the awareness of being a woman is likely to emerge when gender becomes a source of adverse attention from others (discriminatory behaviour, harassment in the street) or indeed of positive attention. Similarly, the awareness of being a man may be heightened where masculinity is under threat (a challenge from a wife to her husband's authority, derogatory comments from other men) or strongly affirmed (in activities featuring 'male bonding', such as sport or drinking). In these circumstances men may demonstrate their sense of manhood through demonstrations of expected masculine behaviour, such as violence, fighting, physical feats, sexual assertiveness or sexist banter. But there are many ways to be a man and masculine identities are cross-cut with different expectations linked to ethnicity, age, sexual orientation and so forth. For example, it has been suggested that African American and Afro-Caribbean British men adopt an exaggerated form of machismo, often manifested through the assertion of control of physical spaces seen as 'their' territories. This streetwise masculinity is their response to racism and denigration by white society, and offsets their sense of being considered inferior to white men (M. Wallace, 1990; Westwood, 1990).

Sexuality is also an important aspect of gendered identity. The gay and lesbian movement has promoted homosexual identification of a highly active and politicized kind. By contrast Kitzinger and Wilkinson (1993), commenting on a collection of writings by heterosexual feminists, suggest that heterosexuality is another taken-for-granted default identity. In fact within the feminist movement heterosexuality has been seen as problematic and may even be stigmatized, counterposed to the assertion of woman-centred values and the espousal of lesbianism as a political strategy. But for non-feminist women, heterosexuality may be an important source of self-affirmation. This illustrates the way identities are highly informed by political contexts. It also points again to the multiple nature of gendered identities which must be viewed within the logic of interacting dynamics.

Interacting dynamics: gender, ethnicity, class and age

Ethnicity

While all women experience some aspects of gender inequalities (responsibility for domestic work, restricted opportunities and subjection to male authority in waged work, the threat of male violence), the specific nature of gender inequalities is different for different ethnic groups, classes and age groups.

For example, in Britain women of colour face specific restrictions in the labour market because of their long-term exposure to processes of individual and institutional racism. In schools, young Asians and Afro-Caribbeans face racial harassment from white pupils and stereotyping from teachers which may affect their educational progress (Fleming, 1991; Mirza, 1992). Asian and Afro-Caribbean women enter a racialized as well as gendered labour market (Brah, 1994). Skilled minority ethnic women are twice as likely to be unemployed as white women; they face difficulties in gaining access to some parts of the female labour market, such as clerical work. Afro-Caribbean women are concentrated in lower-grade caring work and public sector jobs, Pakistani and Bengali women in semi-skilled or unskilled factory work, such as textiles and in home-working (Brown, 1984; Allen and Wolkowitz, 1987; Bruegel, 1989). Afro-Caribbean women are more likely than white to work full-time, illustrating the importance of employment to them where black males suffer greater risks of unemployment and where family relationships have promoted an important breadwinner role for mothers.

The black feminist critique promoted research interest in uncovering the ways in which women of different ethnic groups experience gender. Such research is still under way and we know relatively little about the situation of women in some ethnic groups (for example, Chinese and Turkish women in Britain). It is clear that the position of each group is in many ways unique, a point that can be illustrated by referring to one example, that of Muslim women in Britain. The role of religion means that in some ways this can be seen as an exceptional case (it is certainly controversial) but it illustrates admirably the interpenetration of gender divisions, ethnic identity and racial discrimination.

Haleh Afshar's study of Muslim women in Yorkshire (1994) reveals the difficult situation of women, especially unmarried young women, 'who have to tread a tightrope of double identities, double values and double standards' (p. 141). The international revival of Islam has opened up a positive identity and source of solidarity and pride for Muslim women, as opposed to the experience of being the stigmatized 'Other' in the playground. Thus many women willingly embrace Islamic dress styles, such as wearing headscarf or veil. Abu Odeh's (1993) work shows that many women welcome the protection the veil offers them against male intrusion in the form of sexist abuse and sexual harassment. But fundamentalist versions of Islam, just like Christian, Jewish or any other form of fundamentalist religion, involve 'reinvigoration of patriarchy and the control of women' (Brah, 1993, p. 20). Patriarchal rules, which set restrictions on women's participation in various aspects of public life, may create difficulties for women who must participate in the British labour market, which displays different rules on gender. Afshar points out the double standard whereby males may share aspects of Western lifestyle (drinking, smoking, flirtations, wearing Western fashions) while women must bear the burden of displaying proper Islamic behaviour and maintaining family 'izzat' (honour). Women's limited labour market chances may be further restricted both by the adoption of Islamic identity and by the heightened racism which is the likely effect of the fear and suspicion with which many Westerners respond to Islamic revivalism. The wearing of Islamic dress, however positively experienced by the wearer, by its visibility marks her out as 'different' and exposes her to assumptions surrounding stereotypes about 'oriental' women. Those who reject the rules may well face ostracism by their families and communities. Afshar's finding that the women she studied were more preoccupied with the issues of marriage and motherhood than with education and employment illustrates the variability of the experience of gender for women of different ethnic groups.

Class

Afshar suggests that middle-class Muslim families are more likely in the past to have 'integrated' into the British way of life; middle-class Muslim women may use qualifications and economic privilege to negotiate their way through gendered and racialized barriers. White middle-class women, too, can buy out of some of the effects of gendered inequalities.

Anne Phillips (1987) has traced out the way the feminist movement has faced disunity because of the 'divided loyalties' of class and gender. The experience of gender is class-specific. It can be argued that in the nineteenth centuries upper- and middle-class women suffered greater restrictions from gender differentiation as they were more subject to the doctrines of domesticity and 'separate spheres' which justified their exclusion from paid work. The frustrations of life in the 'gilded cage' gave impetus to the Victorian feminist movement which eventually helped to open up educational and career opportunities for middle-class women. Meanwhile the realities of working-class life meant that for many families the breadwinner/housewife family remained an ideal. Working-class women faced exceptionally hard lives as they struggled both with paid work and having to maintain often large families, but at least the experience of wage labour gave them a modicum of independence and authority in the family.

In the contemporary world, the situation is reversed. Women from the service and capitalist classes are able to use the 'qualifications lever' to pursue managerial and professional careers, thereby achieving financial independence and near equality with men (Crompton and Sanderson, 1990; Witz, 1992). They can use their wealth to buy out of the 'double shift' of paid labour and housework through employing cleaners and childminders. By contrast working-class women are encumbered by increasing workloads in the home and in employment; their labour market opportunities are often restricted to low-paid service work. It is more difficult for them to gain full financial independence from their menfolk, which leaves them more vulnerable to violence in the home.

Recent decades have seen increasing economic polarization between a middle-class professional elite and working-class women. That effect is heightened if we consider the position of women in the labour surplus class (see chapter 4). Such women face poverty and are often responsible for holding the family together. They bear the brunt of current conflicts over social definitions of parenting, as manifested by the controversies over the Child Support Agency and its attempt to recoup the costs of state benefits from absent fathers. Despite the growing numbers of women who shoulder the task of bringing up children alone, the state is reluctant to abandon the gender norms which decree that a family must have two parents, or to accept that the support of children should be a public as opposed to a purely private function. At the bottom of the class hierarchy, the weight of gendered inequality is disproportionately felt (Glendinning and Millar, 1992).

Age

The effect of age on gender is an under-researched topic, especially with regard to older women (Arber and Ginn, 1991a). Indeed, it could be argued that feminism has replicated the ageism of society as so much of its analysis deals with the experience of women of child-bearing age. We know, though, that older women face particular economic problems. Growing up in a climate which encouraged women into the housewife role and offered them limited educational and employment opportunities has meant that many face poverty in old age. As Groves argues, 'women's greater share of unpaid domestic work and their labour market position, including low pay, have inhibited their ability to generate an adequate income for old age' (1992, p. 206). Many older women live alone and fear of violence acts to circumscribe their movements. They have benefited little from the achievements of feminism. However, much of the specific gender experiences of older women remains to be uncovered.

We have more information on younger women. It is suggested that young women are often unsympathetic to feminism or consider it of little relevance to their lives (Stuart, 1990; Lees, 1993). Until they enter the labour market or get married their personal experience of gender inequality may be limited; although gender biases operate at school they are less visible than the evident inequalities of class and race. Adolescence is a time marked by clear gender differences and considerable segregation of the sexes in leisure; but these differences are often experienced by young women as pleasurable and exciting rather than as a form of disadvantage.

Yet younger women are particularly vulnerable to the pressures of compulsory heterosexuality. It may lead some to unwanted pregnancies, while most must learn to handle sexual pestering and sexist abuse from boys (Wood, 1984;

Halson, 1991). Young people who do not conform to heterosexual conventions, either because they are lesbian or gay, or because they cannot or will not join in with the adolescent culture of dating and courtship, are marginalized and made to feel misfits.

In fact, childhood and adolescence are crucial periods for gender relations, as times when young women and men have to make many choices which are vital to their later lives. Yet these are made in the context of differentiated gender expectations and of discourses of masculinity and femininity which promote male dominance.

Summary and conclusions

This chapter has explored the analysis of gender inequality largely through an account of feminism. This is because gender was neglected in mainstream sociology until second-wave feminists forced it on to the agenda. Since then, it has become a major research topic within social science.

Classic feminist standpoints provided valuable insights into gender inequality, stimulated a wealth of important research and provided key concepts for thinking about gender. Recently, however, the classic theories have been attacked for their oversimplified view of gender relations and because they reproduce the analytical strategies of modernist theories which are now criticized for foundationalism, essentialism and teleology. In particular, the classic approaches failed to recognize the diversity of experiences among women which were exposed by black feminism; and the theory of patriarchy was considered to rest on a crude and one-dimensional account of power.

What Barrett and Phillips call '1990s feminism' is influenced by postmodernism, post-structuralism and deconstructionism. It is concerned to avoid essentialism by exploring difference and deconstructing the key categories in which we think about gender. Although some of its projects (the study of gendered texts, for example) are rather marginal to the sociological analysis of inequalities, an important issue it raises is that of discourse. Discursive frameworks are seen to constitute rather than merely reflect reality; consequently, it is vital to study the way gender differences and exclusions are created and recreated through language.

Postmodernism has promoted the exploration of gender as an aspect of social identity. Gender is an important element within the 'fragmented identities' characteristic of post-industrial society and it has been argued here that gender identities are themselves multiple; there are many ways of being a woman, a man, a sexed subject.

While postmodernism has rightly pointed to differences in the experiences of working-class and minority ethnic women, there is an irony here. Current preoccupations with 'sexuality, subjectivity and textuality' may well serve to alienate these newly discovered constituencies further from middle-class feminism, as women lower down the social hierarchy remain concerned with problems of poverty and over-work. Feminism would do well to recover some of its initial zeal in exposing material inequalities rather than retreating too completely into academic theoreticism.

The lived relations of gender are complex and volatile, operating at all levels of society. Classic feminism attempted to link the different aspects of gender together through the concept of patriarchy, as exemplified by the work of Walby. However, in line with the theoretical framework espoused in this book, I suggest it may be preferable to adopt a looser approach, conceiving gender as interconnected and evolving sets of relations, both material and discursive, which create and recreate gender and sexual difference; some of these can be described as patriarchal. There is still a need to develop a more adequate and multi-dimensional theory of gendered power, which may be used to integrate the discussion of the diverse aspects of gendered reality.

Further reading

Three useful books which provide a general overview of the varied aspects of gender relations are: Sylvia Walby, *Theorizing Patriarchy* (Blackwell, 1990); Diane Richardson and Victoria Robinson (eds), *Introducing Women's Studies* (Macmillan, 1993); and Beth Hess and Myra Marx Ferree, *Analyzing Gender* (Sage, 1987). Rosemary Tong, *Feminist Thought* (Unwin Hyman, 1989) is the best, most comprehensive introduction to feminist theory, while Maggie Humm, *Feminisms* (Harvester Wheatsheaf, 1992) is a helpful introductory reader. A reasonably approachable introduction to the complexities of post-structural feminism is provided by Michèle Barrett and Anne Phillips, *Destabilizing Theory* (Polity, 1992) (especially the introduction).

5

'Race' and Ethnicity: 'Travelling in the West'

In *The Happy Isles of Oceania* Paul Theroux describes his travels in Australasia and the South Pacific and presents us with a devastating picture of the ways in which European colonialism has adversely affected the lives of indigenous populations. In Australia and New Zealand the aboriginal people, dispossessed of their lands, their culture despised by many whites, live on the margins of society. Many are confined to reservations or eke out a basic existence on welfare payments. Australian aborigines did not receive the right of citizenship until 1967. In the Pacific islands, colonialism has impinged at varying levels. Some islanders have abandoned their traditional cultures and ways of living at the instigation of what Theroux calls 'the unholy trinity of the missionary, the trader and the planter' (1992, p. 291). In common with other populations around the world, they are adopting aspects of Western lifestyles, particularly Americanized popular culture with its videos, slogan-bearing T-shirts, discotheques and fast foods. Various Christian sects, including Methodists, Seventh Day Adventists and Mormons, are militantly active in islands such as Tonga, Fiji and Samoa and have ousted traditional religions and beliefs, as have cargo cults. In the Solomon Isles Theroux found that the native people still lived under the shadow of the Second World War, when the quarrels of other nations were fought out in their waters; they listened in trepidation to radio coverage of the build-up to the Gulf War, believing that if fighting broke out they would once again be sucked into it. The French have used their colonial holdings in Polynesia to carry out nuclear tests. In a few islands, such as the Trobriands and New Hebrides, the peoples have managed to cling on to their lands, and many of their customary beliefs and lifestyles, but the uneasy balance of their lives now faces a new threat from Western and Japanese tourism and business interests.

In such ways the European colonialist drive which commenced in the late fifteenth century has indelibly marked itself upon the globe. The indigenous peoples of the Americas, Africa and Asia were subject to conquest, enslavement and genocide at the worst, at the least to the disruption and transformation of their own economies and cultures. The damage done ranged all the way from the total extermination of tribal groups in the Caribbean, South America and Tasmania, to the subtler psychic damage which still affects the inhabitants of many ex-colonial societies, as movingly described by Amitav Ghosh in his book *In an Antique Land.*

Ghosh, an Indian anthropologist from London, relates his encounters with the Egyptian fellaheen (peasants) among whom he was conducting fieldwork. Despite the very different cultural traditions from which they came (Islamic and Hindu), he describes both himself and the Egyptians as entrapped within the framework of Western ideas: as he evocatively puts it, 'travelling in the West'. When debating their different religious beliefs, they were forced to assess cultures in the discourse of Western economic development, 'the language that had usurped all the others in which people once discussed their differences':

> They had constructed a certain ladder of 'Development' in their minds, and because all their images of material life were of those who stood in the rungs above, the circumstances of those below had become more or less unimaginable. I had an inkling then of the real and desperate seriousness of their engagement with modernism, because I realized that the fellaheen saw the material circumstances of their lives in exactly the same way that a university economist would: as a situation that was shamefully anachronistic, a warp upon time; I understood that their relationship with the objects of their everyday lives was never innocent of the knowledge that there were other places, other countries, which did not have mud-walled houses and cattle-drawn ploughs. (1994, p. 200)

Cultural exchanges around the world are overshadowed by the technological, scientific and military dominance of the West, its 'science and guns and tanks and bombs' (p. 237).

The relationships of colonialism and its legacy are one important aspect of the great web of racial and ethnic relations which binds the populations of the contemporary world together. 'Race' and ethnicity are two of the social categories which we have evolved to explain lived relationships which emanate from territorial arrangements and from the migration of people from different territorially based groups around the world. In Anthias's and Yuval-Davis's phrase, ethnicity is a construct denoting 'collectivity and belongingness' (1993, p. 2). They see 'race' as an aspect of what they call 'ethnic phenomena' (p. 2), processes by which people are divided up into different communities with clear boundaries between them. In recent history, ideas about ethnicity have tended to converge with the related territorial notions of 'nation' and 'nationality'. Benedict Anderson, in a highly influential account, has offered a definition of nation as an 'imagined community': imagined in the sense that 'the members of even the smallest nation will never know most of their fellow-members, meet them, or even hear of them, yet in the minds of each lives the image of their communion' (1991, p. 6). 'Race' and ethnicity, too, can be seen as forms of imagined community – which, however, are linked to lived relations surrounding territoriality and migration.

While people have defined themselves – and been defined by others – as belonging to different groups or communities as long as there has been historical record, the ordering of such communities into a hierarchy of superior and inferior groups, which is a crucial feature of contemporary racial and ethnic relations, has been particularly influenced by migration. Anderson argues (1994) that it was 'exile', the experience of being apart from one's community, which promoted the nationalist fervour of the nineteenth century. Migration of people around the globe, whether undertaken freely in search of new lands or better prospects, or forced on people because of warfare, conquest or economic disaster, has involved the mixing of groups of people from different territorially based communities and is currently manifested in the 'multiculturalism' or 'social pluralism' of societies such as America and Britain where a multitude of ethnic groups coexist.

Migration, however, has historically been bound up with conquest and warfare. It was encouraged by the establishment of the great empires of antiquity, such as those of Greece and Rome, or later by the Islamic conquest of the Mediterranean areas in the medieval period. European colonialism was the successor to these and can be seen as particularly crucial in promoting substantial inter-continental migration. This laid the grounds for the particular racial and ethnic hierarchies which still characterize the post-colonial world. Conquering groups not only themselves travelled around their conquered territories, but moved subject groups around their empires to provide various types of labour and services, a process which was particularly marked under European colonial expansion since it coincided with the development of the system of capitalist production. The movement of enslaved labourers from Africa to work in the plantations of the Americas and the Caribbean, cultivating crops such as cotton, sugar and coffee, was particularly significant for later race relations and was crucial to the successful development of capitalism (Hobsbawm, 1968; Bryan et al., 1985). In the post-slavery period, white European settlers continued to rely on indentured labour, sometimes from the local populace, sometimes brought in from the Indian sub-continent, China, Africa and elsewhere, to carry on agricultural production or to develop industrial enterprises.

Conquest and colonialism marked some ethnic communities out as dominant, others as subjected and subordinate. Linked to such power disparities between different ethnic, racial and national groups has been the formation of ideas in which dominant groups identify themselves as different from the subordinate.

Robert Miles, in a useful survey, traces out the history of such thinking in terms of 'representations of the Other' (1989, p. 11). For example, the Greeks and Romans thought of those outside the ambit of their imperial civilization as 'the barbarians', and both Muslims and Christians in the medieval period stigmatized those of the other faith as 'infidels'. As Hall (1992a) argues, with the development of colonialism, the prevailing version of this became that of 'the West and the rest'. White European societies were presented as the model for the future development of humankind, as Ghosh's account illustrates. Europeans drew on pre-existing ideas about 'the savage' and 'the oriental' to legitimate their colonial rule (Miles, 1989). They represented themselves as shouldering the 'white man's burden', the task of 'civilizing' backward peoples and leading them towards enlightenment, abandonment of superstition, modernization and economic development. Native populations were portrayed both as childlike and simple and as cruel and unruly, 'half-devil and half-child' in Rudyard Kipling's phrase (*The White Man's Burden*). Africans in particular were stereotyped as something 'less than human', to justify their enslavement. Such views continued to be expressed by colonial administrators and settlers throughout the imperial period as exemplified by this quotation from the 1920s:

> The typical African of this race-type is a happy, thriftless, excitable person, lacking in self-control, discipline and foresight, naturally courageous, and naturally courteous and polite, full of personal vanity, with little sense of veracity, fond of music, and 'loving weapons as an oriental loves jewelry'. (Lugard, 1929; quoted in Miles, 1989, p. 103)

Colonialism and slavery are viewed as central to the formation of racial and ethnic hierarchies and of racist ideologies. However, the lived relations of 'race' and ethnicity continually change as patterns of migration shift, national boundaries are contested and reshaped, and ideas about ethnicity are challenged and reformulated. Since the ending of colonial rule, patterns of migration have been complex. There has been movement at times between ex-colonizers and colonies. One example is the post-war immigration of commonwealth citizens (especially from India, Pakistan and the West Indies) into Britain as a response to labour shortages caused by the war and post-war economic regeneration; another is the continued migration, sometimes permanent, sometimes temporary, between France and her former North African colonies, Algeria, Tunisia and Morocco. But the definition of 'race relations' and immigration as 'social problems' has also led many European societies (and the United States) to adopt policies of immigration control. Control of immigration into Britain since the 1960s has been particularly strict. As Gilroy (1987) and Miles (1989) argue, state policy has been based implicitly on racist principles which have defined 'coloured' or 'new' commonwealth immigrants as unwanted citizens, as opposed to applicants from the 'old' commonwealth countries of Canada, New Zealand and Australia.

At the same time, warfare and ethnic conflicts in various parts of the world over the last few decades have entailed the movement of refugees into various parts of Europe and North America. For example, British governments allowed the Asian communities expelled from East Africa in the 1970s to take up residence in Britain. Patterns of migration are set to alter again as the rules of the newly integrated European Community allow immigration between member states; it is suggested that this will lead to increased prohibition against the entry of non-European immigrants (Brah, 1993; Bhavnani, 1993). The recent collapse of the Soviet bloc, along with the ethnic conflicts in the ex-satellites of the Soviet empire such as the former Yugoslavia, add another dimension to the entanglements of contemporary migration patterns. Finally, the spread of global capitalist production itself fosters the continued movement of elements of capital and labour between countries.

In today's multi-ethnic societies the processes of interaction between different ethnic groups are volatile and have sometimes taken a conflictual form. In Britain and America since the 1960s there have been sporadic outbreaks of rioting involving issues of 'race'. In Britain the Notting Hill and Nottingham 'race riots' of 1958 fed in to popular unease about race relations. Such popular fears were fuelled through the 1960s by the acts and campaigns of politicians. Enoch Powell's infamous 1968 speech about the 'swamping' of British cultures by alien elements, with its vision of the rivers of Britain flowing with blood, gained considerable public support (although in the 1990s ethnic minorities still form only 4.8 per cent of the British population). Such events were the context of the 1962, 1965 and 1971 Immigration Acts, which limited the intake of 'coloured' immigrants only. But these events also prompted calls for legislation against racial discrimination and the development of what has become known as 'the race relations industry'. It also promoted the development of race relations as a topic for study within sociology.

The focus of study was those groups seen to be *racialized*: that is, defined as different (and inferior) in terms of ascribed racial characteristics, especially skin colour. Research concentrated on Afro-Caribbean and Asian groups and showed the disparities between 'Black and White Britain' (Brown, 1984). Various surveys, along with what government statistical material is available, have revealed persistent patterns of disadvantage among these groups in the areas of employment, unemployment, housing, health and education (see Daniel, 1968; Smith, 1977; Brown, 1984).

For example, Afro-Caribbeans and Asians are more likely to live in rundown inner-city areas where services are overstretched; in some cases such areas may approximate to the 'ghetto' areas of North American cities. In Britain 60 per cent of Bangladeshis and 47 per cent of Pakistanis are reported to be living in overcrowded conditions as opposed to only 3 per cent of whites (Anthias and Yuval-Davis, 1992). In London, ethnic minority members, especially the young, are four times as likely to be homeless as whites. In the area of health, Afro-Caribbeans are twelve times more likely to be diagnosed as

Table 5.1 Unemployment and Ethnicity

Adult Males (16+)	
White	10%
Ethnic minorities	19%
Young people aged 16–24	
White	15%
Indian	17%
*Black	42%
Pakistani and Bangladeshi	32%

Source: Labour Force Survey, 1994–5.
* Afro-Caribbean, black-African, black-Other (census 1991 categories).

schizophrenic than white people. Black British are over-represented in the prison population: 24 per cent of women in prison or remanded in custody in 1989 were from minority ethnic groups, and in 1991 15 per cent of prisoners in England and Wales were black (Skellington and Morris, 1992). Members of racialized minorities are highly vulnerable to unemployment especially younger people, as shown in table 5.1. In 1994, 28 per cent of Pakistanis and Bangladeshis and 26 per cent of Afro-Caribbeans were unemployed (Social Trends, 1995).

While part of this disadvantage arises from the concentration of Afro-Caribbean and Asian British in the lower class groupings, studies reveal the importance of racism and discrimination in perpetuating disadvantage (for example, Smith, 1977; Jenkins, 1986). Employers attribute characteristics to Afro-Caribbean and Asian applicants which are used to exclude them from better jobs (Wrench and Lee, 1978). Teachers stereotype Afro-Caribbean boys as lazy, troublesome and non-academic, Asian boys and girls as hard-working but over-ambitious (Brah, 1986; Mirza, 1992). Reports on specific institutions and localities have highlighted the way racism operates in many areas of social life. For example, the 1989 Gifford Inquiry into racial discrimination in Liverpool found that black people were confined to certain parts of the city and were targets of hostility and abuse if they moved outside them. Few of Liverpool's 30,000 black inhabitants held jobs in visible 'white' areas such as city centre shops. Most shocking of all, while the city council claimed to be an 'equal opportunities employer', only 490 out of a total 30,410 council employees were black. Nationwide, Asians in particular have been the target of increasing harassment and attacks. The police reported 8779 racial attacks in 1993, nearly a thousand more than in the previous year. Beatrix Campbell in *Goliath* (1993) paints a chilling picture of the everyday harrassment experienced by people living in Newcastle's West End: 57 per cent of black people in Newcastle had experienced racial abuse, 45 per cent attacks on property;

Table 5.2 Ethnicity and Self-employment: Percentage of Labour Force Reporting Themselves Self-employed

	White	Black	Indian	Pakistani/ Bangladeshi
Males	16	9	18	19
Females	7	*	8	*

Source: Labour Force Survey, 1994–5.
* No reliable figures available.

schoolchildren described being regularly submitted to racist insults, sworn at and spat at, bullied, taunted and beaten up at school. Victimization increases if police or teachers are informed of the harassment.

Qualitative and quantitative studies provide ample evidence of racism and the disadvantages suffered by racialized groups in Britain. Recently, however, the trend has been to move beyond the dichotomized model of 'Black and White British' (Hiro, 1992). Postmodern influences have led to an interest in exploring the position of the many diverse minority groups in Britain (the Chinese and Turkish populations, for example, have been little studied). Statistical evidence indicates the different positions of specific ethnic groups, as in the unemployment figures quoted earlier. For example, while all Asians are more concentrated in semi-skilled or unskilled manual work than whites, Bangladeshi employees are most likely to be in these occupational categories (nearly 70 per cent), as opposed to 40 per cent of Indians and Pakistanis and 55 per cent of African Asians (Anthias and Yuval-Davis, 1993). Certain ethnic groups are also much more likely to be self-employed, as is shown in table 5.2.

The emphasis in study, then, has switched from a concern with 'race' and colour to a broader concern with culture and ethnicity (Modood, 1992). In such an approach the investigation of white ethnicities also becomes a task of sociological interest. Being 'British' and white, can mean being English, Scots, Welsh or Irish – and also Jewish, Polish, Australian and so on. In the multi-ethnic world ethnic identities are multi-layered, 'hybrid' or 'hyphenated' (Bhabha, 1990a; Modood, 1992).

Previous chapters have emphasized the importance of difference and contextual specificity for the understanding of social inequality. This is even more pronounced when considering ethnicity than in the case of gender and class. Each society has experienced specific patterns of past migration which inform current racial and ethnic hierarchies. For that reason it is dangerous to make generalizations about race relations from the experience of one society. Subsequent discussion in this chapter looks specifically at Britain, although examples from other countries are dealt with in chapter 7.

The remainder of this chapter outlines earlier approaches which were concerned with racial inequality between black and white groups, before considering the newer positions which emphasize the plurality of ethnic divisions. First, however, it is necessary to confront some terminological problems involved in the study of racial and ethnic differences.

Defining terms: 'race', ethnicity and nationality

Discussion of racial inequality has often become bogged down in debates about the appropriate usage of the key concepts of 'race' and 'ethnicity' and related terms such as racism, racialism and racialization. Disputes also relate to what terms should be used to describe various ethnic groups. Terms like 'coloured' (now thoroughly discredited) or 'black' can be attacked as being themselves racist, or alternatively as being essentialist and covering up real differences among groups so categorized. By and large, sociologists have tried to use the terms which are preferred by members of the various groups themselves. In Britain the term 'black' was adopted by Afro-Caribbean and Asian activists as a chosen political identity. The term 'of colour' was used in the same way in America. But recently it has been claimed that such umbrella terms conceal the distinct situations of the different groups involved (Modood, 1992); the specific experience of British Asian groups is subsumed into 'black' writings which chiefly express the viewpoint of those of African origin. In this book, I have used 'black' and 'of colour' where it seemed appropriate to refer to political alliances across ethnic minorities or because these terms are used by authors whose work is under discussion. Otherwise I specify which particular ethnic groups are concerned.

These debates have been amply explored elsewhere (for example, Miles, 1989; Mason, 1992). Here I merely indicate how the terms are used in this book. I have drawn particularly on the usages proposed by Floya Anthias and Nira Yuval-Davis, whose approach seems to me analytically coherent and practically useful.

'Race'

'Race' as a common-sense usage refers to the idea that human beings can be divided into sub-groups which have different origins and are distinguished by biological differences. Such differences can be seen as 'phenotypical' (relating to physical appearances such as skin colour or hair type) or 'genotypical' (relating to underlying genetic differences). These ideas were given backing in the nineteenth century by scientists who extended the systems of classification developed for the study of plants and animals to distinguish different sub-species of 'homo sapiens': a popular taxonomy distinguished caucasian, negroid and mongoloid races. Modern genetic science generally now rejects the concept of race as invalid (although there are still disputes about it). Even if originally distinct racial types could be distinguished, centuries of migration and interbreeding make the idea that each individual has a specific racial make-up extremely problematic.

Within sociology, 'race' is considered a non-scientific category and for that reason Miles has consistently argued (1982; 1989) that we should reject the concept altogether. He states that it is an ideological construct: its use only serves to give respectability to discredited racist ideas. But other sociologists have pointed out that all forms of social category (such as class and gender) are constructs; since such constructs inform the way people think and act in relation to others the effects of 'race' are very real (Cashmore and Troyna, 1983; Gilroy, 1987). 'Race' can be viewed as *a form of social relationship to which racial meanings are attached by the participants* (Mason, 1992).

Cashmore and Troyna suggest that 'race' should be seen as a stigmatized identity forced on other people (as opposed to ethnicity which is freely adopted and proclaimed). Similarly Modood proposes that 'race' relates to 'mode of oppression' (how a group is categorized and subordinated) while ethnicity refers to 'mode of being' (how it views its own identity, culture, values). But, while the process of racialization often involves imposition and stigma, this is not always the case. Members of dominant groups may assert a racial identity seen as a positive asset and a cause of their own superiority, as happened in Nazi Germany or among British neo-fascist groups with their belief in the 'master race'. Moreover, a stigmatized identity may be appropriated and subverted as a basis for resistance to dominant meanings, and for positive identification as in the case of Black Power and similar movements: 'Say it loud, I'm black and I'm proud!'

The distinctive feature of 'race' as a form of relationship, as opposed to ethnicity or nation, is the imputation of inborn (usually biological) difference (Rattansi, 1992). Race is a way of constructing differences 'on the basis of an immutable biological or physiognomic difference which may or may not be seen to be expressed mainly in culture and lifestyle but is always grounded on the separation of human populations by some notion of stock or collective heredity of traits' (Anthias and Yuval-Davis, 1993, p. 2).

Anthias and Yuval-Davis also believe that race should be seen as a special case of the broader category of 'ethnic phenomena'.

Ethnicity

'Ethnos' and 'ethnicity' are terms with a rather different history. Less common in popular usage (at least until recently), the terms were employed in social anthropology to describe social groups with a shared culture; they could refer to a whole society, but were more commonly used to describe a collectivity within a larger society (Richardson and Lambert, 1985), as reflected in our usage of the term 'ethnic minority'. Ethnic groups may be defined (or define themselves) on the basis of language, religion or nationality, but the idea of shared culture is perhaps the crucial issue. Also very important (indeed Anthias and Yuval-Davis make this central to their definition) is the idea of a common origin. This origin may be mythical or real, based on a religious text, on historical events or the idea of a (sometimes lost) homeland, or a mix of all of these. The crucial point is that it binds the members of the group together in a sense of belonging and constructs boundaries between them and the rest of the world.

The idea of ethnicity was formerly treated with suspicion by many radical theorists of race relations, on the grounds that it gave too much prominence to culture rather than racism (Richardson and Lambert, 1985) and so could be used to blame the victims of discrimination. 'Ethnic ties' and attachments to culture among immigrant groups could be seen as the reason for failure to achieve educational and occupational success. This could easily lead to the view of ethnic minority cultures as deficient or even 'pathological', for example in the argument that the 'weak' structures of Afro-Caribbean families and the prevalence of woman-headed families were causes of school failure and delinquency. Mac an Ghaill (1988) strongly attacks cultural theories of this kind which are used to explain the apparent 'under-achievement' of black pupils in school in terms of 'cultural deprivation' or difficulties of communication arising from language difference. He states that differential achievements between black and white pupils can largely be accounted for in terms of material differences, chiefly the concentration of Afro-Caribbean families in lower class groupings, while racism and stereotyping in schools also affect performance.

Recently postmodern thinking has encouraged a greater appreciation of culture and its impact on social relationships. In addition the notion of ethnicity allows for consideration of conflicts and hierarchies among groups which are not distinguished only on racial grounds but by culture, language or religion (as, for example, between Protestants and Catholics in Northern Ireland, Sikhs and Hindus in India, or Serbs, Croats and Bosnian Muslims in the former Yugoslavia). This has promoted a widespread adoption of the category of ethnicity, which is currently used more or less interchangeably with 'race'. I share Anthias's and Yuval-Davis's view that it is useful to see 'race' as a special case of ethnic division, but also agree with Mason that it is important to employ the term 'race' to distinguish those situations where racial definitions are the crucial feature. Racially defined groups are most likely to suffer exclusion, marginalization and subordination within the social hierarchy. In this text I have followed Mason's usage of 'race', while I use ethnicity more generally to refer to the sense of belonging to a community which may not necessarily be defined in racial terms.

'Race' and ethnicity are social categories used in reference to divisions within a particular society. A final aspect of the lived relations arising from territorial allocations and migration is the global hierarchy between different nations.

Nation

The concept of a 'nation' (although often linked to ethnicity) implies a distinct politically defined territory. Anthropologists have viewed nations as extensions of kinship or clan groupings (as in the usage 'Sioux nation'). But nowadays we more familiarly associate it with the 'nation-state' which evolved in Europe from the eighteenth century in Europe as the prevailing type of polity. The emergence of nation-states is associated both with the rise of democratic political forms and with the overthrow of absolutist monarchies which preceded them. It has been historically connected with nationalist movements, especially where the formation of a nation-state involved the overthrowing of an occupying power or the ousting of colonial rulers. Indeed, Ernest Gellner argues (1983) that nations cannot emerge until a nationalist spirit is present.

Benedict Anderson defines the nation as 'an imagined political community' (1991, p. 6), a view close to that of Gellner, who suggests that nations come into being when people develop the will to be united with 'all those, and only those, who share their culture' (1983, p. 55). Both Gellner and Anderson link the emergence of nations and nationalism to modernity and the development of industrial capitalism. For Gellner, strongly influenced by Durkheim's account of industrial society, the emergence of complex but integrated modern industry demands that all citizens share a sense of belonging and a common culture. In reality, this involves 'the general imposition of a high culture' (Gellner, 1983. p. 57) on all groups of society and the consolidation of impersonal bureaucratic rule; so, for Gellner, nations and nationalism are essentially illusions by which divided people develop a sense of false unity. By contrast, Benedict Anderson suggests that all types of communities are essentially 'imagined' or invented, and emphasizes the positive features of national identification, in terms, for example, of cultural productions or of the self-sacrifices made by people in nationalist causes. As opposed to a sense of common origin, what unites the nation is a sense of common destiny. Anderson argues that capitalism, together with the development of the technology of printing, created the conditions for the emergence of nations, and allowed the communication of ideas to the mass of people which could inspire a 'national imagination'.

Despite Anderson's stress on the positive features of national development, many radical thinkers, especially Marxists, have taken a negative view of nationalism. For example, Perry Anderson has emphasized how in nineteenth-century England nationalist ideology and jingoism were used by the ruling bloc to consolidate their social hegemony and pacify the working classes (P. Anderson, 1964). Gilroy (1987) stresses the way in which British nationalism has been built upon racist definitions of who 'the British' are.

In the past, nationalist movements served to unite groups who had formerly been separated on the basis of class, ethnicity, regional affiliation, religion and so forth. Thus nationalism could be seen as counterposed to fragmentation. In the postmodern cultural world, however, a different form of nationalism has taken hold, one exemplified by events in the former Yugoslavia and the terrible procedures described as 'ethnic cleansing'. The new nationalism is based on the idea that national boundaries should coincide with ethnos: all those, and only those, who share ethnicity (to paraphrase Gellner) should share a common territory. These beliefs, although based on suspect and essentialist premises that it is possible to assign a specific ethnicity to each individual, have inspired many of the recent conflicts in the former Soviet territories and in Africa, and contributed to the rise of racist neo-fascist groups in Europe.

While this book is concerned primarily with stratification within societies, the concept of nation is relevant to our discussion for three reasons. First, the new nationalisms described above inflame racial and ethnic relations on a global scale and exacerbate tensions already existing within nations. Secondly, the term 'nation' can be appropriated by racialized groups as a way of building alliances to challenge the prevailing hierarchies (as in the idea of a 'reggae nation'). Finally, nations are arranged in a 'pecking order' with the advanced capitalist societies of the G7 group at the top of the pyramid and the 'Third World' countries, especially those of Africa, at the base. Such hierarchical ordering of nations reinforces discourses giving sanction to racial and ethnic hierarchies within a society, such as that of the 'West and the rest'. This is the context in which discussion of racial inequalities must be located.

Explaining racial divisions in sociological theory

The classical sociological theorists, in their preoccupation with industrial development, tended to marginalize ethnicity along with gender. Although showing awareness of existing ethnic divisions and conflicts, they assumed that these were forces of the past, which would fade away with the advance of industrialism and capitalism (Pilkington, 1984). This assumption was shared by the functionalist mainstream of the twentieth century and enshrined in the theory of modernization, which suggested that all nations must follow the Western trajectory if they wished to develop. Ethnicity was seen as a characteristic of traditional societies which was becoming increasingly irrelevant in modern rationalized societies. 'Race' then, only became a significant issue in sociology when it entered public speech as a 'social problem.'

We can distinguish three main perspectives in the sociology of racial and ethnic divisions as it evolved in Britain in the 1960s. Both Marxists and Weberians turned to the study of 'race', attempting to extend their theories of stratification to include it. The relationship of race to class was their main theoretical preoccupation. A third position we could describe as a 'race relations' standpoint. This was a less theoretical stance, which was orientated towards policy issues and drew upon concepts from a range of perspectives.

Marxism

Neo-Marxists were drawn to the study of 'race', perhaps because the conflictual nature of race relations confirmed Marxian assertions that relations between dominant and subordinate groups inevitably promoted social conflict. Marxists sought to explain race relations, as they did gender, by incorporating 'race' as an element into the analysis of the capitalist mode of production. Prevailing strategies were to view 'race' as a special case of labour/capital relations or to show the ways in which racial divisions served to further the interests of capital.

American sociologist Oliver Cox (1970) took the latter line in an early contribution which exemplifies traditional Marxism. Cox's arguments reflected the view of class as the primary form of social division. He argued that apparent racial inequalities were in fact manifestations of class relations between bourgeois and proletariat. Capitalists exploited racial divisions to manipulate and divide the working class. In this view, racism is seen as a product of capitalism and serves to shore up capitalist power. In Britain Sivanandan (1982) developed similar ideas. A theoretical stance which carries this one stage further suggests that race and racism are merely ideological constructions, in the Marxian sense. That is, they are ideas which function to mystify and conceal real material formations and to legitimize and perpetuate prevailing relationships of exploitation and domination (Gabriel and Ben Tovim, 1979).

Such approaches minimize the distinctiveness of racial oppression and imply that racial divisions arise as a by-product of class exploitation. But as has been suggested, the forms of lived relations of territory and migration are heterogeneous and can be found in all types of historical epoch. A more satisfactory type of Marxist approach, which gives more weight to the specific nature of racial disadvantage, treats racialized groups as distinct types of labour. The work of Robert Miles typifies this approach. He suggests that the majority of Afro-Caribbean and Asian workers in Britain can be viewed as a 'racialized fraction' of the working class (Phizacklea and Miles, 1980; Miles, 1982). Miles, as we have seen, does not believe that 'race' has any 'real' existence; but he believes that the stigmatizing of ethnic groups by imputing racial differences to them allows them to be discriminated against and used to fill the kind of jobs that are rejected by the white majority. Black workers occupy distinct labour market positions, are more disadvantaged than their white fellows, and form a distinctive sub-group within the working class. However, they are still part of the proletariat, and Phizacklea and Miles argued that the consciousness of class as well as racial disadvantage led many black working people to be active within the labour movement.

Another concept, also utilized by Miles, is the notion of 'migrant labour'. This links the experience of settled immigrant populations (such as Afro-Caribbeans in Britain) to the broader processes of international migration within colonialism and capitalist development. It is argued that colonial powers and capitalist employers both used migrant labour as a source of cheap, highly exploitable labour. Castles and Kosack (1973) employed this concept to analyse the situation of ethnic minority workers in Europe, epitomized by the Turkish and North African 'guest-workers' in Germany. Migrant labourers, they argue, are used as an international reserve labour force to supplement the indigenous proletariat, especially in the 'dirty' jobs which are hard to fill. Because of their migrant status such workers can be expelled to their home countries when their labour is no longer needed, without any cost to the state (it does not have to pay them unemployment benefit, for example). Miles argues this concept can be applied to Afro-Caribbean and Asian workers in Britain, even when they are permanently settled in Britain and have citizen status (unlike the guest-workers). This is because their former immigrant status and their experience of different conditions in their countries of origin make them particularly vulnerable to exploitation. Miles also emphasized how frequently the black workers he studied held to the 'myth of return' to the Caribbean or India, which helped to give meaning to the circumstances of their lives in Britain. The rather similar notion of 'internal colonialism' has been employed by Blauner to explain the position of black workers in America; they form a pool of workers who are differentially viewed and utilized by employers because of the past history of slavery and colonialism (1969). Unlike other immigrant groups their labour-market situation has always been circumscribed by compulsion and coercion rather than free choice.

The advantage of the concept of migrant labour is that it extends the focus of analysis from contemporary capitalism, connecting it firmly to the past history of international relations and colonialism. It draws closer to the framework of territorial relations and migration which I have suggested is the context of racial and ethnic divisions. However, it still restricts the concept of 'race' to situations involving 'labour'.

An attempt to move beyond this economistic framework was made by Stuart Hall and his colleagues at the Centre for Contemporary Cultural Studies (for example, Hall et al., 1978; Centre for Contemporary Studies, 1982). Their brand of cultural Marxism was strongly influenced by the work of Gramsci. They considered the way racism and imperialist dogmas had been used to strengthen the cultural hegemony of the ruling bloc in British society. For example, the state's highlighting of 'problems' brought by immigration, such as the social panic over mugging which focused especially on young Afro-Caribbean men, served to divert attention from the real causes of Britain's social and economic problems (which they saw as rising from capitalist development and the fiscal crisis surrounding the funding of the welfare state). They view racism as deeply entrenched in British society. It does not merely serve to legitimate class domination but also informs the meanings working people impute to their experiences and the way they live out their own class position. In Hall's words 'race is thus . . . the modality in which class is "lived" . . . the form in which it is appropriated and "fought through"' (1980, p. 341).

The Marxist approach to race is undoubtedly useful in illuminating the specific ways in which colonialists and capitalists have exploited the labour of racialized groups and in showing how racist policies have been promoted by the state. But it shares the limitations of the Marxist analysis of gender. Other forms of division are seen as ultimately less important than class relations, and as determined by them (if not reducible to them). Moreover, there is a tendency to talk of racialized groups as analogous to 'labour' as though they were all part of the proletariat. While it is true that immigrant groups (especially those of colour) are disproportionately concentrated in lower occupational groupings, the past decades have seen the development of an extensive Asian petite bourgeoisie in Britain and of a 'black bourgeoisie' in the United States. In Britain some Asians and Afro-Caribbeans can be found at all levels in the class structure (for example among the professions). This suggests that rather than viewing racialized minorities as a distinct class, or class fraction (or even a separate class fraction within each broader class as suggested by Miles in his later work), it is better to think in terms of race and class dynamics interacting to produce a racialized labour market.

Within Marxism, racial divisions, like gender divisions, are viewed primarily from the standpoint of their contribution to the maintenance of capitalism. Because of this the importance of racist attitudes and practices among the white population as a whole tends to be underplayed. More fundamentally, as I have argued, racial and ethnic relations have a different existential location from class relations. They cannot be reduced to economic factors. Therefore Marxist approaches offer only a partial view on racial divisions.

Weberianism

The same criticism can be made of neo-Weberian approaches. Indeed, it is plausibly argued by Sarre (1989) and Anthias and Yuval-Davis (1993) that there is considerable overlap between Weberian and Marxist thinking on 'race'. Both perspectives see racial inequality in primarily economic terms and analyse 'race' in terms of its link to class.

Weber's own framework allows for a more flexible approach to race, in terms of his view of stratification as deriving from the distribution of power in society. This could be used to distinguish different kinds of groups within any particular society. There is no need to reduce everything to class. Indeed, Weber's concept of status provides one way of conceptualizing racial and ethnic divisions. Parkin (1979) suggests that ethnic groups could be seen as negatively privileged status groups. Processes of 'social closure', involving exclusion and demarcation, are used to mark out the social boundaries between groups and maintain the hierarchical ordering of the society. In this way, black groups might be kept out of jobs seen as reserved for whites, confined to lower ranks in the occupational hierarchy or excluded from certain areas of social life. This applies well to societies which are highly racially segregated, such as South Africa before the ending of the apartheid system or the Southern states of the USA prior to the successful campaigns of the Civil Rights movement. It can be objected, though, that this is merely descriptive and does not explain why such status differences come about. Castles (1984), moving away from his former Marxist position, tries to do this by combining Marxian and Weberian concepts. He explains the position of minority ethnic workers in Britain in terms of a mixture of class position, capitalist needs and minority status, arising from the colonial past.

The major contributor from the Weberian school, however, has been John Rex, who has put more weight on the economic as opposed to the status position of ethnic minorities. Rex firmly links 'race' disadvantage to class, although employing the latter term in the broader Weberian sense which embraces lifestyle differences. For example, he has pointed to the different consumption patterns of minority groups, particularly in housing. Research carried out with Moore in the Sparkbrook area of Birmingham was used to formulate the idea of distinct 'housing classes'. The study found that black immigrant groups were confined to certain types of housing (decayed inner-city properties, rented accommodation and lodging houses); access to housing was bringing the different ethnic groups into conflict with each other as an aspect of 'class struggle' (Rex and Moore, 1967, p. 273). In another study, with Tomlinson, of Asian and Afro-Caribbeans in Birmingham, Rex suggested that black minorities may form a distinct underclass because of disadvantage in the key areas of employment, education and housing (Rex and Tomlinson, 1979). White racism (among the white working class as well as employers) has helped to marginalize black minority groups, confining them to a distinct class location. Rex and Tomlinson also employed the Weberian concept of the dual labour market (see chapter 4) in their analysis of the employment situation of Afro-Caribbeans; their research indicated that whites and blacks were segregated into jobs with different characteristics.

In his many writings Rex has seemed to vacillate between the broader Weberian approach, as advocated by Parkin, and a position with many similarities to Marxism. He offered a well-known definition of a 'race relations situation' as one in which different unequal groups are in conflict with one another, and where the membership of the groups is fixed and ascribed (as opposed to achieved) on the basis of deterministic belief systems, involving for example a biologistic view of race (1970). Such a definition provides a foundation for analysing 'race' as an aspect of stratification quite distinct from class. However, as demonstrated above, in his research studies Rex drew on concepts from class theory to explain the specific position of black minority groups. In his more recent work he still states that class theory should be central to the explanation of ethnic and racial differences: 'class theory is useful – perhaps it is the most centrally useful theory – in approaching major problems of race and ethnic relations' (1986a, p. 83).

The reason for these beliefs appears to be that he shares Miles's view that 'race' is an unreal category. For this reason it cannot be a base for action in the way that class is: therefore the formation of racialized groups must be linked to broader economic processes:

> Since what are called racial and ethnic groups are groups (or quasi-groups) to whom common behavioural characteristics are imputed, rather than groups which have such characteristics, it is clear that the creation of such groups may depend upon the non-racial non-ethnic context and the motivations to which it gives rise. The study of race relations is therefore inextricably tied up with the study of group formations generally and with the study of social class and status. (Rex, 1986b, p. 17)

The Weberian approach allows for a multi-dimensional theory of stratification in terms of interaction between different types of group competing for power and resources. But perhaps because Weber himself did not make it entirely clear how race and ethnicity might be accommodated in his model (as status groups? as economic groups?), neo-Weberian sociologists of 'race' have tended to draw on class concepts. While Rex and Parkin move beyond the view of racial divisions as a product of capital needs, by giving far more weight to white racism, the status of 'race' as a separate aspect of inequality is still imprecise. As Anthias and Yuval-Davis argue, there is consequently remarkable similarity in the explanations offered by Rex and by Marxists such as Miles. Class still plays too prominent a role in this analysis.

The race relations approach

This criticism is not so relevant to the 'race relations' group which grounds itself on the distinctiveness of 'race' as a sociological topic. As stated earlier this approach is not a distinct theoretical position so much as a standpoint from which to think about 'race'. It is particularly associated with the work of Michael Banton, but many other sociologists worked broadly in this tradition.

The race relations approach was based on the proposition that race should be an autonomous and distinct topic for sociological enquiry. Adherents advocated the use of a broad range of applicable concepts from different areas of economics, sociology, social anthropology and elsewhere (Richardson and Lambert, 1985). Such borrowings might include concepts derived from Marx or Weber. From this standpoint, the broader topics of ethnicity and culture were seen to be of interest, in contrast to the tendency of Marxists and Weberians to concentrate on the dichotomous relations of 'black' and 'white' groups. Studies looked at the way distinct cultures were evolving among the various ethnic minority groups in Britain; these might be viewed in relation to debates about assimilation, integration or ethnic pluralism and multi-culturalism as possible outcomes of processes of immigration. However, the position of black minorities in Britain was still central to the race relations endeavour, especially as the orientation of this tradition was strongly towards social policy.

This policy orientation led to concern with the role of the state. Research dealt with topics such as the history of migration to Britain and elsewhere; immigration laws; the history of racist ideas; race relations legislation and equal opportunities; the ways in which minority groups in Britain experienced disadvantage and discrimination. Much of this research was descriptive and empirical rather than theoretical; but it provided a rich pool of information which could aid in the construction of theories.

Despite its lack of specific theoretical allegiance, we could see the 'race relations' standpoint as an example of classic mainstream liberalism. Indeed it shares many features with the liberal feminist standpoint: the theoretical eclecticism; a reformist political stance, advocating change within the existing system; and a particular concern with legislation, legal reform and education. For Marxist critics, this approach appeared insufficiently radical; there was a tendency to focus on individual racist attitudes and prejudice, rather than on how racial divisions are linked to broader social processes of capitalist and colonial or post-colonial development. However, the eclecticism of the race relations standpoint was useful for opening up wide areas of research. Indeed, its eclecticism is more compatible than the stricter frameworks of Marxism and Weberianism with the newer approaches currently evolving in the study of racial and ethnic divisions.

Newer developments: the 'new sociology of ethnicities'

Since black feminists had taken the lead in challenging the premises of classic feminism, it is not surprising that the study of 'race' and ethnicity is being influenced by similar ideas. Many new texts show the influence of postmodern and post-structuralist ideas (for example, Mercer, 1990; Donald and Rattansi, 1992; Gilroy, 1993). Within literary and historical studies a parallel new perspective, that of 'post-colonialism', has been developed as a corrective to what are seen as ethnocentric and distorted Western views of culture and history.

Postmodernism, post-structuralism and ethnicity

Like feminists, theorists of 'race' and ethnicity have been attracted to the postmodern perspective because of the critique it offers of one-dimensional modernist theories. While theories derived from class analysis tended to portray 'race' and ethnicity as secondary aspects of stratification ultimately determined by capitalist relations, a postmodern approach allows for the development of multi-dimensional accounts of inequality, *in which each dimension can be accorded equal weight*. 'Race' and ethnicity are considered crucial aspects of social differentiation in their own right.

New writing on 'race' and ethnicity has incorporated or found useful many of the features of postmodern and post-structural thinking which have been utilized in the analysis of gender. These include the following:

1 *The stress on difference and diversity* (Brah, 1992). Each ethnic group experiences different patterns of disadvantage and has developed distinctive responses within its own culture and community. Tariq Modood (1992) has been critical of the way previous studies featuring the experience of 'black' Britons concealed the specific concerns of the diverse Asian groups and subgroups, such as Pakistanis, Bangladeshis, Asians from East Africa, Gujaratis, Punjabis, Muslims, Sikhs and Hindus. Modood also argues that too much attention has been paid to skin colour as the base of racism, whereas he suggests that racism directed against Asians features themes of cultural and religious difference. The stress on diversity gives more weight to the concepts of ethnicity and culture as opposed to 'race'. The image of Britain and other societies now is that of a patchwork of heterogeneous ethnic groups (Anthias and Yuval-Davis, 1993; Afshar and Maynard, 1994).

2 *The attack on essentialism* (Donald and Rattansi, 1992). Traditional approaches, even radical ones, are criticized for essentialist views of ethnicity. There is an attempt to deconstruct the categories of 'black' and 'white' to show the divergent experiences of the various groups and individuals included. Such categories, like 'race', are seen as social constructs which cover as much as they reveal. Even the uncovering of the specificity of ethnic experience runs the risk of new forms of essentialism, as Yuval-Davis (1994) warns; it may be implied that 'all Pakistanis' (or Irish, or Cypriots) think or feel in certain ways or share experiences, or should do. Gilroy (1987; 1993) has termed this 'ethnic absolutism' and campaigns against its manifestations, which, he points out, can lead to such atrocities as have occurred in Bosnia, Rwanda and elsewhere. Closer to home, it promotes the kind of thinking, portrayed tragically in Spike Lee's film *Jungle Fever*, that it is a betrayal of one's 'brothers and sisters' to form a relationship with someone from a different ethnic community. By contrast, postmodernists see ethnicity as fluid and complex. Ethnic purity and the search for 'roots' are delusions; to some extent we are all mongrels.

3 *Rejection of the presentation of racialized minorities as victims* (Gilroy, 1987). Black groups are not passive recipients of racism and discrimination, but have a longstanding history of political and cultural resistance. Even in the appalling conditions of slavery, African exiles managed to develop their culture (songs, music, dance, rituals, diaries, literature) as a counterpoise to imposed Western values and a base for opposition and critique. In recent history oppressed and racialized minorities have been active in opposition to

their own subordination, not only through the more obvious forms of anti-racist and civil rights political activity, but also through the elaboration of counter-cultural forms, such as popular music.

4 The analysis of discourse (Bhabha, 1990b; Hall, 1992a). Various forms of discourse which perpetuate racist ideas and Western images of the 'Other' have become a topic of investigation. Studies of academic, literary and popular texts show how deeply embedded images of white superiority and non-white 'difference' have been within Western culture. In line with post-structuralist thinking, it is argued that such discourses not only reflect but help to constitute hierarchies between nations and ethnic groups. For example, Edward Said's famous account of *Orientalism* (1985) demonstrates how cultural representations of the relationships between Europe and Asia and the Middle East portray the 'Oriental Other' as exotic, seductive, but wily and untrustworthy. Discourses of this type are not just images; they have vital effects in terms of how different nations relate in a diplomatic and military context. Indeed, they become deeply embedded into the everyday relations between people of different ethnicities, as demonstrated in the wry description offered by Indian writer, Amit Chaudhuri, of the Indian restaurants in the Cowley Road area of Oxford:

> The furniture, selected with some tender and innocent idea of opulence in mind, was cheap and striking. Honest Englishmen sat being served among fluted armrests and large mendacious pictures of palm trees and winding rivers, helplessly surrendering to an inexhaustible trickle of eastern courtesy. Everything . . . from the silvery letters of the sign on the outside, to the decor within was a version of that style called 'the oriental'. (*Afternoon Raag*, p. 37)

Paul Gilroy's admirable work offers a good example of these newer approaches which we might call the 'new sociology of ethnicities'. *There Ain't no Black in the Union Jack* (1987) was written as the newer ideas took hold. In it he still uses the concepts of class and class formation, displaying the influence of the cultural Marxism of Hall. Indeed, unlike the postmodern feminists, writers concerned with the 'new ethnicities' (Hall, 1992c) have not abandoned the concept of class, which, they argue, must be understood as part of the process of social differentiation. But Gilroy criticizes existing accounts of the relationship between class and 'race', either for reducing it to economic issues or for portraying race as merely an ideological effect. He attempts to give more weight to 'race' as a separate factor by focusing on 'racial meanings, solidarity, and identities' (p. 27), suggesting that 'race' should be viewed as a political category (p. 38) and different racial groups as 'political collectivities', (p. 149). In empirical chapters he traces out a discourse of black criminality which has developed in Britain over the post-war decades; and he studies various forms of autonomous political and cultural forms through which black minorities in Britain and America have resisted racial oppression. He argues that black 'expressive cultures', such as the popular music forms of reggae, hip-hop and rap, can be read as an indictment and critique of capitalism. These chapters display the interest in language and culture which we have noted as typical of postmodern feminism and which is extended in Gilroy's later work (1993).

Anthias and Yuval-Davis (1993) criticize Gilroy for never providing a very clear account of the precise relationship of class and 'race' (is class, too, a political category?) and for the ambiguity of his view of how 'race' is to be grounded. Nonetheless, his work can be seen as a very important (if not totally successful) attempt to combine a structural approach (to class formation) with an account which draws on the postmodern interest on meaning, culture, discourse and the social construction of identities. Anthias's and Yuval-Davis's own theoretical position is an extension from this. They view ethnicity, gender and class as different aspects of the social processes by which boundaries between collectivities are drawn and social differences are constructed. Each has its own separate 'existential location', but, they argue, they should not be seen as separate since all intersect with one another in any specific context. This resembles the framework presented in this book.

It is noticeable that many of those involved in the new sociology of ethnicities are sociologists of colour. With some exceptions (such as Hall, Sivanandan and Cox), most of the previously prominent figures in the sociology of race relations were white. This may reflect the desire of black intellectuals to develop their own ways of thinking rather than rely on adapting concepts from the dominant Western metanarratives which were shaped by Western preoccupations and assumptions. There is an attempt to move out of the framework of Western thought and its ethnocentric values, to escape from 'travelling in the West'. This is the thinking that informs the notion of 'post-colonialism'.

Post-colonialism

The name 'post-colonial' implies a link with postmodernism, post-structuralism and so forth; and, indeed, like postmodernism the term originated within cultural studies rather than sociology. It refers to the attempt to develop a critique of Western culture and thought, led by academics from 'Third World' societies and from minority groups within the West. Thus, for example, there is an attempt to approach the analysis of classic literary texts, or to reconsider the history of a particular country, from a post-colonial point of view.

Dirlik (1994), in an article critical of the concept of post-colonialism, suggests that the term is ambiguous but distinguishes three key usages:

1. To describe current conditions in former colonial societies.
2. To characterize the global situation in an era after colonialism had ended.

3. As a critical form of discourse informed by the experience of post-colonial living with which to approach the study of post-colonial societies and cultures.

The former two more sociological usages would refer to study of relationships between societies and between different ethnic groups within societies which would take account of the colonial past. In that sense, most of the theoretical positions set out in this chapter could be labelled 'post-colonial'. However, the more common usage of the term is the third. Post-colonialism, in this usage, refers to a standpoint from which to carry out sociological, historical and cultural analysis, similar to a feminist standpoint.

The post-colonialist approach has largely been developed within the study of literature (Bhabha, 1990b; Said, 1985). It can be seen as another instance of the postmodern 'cultural turn'. For example, Gilroy in his later writing has turned to more extended study of aspects of black culture, such as writing and music. He analyses this through the concept of the black 'diaspora' (using a term more commonly applied to the situation of the Jews): that is, the scattering of people of African (or Jewish) descent throughout many countries of the globe. He describes a cultural formation that has arisen from the diaspora which he names the 'Black Atlantic' to convey the idea that it is a hybrid, a mix of elements from Western culture (both American and British), from the Caribbean and from the homelands of the African slaves. Just as capitalism was founded on the trade between these locations, so is the culture shaped by journeys (actual, spiritual and symbolic) between the areas. Gilroy (1992) uses the idea to attack the ideal of the recovery of a 'lost' or 'original' African culture (an aspect of his critique of 'ethnic absolutism).

The sociological issue that arises from this is the notion of 'hybridity' which has been developed by Homi Bhabha to describe contemporary ethnic identities (1990a). For example, Indian people settled in Britain are affected by aspects of both, or all, the cultures to which they are exposed. They are not simply Indian, or simply British, but Indian-British, having what Modood (1992) calls a 'hyphenated' identity – which is different from that of an Indian who has never left India. However, Bhabha points out that in the global society in which we live *all* cultures and societies are hybrid. There is no such thing as a 'pure' culture, since all have been inevitably affected by processes of migration, travel and tourism, cultural exchange and communication. As stated in chapter 3, theorists of globalization assert that developments in mass media and computer technology are speeding up this international interchange. Bhabha views hybridity positively, arguing that it provides a 'third space', a freedom from total submission to either set of cultural values, from which a critical stance or an opposition to hierarchy can develop.

Bhabha's analysis suggests ways in which the post-colonial framework is useful in analysing racial and ethnic differentiation. The notion of hybridity helps us to explore the complexity of the ethnic dynamic in post-industrial societies (in a post-colonial world) and adds another dimension to theories of fragmentation. It can also serve as a critical commentary on discourses and ideologies which feature the notion of 'races' as absolutely distinct and incompatible entities. The post-colonial framework brings to the fore the notion of racist discourses, which is another very important element within the 'new sociology of ethnicities'.

Racism

The analysis of racism has been a strand in all the theoretical perspectives discussed here. The classic Marxist approach is to see it as an ideology: that is, as a set of ideas which is slanted by the interest of particular groups in society. Dominant forms of ideology are used to justify the status quo and legitimate the power of socially dominant groups. Miles (1989), for example, views racism as a set of ideas which helps to obscure the reality of class relations. This usage follows one of the key principles of Marxian analysis, which is to make a sharp distinction between material reality and ideas.

Writers such as Anthias and Yuval-Davis (1993) use racism in a wider sense, not just to refer to ideas or ideologies but also to behaviour and practices. This is in line with the post-structuralist position, which refuses such a sharp distinction between 'words' and 'things'. We saw in chapter 4 that there is ambiguity as to whether the term discourse refers simply to ideas and 'talk' or whether it also covers practices and material relationships. Miles, however, describes this broader usage of racism as 'conceptual inflation' (1989, p. 41). He contends that this usage of the term becomes so comprehensive as to lose its analytic utility and clarity. Almost anything can be described as 'racism'. Perhaps one way to get round this difficulty is simply to specify in each case whether racist ideas, attitudes, or practices are under consideration.

Another debate concerns historical change in the operation of racism. Martin Barker (1981) offered an influential account which suggested that older forms of scientific racism were being replaced by what he termed 'the new racism'. Scientific racism is the view, discussed earlier, that distinct races can be isolated on the basis of biological and genetic differences. However, since the scientific backing for this has been questioned, a new sort of racism has emerged which does not focus on innate differences but on the notion of cultural incompatibility. This view, which Barker claims was developed by the New Right and has been employed by the Conservative party and by ultra-right nationalist groups, suggests that it is natural for people to wish to live only among their 'own kind': 'birds of a feather flock together'.

Though these ideas are certainly politically current around Europe at present, it can be questioned whether such a transformation has occurred. David Mason (1992) claims that the notion of cultural incompatibility was always an aspect of the biological view of 'race', and Brah (1993) notes its common use in colonial thinking, in India for example. Moreover, as Mason points out, ideas of biological determinism linger on. For example, American social scientist Charles Murray, well known for his arguments about the rise of the underclass in Britain and America, is now reviving the idea that intelligence is genetically transmitted and that African Americans are innately less intelligent than whites (Herrnstein and Murray, 1994). Such views are still commonly voiced in popular thinking. Rather than talking of a shift from one type of racism to another, we need to grasp that many forms of racism coexist: we should be speaking of racisms, rather than racism.

For example, Philip Cohen (1988) suggests that different classes use different 'codes' embodying different strands of racist thinking. Among the upper class there is a stress on 'breeding' and purity which reflects historical concerns over inheritance and lineage. Working-class racism hinges round notions of territoriality: what Cohen terms the 'nationalism of the neighbourhood; racialized groups are seen as 'invading our space', 'dating our girls' and 'taking our jobs and houses'. Finally, the 'bourgeois' code emphasizes inherited intelligence and aptitude, drawing from the tenets of scientific racism. Specific and quite localized situations will produce different types of racist discourse. Brah (1993) points to the rise of multiple racisms in Europe in the 1990s, with, for example, the revival of anti-Semitism in many countries, a revival manifested in the desecration of Jewish cemeteries; the neo-Nazi dogmas of young German skinheads; and attacks in various countries on specific ethnic groups, such as Turks in Germany. North Africans in France and South Asian Muslims in Britain. Brah concludes, 'What is new about the 1990s is *not* that there is a single neo-racism in Europe but that a variety of racisms (some of which had become less salient) are being reconstituted into new configurations' (1993, p. 20).

And we might add that this variability itself is not new. Racism has always been multi-dimensional and specific to different contexts. The same is true of ethnic identities.

Ethnicity and identity

'Race' and ethnicity are generally seen as more powerful forces than class in promoting identification in present-day societies. They are more likely to engender active or politicized identities. This is partly because of the visibility of 'race' where skin colour is an issue. But since some white ethnicities are also strongly felt (as in Serbia, Croatia and Bosnia) this is clearly not the whole story. One factor is the experience of discrimination. As Modood points out, 'the present ferment amongst Asian Muslims illustrates how the sense of being humiliated and marginalized enhances traditional forms of solidarity' (1992, p. 43). Also 'race' and ethnicity have become bases of political activity over the past decades, heightening awareness of ethnic affiliation even where it was lacking in the past.

The current emphasis within the new sociology of ethnicities is on the complex and fluid nature of ethnic identity. Allen (1994) stresses that awareness of ethnicity is not constant through an individual's life; it emerges only in specific contexts in which, for reasons such as those given above, it assumes significance as an aspect of individual experience. Hall (1990), espousing a postmodern position, emphasizes the role of discourses about 'race' and ethnicity in creating identities. As Hall puts it, over the course of a lifetime the 'imagined communities' with which we identify change. He warns against seeing ethnic identities as fixed (sometimes hidden) entities, waiting for us to discover them and our 'roots' and 'our true selves' in the process. Rather, identities change as discourses about ethnic relations change:

> Instead of thinking of identity as an already accomplished fact, which the new cultural practices then represent, we should think, instead, of identity as a 'production' which is never complete, always in process, and always constituted within, not outside, representation. (1990, p. 222)

The example of racialized minorities in Britain and America shows the volatility of politicized racial and ethnic identities. The Black Power movement of the 1960s led many Afro-Caribbean and Asians to adopt the identity 'black' as a statement of a political affiliation, uniting the diverse racialized ethnicities in a struggle against the white oppressors. Then, in the 1970s, an interest in the history of slavery and the African past led those of African origin to locate themselves more specifically in relation to that past. West Indian became Afro-Caribbean; Black American became African American. In the 1980s the move towards ethnic particularism might lead people to identify more narrowly, say with a specific Caribbean island or region in the Indian sub-continent. In the 1990s, political thinking which emphasizes the idea of 'post-colonial subjectivities' may encourage people to adopt 'hyphenated' identities: Mexican–American, British–Indian and so forth.

Modood's work also alerts us to the important contribution culture and religion may make to identification, citing the case of the Islamic revival and its effects on Asian Muslims resident in Britain. This caused a major reorientation of identity. British Muslims stopped seeing themselves, and being seen, in terms of 'black', 'Pakistani' or other racialized and stigmatized identities. The attacks on Islam in the wake of the turmoil surrounding Salman Rushdie's *The Satanic Verses*, and other controversies concerning Islamic observance in Britain, promoted a more confident assertion of identity in terms of being a Muslim. As Modood says, 'any oppressed group feels its oppression most according to those dimensions of its being which it (not the oppressor) values the most' (1992, p. 54). Religion became the focus for racism, but also a source of pride and self-assertiveness for supporters of Islam, even as they were becoming the latest in a line of 'demons' denounced by the West. This example also illustrates the need to take into account events that occur outside any given society (here the strengthening of traditional Islam which initiated outside Britain). Mukta (forthcoming) makes the important point that internal relations in migrant ethnic communities are often influenced by changes in class, gender and ethnic power relations in countries of origin.

The interplay of all these factors means that the identity of the 'post-colonial subject' can be confused, especially for those who move between countries of origin and Western societies. This is illustrated in the subtle accounts provided by post-colonialist writers, Amit Chaudhuri and V. S. Naipaul, of their own attempts to locate themselves in different contexts. Naipaul describes the strangeness of his return from Britain to Trinidad:

> All the people on the streets were darker than I remembered: Africans, Indians, whites, Portuguese, mixed Chinese. In their houses, though, people didn't look so dark. I suppose that was because on the streets I was more of a looker, half a tourist, and when I went to a house it was to be with people I had known years before. So I saw them more easily. (*A Way in the World*, p. 1)

Chaudhuri describes how in England he studied his compatriots as if through white eyes:

> Only a little way away from me sat the Indian bus driver in his uniform, but for some reason I thought of him as 'Asian' and he became for me mysterious and unclassifiable. (*Afternoon Raag*, p. 35)

Chaudhuri's ironic account illustrates how the white viewpoint becomes the 'natural' one. As we saw in chapter 4, majority status invokes 'default' identities. Since they are seen as 'normal', the 'natural' way to be, people give little thought to them. Thus, in Britain, minority white ethnicity (Scots, Welsh, Irish) may be the source of a strong politicized identity, as in the case of the various nationalist movements associated with these ethnic groups. The post-war period has witnessed intermittent attempts by Welsh and Scottish people to revive their cultural traditions and their own languages and to demand relative or complete autonomy from the British state. However, white ethnic identification as English, or as American, is evoked only in the international context (as against German, French, Russian and so forth). That is, English and American identity takes a nationalist, not an ethnic, form.

Frankenburg, however, has produced some interesting pioneer work while studying white ethnic identity in America and trying to dig out the meaning of 'growing up white'. She argues that 'whiteness' has three dimensions: structural advantage; a particular way of looking at the world; and an assumption that cultural practices employed by the white majority are 'normal' and universal. Other forms of cultural behaviour are defined as odd, deviant or exotic. Whiteness becomes, in the words of one of her interviewees, 'a privilege enjoyed but not acknowledged, a reality lived in but unknown' (Frankenburg, 1993, p. 51).

This discussion reveals the multiplicity of identities relating to territoriality and migration. If we return to the imagined Afro-Caribbean young woman of earlier chapters, she has available to her identities as British, Afro-Caribbean or 'black'. She may think of herself in terms of the particular island her family came from, such as Jamaica or Barbados, or hark back to the distant past in Africa. She may also see herself in local terms, belonging to Birmingham, or to a particular area, Sparkbrook or Handsworth, within it. Her identity may involve any, or all, of these. And that is without considering the way other stratification dynamics impinge upon her consciousness.

Interacting dynamics: ethnicity, class, gender and age

Class

Incomer migrants enter the labour market on disadvantaged terms, reflecting their relative powerlessness. Moreover, many come from working-class or rural peasant backgrounds in their countries of origin, and are driven by poverty and the hope of achieving economic success abroad. Those who do have qualifications and training for higher occupational positions often find these devalued or disregarded in their new country, as was the case with many Asians from East Africa. But as migrant populations become settled, the new generation can compete for upward mobility through the mass education systems of the West, and some achieve it.

Racialized minority members in Britain and America are likely to be disproportionately concentrated in working-class locations. In Britain, this is especially true of Afro-Caribbeans, in America of African Americans and Chicanos. Modood (1992) gives an account demonstrating the complexity of class and ethnic stratification among British Indians. He distinguishes four groups. At the bottom of the socio-economic scale are Muslim Gujaratis from rural areas, mainly filling unskilled jobs (as do Pakistanis and Bangladeshis). Punjabis, mainly Sikhs, are the longest-settled group, and Modood suggests that their class profile is equivalent to that of the white population, as is that of Hindu Gujaratis. The East African refugees, who came predominantly from urban middle-class occupations, he sees as beginning to regain their lost class position, after the original setback. Finally there is a small group of successful urban professionals from a variety of ethnic backgrounds who often act as leaders in their own ethnic communities.

Recently attention has focused on two privileged groups: the black bourgeoisie and the Asian petite bourgeoisie. In America, a 'black bourgeoisie' is now well established, holding top posts in the professions, the media, the business and financial world and especially in government agencies and the law. Their social prominence and the power they gain through involvement in the political process can be seen as an important advance for racialized minorities and a challenge to negative stereotyping of black groups. However, it is argued that the black bourgeoisie has turned its back on the rest of the black population, fearing to be dragged down by association with them. This is well portrayed in *Jungle Fever*, where the film's black 'yuppie' architect hero shrinks from contact with his 'no-good' crack-addicted brother. There is growing polarization between the black elite and the demoralized ghetto underclass. The idea of the 'black underclass' has been put forward both in Britain and America. Generally in Britain, where racialized minority members are distributed more broadly through the class structure, this idea has been rejected (Pilkington, 1984). But in America the idea of the ghetto underclass has gained considerable acceptance, as will be discussed in chapter 7.

A black bourgeoisie has not consolidated in Britain. Gilroy (1987) refers to it as a 'grouplet' as yet in embryonic stage. There are, however, growing numbers of Asian and Afro-Caribbean people in professional and media jobs (although there is ample evidence of discrimination in areas like law) and a small group of very wealthy and successful Asian businessmen, such as Shami Ahmed, the multi-millionaire owner of the Legendary Joe Bloggs clothing company. But more numerous are the self-employed people who are described as constituting an Asian petite bourgeoisie. Table 5.2 showed that Indian males were most likely to be self-employed than any other group. While some interpret this as the result of Asian values of hard work, self-sufficiency and enterprise, others suggest that the rise of Asian enterprise can be linked to racism and lack of opportunities to gain employment (Cashmore and Troyna, 1983; Jones and McEvoy, 1986). Success depends greatly on the use of family resources (capital from savings and loans, goodwill and, crucially, family labour) and on degrees of self-exploitation (working very long hours in poor conditions). The businesses are orientated to community needs (restaurants, sari shops, travel agencies dealing with the Far East) and are dependent on the community for custom.

Despite their vulnerable position, Asian entrepreneurs have attained a class and status position above others in their ethnic group. Will such differences of class start to split hitherto integrated ethnic communities and weaken ethnic loyalties? Anthias and Yuval-Davis believe not, because of the strength of ties that rise from shared experience of discrimination: 'In the currency of a racist society, ethnic solidarity is likely to be retained at the expense of class consciousness in differentiating within racialized populations' (1993, p. 88). But Blakemore and Boneham (1994), in their research on Asians and Afro-Caribbeans in Birmingham, suggested that many had developed strong ties to their working-class communities.

Gender

The writings of black feminists also emphasize the commitment of women of colour towards their ethnic groups. Ethnic solidarity is seen to transcend gender as well as class consciousness. That does not mean that there are no gender inequalities in ethnic communities. However, it is important to avoid stereotyping ethnic minorities as patriarchal and backward in gender terms, in contrast to a more egalitarian white majority. This was the reason for the black critique of the white feminist portrayal of issues such as arranged marriages (Amos and Parmar, 1984; Carby, 1982). Rather, we must develop an understanding of how gendered power operates differently in different ethnic groups.

The example of British Muslim communities was discussed in chapter 4. A rather different situation is that of Afro-Caribbean women. Within Afro-Caribbean families and communities women have traditionally been seen to occupy an influential role. They usually work full-time, often assuming responsibility as breadwinners in what is seen as a typically Caribbean family form, the matrifocal or woman-headed family. (The majority of British Afro-Caribbean families, of course, are of the conventional nuclear kind). Young women are strongly encouraged by their families to work hard at school and develop careers, and appear more committed to educational achievement than their white peers (Mirza, 1992). From this arises what Wallace (1990) calls the myth of the black 'superwoman', powerful, strong-minded and nurturant. However, this ignores the way family responsibilities act as a particularly heavy burden on Afro-Caribbean and African American women who are expected to hold down a full-time job, do the housework and keep the extended family together. Men exercise their male power by refusing domestic labour, expecting their wives to carry the major responsibility for family subsistence and at times by resorting to violence. As Fuller argues, 'matrifocality may allow women to develop with a definition of femininity that includes strength, competence and so which enables them to challenge patriarchal relations of sexual domination, but it does not thereby do away with patriarchy' (1982, p. 98).

Afro-Caribbean women also face racism in the labour market. Racialized minority women in Britain suffer a triple disadvantage of 'race', sex and class. Phizacklea (1990) has shown how these three dynamics have combined, in the context of the Midlands textile industry, to produce a low-paid female work-force often labouring in sweatshop conditions. Subject to discrimination in the labour market and dependent on males of their own community because of immigration rules, women – stereotyped as 'naturally' suited for machine work because of their 'nimble fingers' – are at the end of a chain of subcontracting which has developed because of the power of multi-national companies within the global market.

There has been disagreement as to the relative effects of 'race' and gender. Data analysed by Brown (1984) and Smith (1977) appeared to show that the gap between white and black men was greater than between white and black women. Thus the poor situation of racialized minority women in Britain was ascribed more to class and gender than race. However, Bruegel (1989), re-analysing employment data, refutes this. She argues that aggregate data conceal the differences between white and black women's employment situations. For example, black women's apparently high average wages relate to the fact that they work longer hours and that their employment is concentrated in London, where all workers are more highly paid.

We can conclude that it is futile to attempt to disentangle the effects of the three dynamics. All act together to confine racialized minority women to the least privileged sections of the employment structure.

Age

On the face of it, one might assume that older migrants, such as those who arrived in Britain in the immediate post-war years, had faced greater handicaps and hardships. They will have experienced sharp segregation in the labour market and more overt forms of racism, for example in housing. Their position was made more difficult by lack of British qualifications and for some by lack of expertise in the English language. The second generation, growing up in England and participating in the British education system, were expected to have better economic prospects. There is certainly evidence of considerable poverty among some older people who were first-generation immigrants. But Ken Blakemore and Margaret Boneham (1994) point out that the specific situation of emigration meant that people expected to undergo hardships and were pleased with any kind of improvement in their standard of living.

In contrast, second-generation immigrants have higher expectations, while bearing the impact of recent recessions. Many of these young people have reacted more aggressively against discrimination than their parents. The feeling that special difficulties were faced by young Asians and, especially, young Afro-Caribbeans is mirrored in the title of Cashmore's and Troyna's book, *Black Youth in Crisis* (1982). Concern surrounds the numbers of alienated minority youth (especially Afro-Caribbean males) who are rejecting school and its values, possibly immersing themselves in a street culture of drugs, petty crime and hustling. Although Asian teenagers are stereotyped as conformist and hard-working, Martin Mac an Ghaill's ethnographic study (1988) revealed that Asian boys, too, are developing anti-school cultures. Girls, however, seem more prepared to play along with school and its values, despite their awareness of racism (Fuller, 1982); whereas their brothers' response to the experience of racialization can be confrontational, their solution is to work hard to gain the educational qualifications needed to help them succeed against the odds.

It is important not to overstate this problem. Many young people from ethnic minorities in Britain are conformist, successful and committed to education. Indeed, they are more likely than their white compeers to go on into further or higher education. In 1984–6, 10 per cent of South Asian and 7 per cent of Afro-Caribbean males of employable age were students, as opposed to only 4 per cent of whites; the figures for women were 7 per cent, 9 per cent and 4 per cent respectively (Social Trends, 1988). As O'Donnell points out, most young blacks share with their white peers respect for the law and a desire for a 'good life'; the difference is that they face more obstacles in achieving this (O'Donnell, 1985, p. 79).

However, there is anxiety that if young people of colour continue to face discrimination and exclusion, the situation may deteriorate and the problems experienced in some cities in the United States, such as New York, Los Angeles and Chicago, could be replicated in Britain. Young African Americans and Latinos in their early teens and younger are dropping out and being sucked into a world of gangs, crime and violence, drugs and guns. One result is that the death rate among young black males is extremely high. United States Bureau of Trade statistics for 1989 revealed that while American citizens have a 1 in 133 chance of being a homicide victim, for black males the rate falls to 1 in 21. Homicide was the major cause of death for black males aged between fifteen and twenty-four. Although the reporting of the ghetto culture of drugs and violence may sometimes be exaggerated and sensationalized, it appears that young people of colour in America are the victim of an extreme trend towards racial polarization. Unfortunately with widespread unemployment attendant on global restructuring of capital, the position is set to get worse.

Summary and conclusions

There has been a growing interest in the study of 'race' and ethnicity in Britain over the course of the twentieth century. This has been influenced by definitions of race relations as a social problem and source of social conflict. But more recently it has also been promoted by the rise of nationalist and ethnic politics and a worldwide assertion of ethnic identity.

Early approaches to the study of 'race' and ethnicity centred on the division between 'white' and 'black' groups and drew largely upon concepts from class analysis to explain those divisions. These approaches shed considerable light on the use of the labour of migrants and of racialized minorities within colonialism and capitalism. But because of the one-dimensional nature of classic development theories, both Marxian and liberal, these approaches often treated racial divisions as subsidiary to class.

What I have called 'the new sociology of ethnicities' has supplemented these initial accounts with a broader perspective on ethnicity. Influenced by postmodernist and post-structuralist thinking, these writers focus on the 'postcolonial subject' and are particularly concerned with identities, cultural practices and racist discourses. However, unlike some of their feminist counterparts, they have not turned away from the study of material disadvantage and power disparities; they do not celebrate diversity at the expense of ignoring inequality. They also see class as an important element of the social processes which create racial and ethnic difference. Writers such as Gilroy, Phizacklea and Anthias and Yuval-Davis have led the way in exploring the intersection of ethnicity, class and gender. Although there is sometimes an apparent tension between structural analysis of class, and constructionist and discursive accounts of 'race' (as in Gilroy, 1987), the new sociologists of ethnicity appear to have negotiated the crossing of the structuralist/post-structuralist divide.

Our world is currently characterized by increasing ethnic and nationalist tension on a global scale, and by polarization of racial inequalities often exacerbated by the whipping up of race hatreds within nations. While the international dominance of the advanced capitalist nations continues to shape race relations, the whole world is still 'travelling in the West'.

Further reading

Among a number of text books dealing with more traditional perspectives on 'race' are Robert Miles, *Racism* (Open University, 1989); Andrew Pilkington, *Race Relations in Britain* (University Tutorial Press, 1984); and Ellis Cashmore and Barry Troyna, *Introduction to Race Relations* (Routledge, 1983). The best introduction to newer approaches is Floya Anthias and Nira Yuval-Davis, *Racialized Boundaries* (Routledge, 1993). Paul Gilroy, *There Ain't no Black in the Union Jack* (Routledge, 1987) is more difficult but rewarding. Annie Phizacklea's *Unpacking the Fashion Industry* (Routledge, 1990) exemplifies an approach which looks at the interaction of 'race', class and gender in a particular context.

6

Age: the Neglected Dimension of Stratification

> No one could fail to notice Joseph's standing in the community. Dealings with him (as with the elderly in many societies) are marked by a jocular respect, a celebration of an old man's importance and authority. To tease the elderly is to show that you are on terms of happy intimacy with your own heritage . . . And from time to time the young men call on his authority: Is this as far as the fence rails should extend? Is this the line along which to cut a horse's hooves? Do you ever find lynx on such and such a hillside? . . . He had not only the expertise but also the authority of his eighty-some years. But his composure and eloquence were not those of an old man; they expressed the completeness and distinctiveness of a culture. (Brodie, 1986, pp. 2, 4)

Joseph is an elder of the Beaver tribe of British Columbia in the north-west of Canada. As in many tribal and clan-based societies, elders are treated as an important social resource because of their fund of knowledge and long experience of living; often they act as repositories for myths, folk-wisdom, songs and stories of the society's past. In contrast, it is argued that in industrialized societies, where wealth and power are linked to participation in capitalist production, the social standing of older people has declined (Cowgill and Holmes, 1972). Ironically, the institution of retirement, though promoted as a way to ease the lot of older working people, has contributed to a view of them as redundant to society's needs or even a burden upon society. The feeling of 'being on the scrap heap' is reflected in this comment from an elderly man born in Jamaica, speaking of his desire to return to the Caribbean: 'I want to go by 1985 or I'll end up in a mental home . . . I feel that the elderly black person should try to go home, you have no use as an elderly person' (quoted in Fenton, 1987, p. 25).

On the other hand, historians and sociologists of old age have warned against rosy views of the status of older people in non-industrial societies (Fennell et al., 1988). They argue that in many societies negative attitudes have surrounded elderly people. Featherstone and Hepworth (1990) note the long history of distaste for ageing bodies. Younger people have commonly distanced themselves from elderly relatives, considering them a burden rather than willingly taking on the duty of caring for them. Thomas (1976) and Laslett (1977) provide evidence that this was the case in pre-industrial Britain. Age does not *on its own* automatically bring high status, which is often only accorded to those who as younger people were powerful or wealthy or community leaders (Featherstone and Hepworth, 1990; Blakemore and Boneham, 1994). Nonetheless, Brodie's account (1986) of Joseph illustrates the way that in *some* contemporary communities and societies, such as among native Americans and Canadians or in African tribes, *some* older people still occupy a vital and special place.

This contrasts with Janet Ford's and Ruth Sinclair's study of older women in Britain today and the ageist attitudes which serve to render them almost invisible in our society:

> From 60 onwards we shall in all probability be referred to as 'elderly', 'retired' and 'OAPs' by the rest of society. In the west these terms form part of the stereotype about older people, who are seen as unproductive, dependent, restricted in their lives and therefore not very interesting. We . . . have successfully deprived age of authority and of interest. (1987, p. 1)

Although their research revealed tremendous variety in the ways people adapt to age and cope with its limitations and physical restrictions, most of their respondents were aware of the negative images of elderly people held by younger age groups: 'other people think age is a write-off' said one, while another believed older people were considered 'finished and boring' (pp. 95, 107).

Such a contrast reveals that meanings attached to specific age groups differ between societies. While we tend to think of age in common-sense terms as a biological fact relating to the number of years an individual has lived since birth, as Harris (1987) points out, chronological age has in itself no intrinsic significance; it only gains meaning from the behavioural characteristics imputed to it, so that the idea of a person 'being elderly' or 'being adolescent' triggers off certain expectations about how that person will act, feel and think.

Age, then, as studied here, is a sociological rather than a chronological phenomenon. It relates to social categories, such as childhood, youth, adolescence, middle age and old age, which have been developed to describe lived relationships between individuals and groups as they move through the life course. The term 'life course' as opposed to 'life cycle' is used here, because in biology the latter term is often used as an equivalent to the 'reproductive cycle' which terminates when an individual of a natural species has achieved successful procreation (Harris, 1987). By life course in contrast I am implying the progress through socially defined life stages, which may be distinguished by *rites de passage* or simply by the different social roles associated with them. For example 'adolescence' or 'youth' in current societies are deemed to end when a young person 'settles down', as indicated by securing a permanent job, getting married, establishing a home or starting a family; although the chronological age at which these events occur is variable they are taken to be social activities associated with the status of 'young adulthood'. Each stage in the life course is differentiated by the social meanings, expectations and imputed activities associated with it. Social rules suggest what forms of behaviour are suitable for each age-group, so that, for example, it is not considered appropriate in our society for children to have a full-time job or be involved in sexual relationships or for elderly women to bear children or to have relationships with teenaged boys. Many activities are quite strictly segregated by age: we would get a shock if we saw a sixty-year-old sitting at a classroom desk or dancing in a mini-skirt at a discotheque. Nor would we expect to see a twenty-year-old at a boardroom table or on the benches of the House of Commons.

Age is viewed here as a dimension of inequality because, like class, gender and ethnicity, it involves the construction of social differences which in turn brings differential access to social resources, such as wealth, power and status. In our society, there is an 'age elite' of middle age-groups, with the young and the old being relatively powerless. As we shall see, it is claimed that a distinctive feature of the lived relationships of age in Western capitalist societies is that the old and the young are forced into social dependency on the middle groupings. However, all age-groups are affected adversely by ageism. Ageism refers to systematic stereotyping of people and discrimination against them on the basis of characteristics, abilities and limitations which are imputed to them simply because of their age (Bodily, 1994). Thus *all* older people are seen as less suitable for employment on the grounds that they are physically slow, lacking in dynamism, and not very adaptable to change; *all* younger people are suspected of being unreliable, reckless, undisciplined and prone to drug-taking and promiscuity.

While this kind of stereotyping acts particularly against the young and the old, middle groupings too may suffer from aspects of it. For example, middle-aged women applying for jobs as secretaries, receptionists or computer operators may be told they are 'too old for the job'. Where youth and glamour are associated with particular forms of employment, the middle-aged find themselves faced with ageist exclusion. Surveys carried out by the Institute of Personnel Management and the Metropolitan Authorities' Recruitment Agency revealed that in many workplaces age discrimination begins for men at forty and for women at thirty-five; 30 per cent of employers explicitly specified upper age limits and 40 per cent of employers believed that age was a crucial factor in recruitment (Richards, 1994). Bodily (1994) points out that simply trying to remove the negative stereotypes associated with particular life stages is insufficient. A thorough attack on ageism involves breaking the link between life stage and imputed characteristics, good or bad; the assumption that time in itself (as embodied in chronological age) is a causal factor must be challenged.

The specific categories of age vary from society to society, and there is considerable debate as to how to categorize age relationships in contemporary societies (Cain, 1975; Murphy, 1987). Generally, sociologists tend to distinguish five broad groupings: childhood; youth (sometimes more narrowly defined as adolescence); young adulthood; mid-life; and old age. Sub-groups can be delineated in these broad groupings. For example it is now common to distinguish between the 'young old' (sixty or sixty-five to seventy-four) and the 'old old', those aged seventy-five and over (Arber and Ginn, 1991b). Problems of poverty, isolation and physical deterioration are particularly severe among the latter (Gilbert et al., 1989).

It has already been stressed that age has been a neglected topic within sociology. Arber and Ginn (1991a) argue that, although lip-service is frequently paid to age as one of a number of bases of stratification, older people continue to be excluded from study. Harris (1987) points out that in sociological research age is commonly treated as an independent variable, something that data has to be 'controlled for', which often means screening it out. But with a few notable exceptions (Mannheim, 1952; Eisenstadt, 1956), age has not been analysed as a general category or framework for analysis. Rather, research has focused on the experience of specific age-groups, such as children, adolescents or older people. The study of these groups has developed as distinct academic specialisms, such as, for example, the social history of childhood, the sociology of youth cultures or gerontology (the interdisciplinary study of old age). While these have provided important insights into the inequalities associated with youth and age, they are rarely incorporated into a general theory of age and inequality.

The neglect of age, as with gender and ethnicity, goes back to classical sociological theory. This may be because age was viewed as a natural phenomenon. Since it was assumed that all individuals would pass through all the stages of the life course it was not seen as a crucial source of *social* disadvantage. Moreover, the preoccupation of the classic theorists with work and the public sphere meant that social groups who were less likely to be involved in production or in political activities (children, older people) received less attention. However, age was treated as a crucial factor in the discipline of social anthropology. Anthropologists writing about non-industrial pre-class societies observed that age and gender were the basis of the social division of labour. But within classical sociological theory and subsequently within functionalism,

Table 6.1 Percentages of Elderly People (aged 65+) in Selected Countries in 1988 with Projections for 2010

	1988	2010
UK	15.5	15.9
USA	12.1	13.9
Denmark	15.4	16.7
France	13.6	16.9
West Germany	15.4	20.5
Italy	13.7	20.2
Ireland	11.0	12.8

Source: Arber and Ginn, 1991b, Table 1.3, p. 8.

the assumption was often made that occupation or class-based stratification systems had replaced those based on 'ascribed' characteristics like age and gender.

As in the case of 'race', age emerged as a topic of sociological interest through its definition as a 'social problem'. Three particular developments were involved here. The first was the increasing attention given to the demographic phenomenon of an 'ageing population'. This refers to the growing proportion of the population who are in the older age groups. In Britain, the proportion of the population over pensionable age (sixty-five for men, sixty for women) has risen from 5 per cent at the beginning of the century to 16 per cent in 1993. The ageing population is linked to industrialization, because of the decline in infant mortality which characterizes industrial development, along with general improvements in health care which help people to live longer. Falling fertility rates in the post-war period have also been a major factor. Ageing of the population is a characteristic of all advanced Western societies, as is indicated in table 6.1. In Europe as a whole, 13 per cent of the population is over sixty-five (Clarke, 1993).

As a result of the ageing of the population there are more older people about, which forces them into the public eye. In addition, the growing proportion of retired people has been interpreted as a social problem for the advanced societies because it increases the 'burden of dependency' on the working population, and creates an ever growing demand on the welfare state, in terms both of pensions and the cost of health and personal care. While this can be contested (for example, the burden of dependency has been eased at the other end by falling birth rates and declining family size), social concern about the effects of ageing population has been a key interest within gerontology and social policy.

At the other end of the life course, two issues have contributed to the view of youth as a 'problem period' and to growing interest in the idea of a 'generation gap'. The first is the development since the Second World War of a series of spectacular and highly publicized youth cultures; teddy boys, mods and rockers, skinheads, hippies, punks, ravers, New Age travellers, and so forth. Often youth cultures are associated by the public with drug-taking, violence, sexual permissiveness and other kinds of behaviour which are seen by older age-groups as unacceptable or threatening. Sociologists have charted the long history of the 'moral panics' about young people, which are fostered by the media and portray the stability of society as threatened by waves of delinquent behaviour among teenagers (Cohen, 1972; Mungham and Pearson, 1975; Pearson, 1983).

A linked phenomenon was the student protest movement which arose in the 1960s in America, Britain, France and Germany and other countries. Since this involved many young people from middle-class backgrounds it appeared even more socially disturbing than the youth cultures which had been predominantly associated with working-class youth. As well as occupation of university buildings, mass demonstrations against the Vietnam war and other forms of political radicalism, student protest was manifested in a link with the hippie 'counter-culture' of 'dropping out', soft drug use and sexual experimentation, particularly in America. To anxious parents it seemed that a whole generation were rejecting their elders' values and lifestyle. Although the student movement turned out to be relatively short-lived, the moral panic surrounding it was a spur to the sociological study of generational conflict. This was particularly the case in America, where the apparent lack of major class conflict pushed other kinds of structured conflict to the fore; there was growing interest in elaborating an account of age as a distinct dimension of stratification (Feuer, 1969; Riley et al., 1972; Foner, 1975). In Britain, the sociological preoccupation with class was at its height in the late 1960s and the events of the student protest were interpreted in the light of Marxist theory. Youth protest was seen as largely an aspect of class relations (Hall and Jefferson, 1976; Brake, 1980; 1985). A continuing preoccupation with class has recently been supplemented by an interest in gender (McRobbie and Nava, 1984; S. Griffin, 1993), while, because of the recessions of the 1980s and 1990s, employment, training and unemployment are replacing subculture and protest as key themes in the study of youth: in 1993, 21 per cent of males aged between sixteen and nineteen and 16 per cent of females were unemployed.

The remainder of this chapter looks at these themes in more detail. It is constructed differently from previous chapters, because of the relative lack of general theories of age as a form of inequality. What theories do exist are surveyed in the next section. Since most of the study of age-groups has been carried out within disciplinary sub-specialisms, I discuss accounts of age inequality developed within these. I have chosen to concentrate on two of the five age-groups listed above, youth and old age. This is partly because these groups are most disadvantaged by the lived relations of age; and partly because, for the reasons given above, they have received most attention within sociology.

Sociological frameworks for considering age

Since classical theory provided few clues about the analysis of age, sociologists turned to the ideas of anthropologists when they began thinking about age differences in contemporary societies (Eisenstadt, 1956; P. Abrams, 1970; Foner, 1975). From anthropology they drew the concepts of 'age grades', 'age sets' and 'age spans' which have provided the basis for theorizing age stratification.

Age stratification theory

An age grade was defined by the functionalist anthropologist Radcliffe Brown as

> The recognized division of the life of an individual as he passes from infancy to old age. Thus each person passes successively into one grade after another, and, if he lives long enough through the whole series – infant, boy, youth, young married man, elder. (Quoted in Davis, 1990, p. 25)

Anthropologists distinguished a number of such phases tending, as the quotation demonstrates, to focus on male age-groups. Specific expectations and social functions were associated with each age grade; this was seen as a way to stabilize society and integrate the different grades into the whole. Since each individual would pass through each grade, there was no reason for young people to rebel against the power of the elders. In this way age stratification differs from the dynamics of stratification of gender and ethnicity, where movement between differentiated groups is virtually impossible, or even class, where movement, though possible, is constrained. This fluidity works against potential conflicts of interests between age-groups. As Philip Abrams puts it:

> This allows the ruling class, adults, to persuade most of the oppressed class, the young, to accept their lot cheerfully. By agreeing to be a good child one can hope to become a successful adult. The child is led to tolerate the childishness that permeates his present role by learning to see it as a precondition for access to the more desirable role of adult. (1970, p. 182)

The movement from one age grade to another was often marked by *rites de passage*. Such rituals bound together all those in a particular age grade into a collectivity. Anthropologists also used the term 'age set' to distinguish a group of young people who went through initiation ceremonies (marking the passage to adulthood, or perhaps to warrior status) at the same time. Members of an age set might come together on further occasions of ritual or celebration to affirm the bond between them. Although there are few formal *rites de passage* in modern society (christening and marriage ceremonies being important exceptions), customs such as American and British class reunions of school or university students who graduated in the same year can be seen as a version of these tribal rites; and in Japan it is customary for employees who join a firm in the same year to meet as a group for drinking parties and other social events.

Age-groups in modern societies are less formally marked than the age grades of tribal societies (O'Donnell, 1985). But age stratification theorists distinguish groups on the basis of the different cultural definitions and social expectations, roles and identities associated with them. Age stratification theory developed in America and was specially concerned with youth. For example, Parsons (1954) described the evolution of a distinctive teenage culture. He saw this as a transitional stage between childhood and adulthood, marked by its own values which focused on 'having a good time', dating and sporting prowess: 'swell guys' and 'glamour girls' were the heroes and heroines of this culture; youth culture has 'important positive functions in easing the transition from the security of childhood in the family of orientation to that of full adult in marriage and occupational status' (1954, p. 101).

Youth and adolescence are commonly understood in terms of 'transitional status'. John Davis suggests that since the end of the nineteenth century, youth has emerged as 'a transitional but nevertheless distinct age grade between childhood and adulthood' (1990, p. 821): the period immediately after the Second World War was crucial in consolidating this process, with the lengthening of the period young people spent at school and therefore in financial dependency on their parents; at the same time post-war affluence and full employment allowed the emergence of a commercialized youth consumer culture.

Parsons also considered old age as an age grade, characterized by social isolation from kinship, occupational and community ties. Like others, he linked decline in old people's status to retirement: 'retirement leaves the older man in a peculiarly functionless position, cut off from participation in the most important interests and activities of the society' (1954, p. 103). He noted the emergence in America of segregated retirement communities, such as those of Florida and South California, where older people (of the more privileged classes) huddled together as a group. Similarly, in Britain there are 'colonies' of retired people in the south-coast seaside resorts such as Bournemouth and Hastings (Phillipson, 1982).

Parsons characterizes age grades in terms of particular structural problems (transition and insecurity, social isolation and lack of function). There is a similarity here to the psychological framework developed by Erik Erikson (1965). Erikson distinguishes eight stages of human development, each of which is marked by specific psychic dilemmas or crises which confront individuals; for example, for adolescents it is the search for a stable adult identity, while for elderly people it is the need for 'ego integrity'. This involves making sense of life histories, shaping them into some satisfactory pattern which resolves the difficulties and failures of the past. A quotation from a retired farrier taken from Blythe's study of old people (1979) nicely illustrates this latter process:

> My wife, she died four year agoo . . . I did properly miss my wife, and no mistake, but I had my daughters and that took it off. When you've spent your whol' life a-usin' of your hands, like I have, you don't know what to do when you can't . . . I have two nice daughters and grandsons that are gittin' on well, an a granddaughter that is at the teachers' college at Canterbury. I balance things up when I can. I've got no work and no wife, but I've got what I've done, haven't I? (p. 76)

Such views of age-groups as characterized by distinct structural or individual dilemmas are interesting but insufficient in sociological terms. Parsons's functionalist account presents age as a source of social differentiation, but fails to conceptualize this in relation to power and inequality. Ann Foner (1975) advances on this by presenting age stratification in terms of inequality and potential conflict. She views age as part of a 'family of social stratification systems' (p. 14) which involve inequalities of wealth and power, and draws an explicit analogy between age and class as parallel forms of stratification. Thus, age-related inequalities generate conflicts of interests leading to the emergence of age consciousness and age solidarity, as demonstrated by the activities of the student movement or the Gray Panthers, or, on a more everyday level, the characteristic clashes between parents and teenagers.

Foner's account illustrates the potential of a systematic theory of age stratification and shows a sensitive awareness of the way age interlocks with other aspects of stratification. However, the age stratification approach did not find particular favour in Britain, perhaps because of its association with functionalism, which is seen to gloss over the divisive aspects of stratification and to legitimate social inequality as serving positive functions. This is exemplified in S. N. Eisenstadt's functionalist account of age groups. He states that 'the function of differential age definitions is to enable the individual to learn and acquire new roles . . . and in this way to maintain social continuity' (1956, p. 28). While Eisenstadt recognizes the asymmetry of power between age-groups, he argues that this is necessary to ensure acceptance of and respect for authority.

The major criticism of age stratification theory. however. has been that it assumes a homogeneity of experience across the strata, neglecting differences of class, gender and ethnicity. Parsons's accounts of youth cultures and of the segregated old-age communities, for example, are based on the experience of middle-class Americans and assumes that such behavioural patterns are typical of the populace as a whole; elderly African Americans and Chicanos are less likely to be found in the retirement blocks of Florida. The dominance of class theory in British sociology in the 1960s and 1970s meant that age differences were interpreted as an aspect of broader capitalist relations. The political economy perspective within the study of older people and the radical approach to youth subcultures, which will be discussed later in the chapter, both drew substantially on Marxist theory. Thus a separate theory of age stratification has been little developed in Britain.

Generations and generation units

Another criticism of some versions of age grade theory is that they are essentialist, presenting age differences and conflicts as universal constants, as in the case of Erikson's stage theory. A different conceptualization that avoids this is the notion of generation. The best-known version of this is provided by Karl Mannheim in a famous paper, 'The problem of generations' (1952). He develops an analysis of generation as a distinct type of 'social location' using, like Foner, a direct analogy with class. However, Mannheim is concerned to link the notion of generation to processes of social change and of intellectual and cultural development: his view of age-groups, though rooted in biology, is informed by the role of history:

> Generation location is based on the existence of biological rhythm in human existence – the factors of life and death, a limited span of life, and ageing. Individuals who belong to the same generation, who share the same year of birth, are endowed, to that extent, with a common location in the historical dimension of the social process. (Mannheim, 1952, p. 290)

A 'generation' is a group of people who are born at around the same time; the term 'cohort' is often used by empirical researchers in a similar way. It is conventional to regard a generation as lasting thirty years, the time from the birth of an individual to adult maturity and parenthood. Each generation grows up in a specific historical context, entailing exposure to different experiences and intellectual influences, which will inform its members' feelings, behaviour and beliefs. In this way new cultural formations come into being as each generation achieves a position of social dominance.

Mannheim recognized that a generation does not necessarily act as a unified social collectivity (any more than classes necessarily do). There might be divisions and opposing currents within a generation. When a generation (or a large part of it) did develop some sense of itself as sharing interests and experiences, Mannheim defined it as constituting a 'generation in actuality' (the analogy to class consciousness is clear here). Mannheim also distinguished a 'generation unit': a group within a generation that develops sufficient awareness to act coherently for itself, to 'work up the material of their common experience' (p. 304). The distinctions Mannheim is making here correspond to what I have previously defined as passive, active and politicized identities.

The virtue of the notion of generation is that it links age divisions firmly to changing historical circumstances and to cultural transformations (Abrams, 1970). However, there are definitional problems in terms of how to distinguish one generation from another. Does it make any real sense to define a generation strictly as all those born in a single year? Such a system of categorization seems arbitrary, to say the least. Used more generally to describe, for example, all those born in the immediate post-war years, the term becomes rather vague and this vagueness is heightened by the fact that at some (unspecified) moment the younger generation inevitably becomes the older generation. This framework, therefore, does not enable us to generate such a clear set of categories for analysing age differences as the age stratification perspective with its notion of age grades. Moreover, the idea of generational change and conflict is often used in a fashion which overlooks divisions of class, gender, ethnicity to suggest that a whole 'younger generation' share common cultures and values.

The concept of generations has not been used to any great extent in contemporary accounts of age. One exception is the work of Abrams who combines concepts from Mannheim and from age grade theory in his analysis of generational conflict and the political rebellions of young people. He solves the problem of definition (to some extent) by distinguishing between a biological generation (chronologically defined) and a sociological generation (which may be made up of many biological generations but crucially is involved in the redefinition of culture). Thus the student radicals of the sixties are viewed as a self-conscious generation unit, standard-bearers of new cultural, political and sexual values.

The concept of 'generation' has slipped into popular consciousness in relation to young people, as witnessed by terms like the 'generation gap' or 'generation X' (used to describe rebellious and disaffected youth in both the 1960s and 1990s!). Sociologists of youth use the term in relation to conflict and change, while Johnson et al. (1989) have developed an interesting if controversial argument about the switch in balance of economic power from the younger generation to the older ones. But little has been done to extend Mannheim's theoretical account.

The life course

Despite this, sociologists are generally aware of the importance of age as a base for differentiated experience and as a vehicle of social change. Age is viewed as a significant variable in social research. Cohort analysis has been an important technique for tracing processes of social change, for example in the study of social mobility or of changing patterns of family formation. In recent years, the postmodernists' stress on diversity in experience has provided an additional impetus to the study of age differences although they have not as yet contributed to any major theoretical re-exploration of age. They do, however, suggest an important role for younger people in the transition to a postmodern culture. Crook et al. (1992) see them as pioneers of the cultural changes associated with postmodernism, especially those related to the mass media and information technology. Young people are disproportionately involved in the 'new social movements'. Older people, on the other hand, are conspicuously absent from the postmodern scenario, although one or two recent accounts have begun to consider ways in which prevailing views of old age could be deconstructed (Featherstone and Hepworth, 1989; Hazan, 1994).

The importance of age as a topic of empirical investigation has encouraged a pulling together of work carried out in the various sub-specialisms under the rubric of the sociology of the life cycle or life course (Allatt et al., 1987; Bryman et al., 1987). This provides an umbrella for those concerned with study of the various stages in the life course to trace out connections and continuities. Featherstone and Hepworth (1989), advocating the use of the term life course rather than life cycle, suggest it can be used to challenge the stage models of age development (such as Erikson's) which present individuals as proceeding through an ordered (and unchanging) sequence of life stages. Using a postmodernist framework, they point out that the life course is historically variable and that phases may blur into one another. Although much work on the life course is concerned only with one particular age-group, there is a basis here for developing an integrated theory of age, drawing on insights developed within areas like gerontology or the sociology of youth. It is to these that we now turn.

Explaining the experience of old age

> Ever-stricter stratification by age has emerged since industrialization. The process has accelerated in the twentieth century and, we argue, reached completion in the twenty years following the Second World War. It entailed the increasing segregation of biological from socially defined old age. In the post-war period, more universally than before, old age, and the socially accepted rules associated with it, was accepted as beginning at a fixed chronological age: the state pensionable age of sixty/sixty-five. (Harper and Thane, 1989, p. 43)

This quotation expresses the radical view of the position of the elderly in the post-war epoch. Ageist divisions have become more entrenched and the experience of old age has been shaped by the institution of retirement. Social research has uncovered the disadvantaged position of elderly people as a group, although it should be stressed that the experience of individuals varies. Townsend's pioneering study of poverty in Britain (1979) found that old people were one of the major groups among the poor. In 1985, 61.3 per cent of all pensioners were on low incomes compared to 19.6 per cent of the population under pensionable age (Walker, 1990).

The problem of poverty is more acute among women and ethnic minority members. In 1987, 35 per cent of older women were living on or below the poverty line (as defined by supplementary benefits) as opposed to 23 per cent of men. Women are much more likely than men to rely on the state pension for the bulk of their income; Arber and Ginn (1991b) give figures from the General Household Survey for 1985–6 showing that 64 per cent of men have non-state pension income as opposed to only 27 per cent of women. Ethnic minority elders are as yet a tiny proportion of the British population, but figures for America where minorities have been longer established show that in 1983, 36 per cent of African-American and 23 per cent of Hispanic older people were living below the poverty level, compared with 12 per cent of whites (Markides and Mindel, 1987).

Financial problems may be heightened by ill health and isolation. A growing proportion of older people live on their own, 34 per cent in 1980 as opposed to 22 per cent in 1962 (Gilbert et al., 1989); because of women's greater longevity they are more likely to live alone, especially as they enter their seventies and eighties. Fifty per cent of all women over sixty-five live alone (Ford and Sinclair, 1987). Women and ethnic minority members have been shown by surveys to be more likely to suffer from chronic health problems and from restricted mobility (Fenton, 1987; Arber and Ginn, 1991a).

Although the British government has encouraged people without occupational pensions to supplement state pensions with private ones, it is likely that the problem of poverty or low income among elderly people will be heightened over the next decades because of the increasing commonness of redundancy and early retirement. There has been a striking decline in male economic activity rates. Between 1971 and 1991 the rate for men aged sixty to sixty-four fell by 32 per cent to 51 per cent. In 1971, 31 per cent of men aged sixty-five to sixty-nine were in employment; by 1981 the figure had halved to 16 per cent. In 1991 only 6 per cent of all men over sixty-five and women over sixty were economically active (Phillipson, 1990; Harris, 1991). Increasingly, retirement is the context for the experience of old age. It is not surprising that it figures so largely in the various explanatory frameworks.

Functionalism, modernization and disengagement theory

The position of the elderly in contemporary society has frequently been explained by reference to economic development. Modernization approaches, closely linked to functionalism, suggested that industrialization had affected the elderly in a number of ways (Cowgill and Holmes, 1972). Whereas in pre-industrial society older people continued working until prevented from doing so by bodily incapacity, under the industrial system the labour of the old became redundant as employers preferred to utilize younger and fitter sources of labour. Thus industrialization inexorably led to the formalization of 'retirement' as a status for older people and the evolution of welfare and security schemes to fund it. The previous role of older people as informal repositories of knowledge within the community was jeopardized by the development of formal mass education systems and by processes of rapid technological change which appeared to make that knowledge outdated. At the same time, improvements in public health and declining mortality meant that in the twentieth century far greater proportions of people lived into their sixties and beyond. All these developments both heightened the visibility of older people and helped to devalue their social status. Blythe (1979) suggests that old age was venerated in the past largely because it was rare.

Such a scenario lies behind the theory of 'disengagement'. The situation of the old poses something a problem for the functionalist theory of age-groups, since it is hard to see how the segregation and relative poverty of the elderly could serve as a mechanism of social integration. Indeed, in his account of the functions of age-groups Eisenstadt (1956) more or less completely ignores the elderly, concentrating on youth groups. However, Cumming and Henry (1961) offered a partial (if not very convincing) explanation in suggesting that the institution of retirement offered a benign way for older people gradually to disengage themselves from active participation in society, making way for younger people to take over their places and thus maintaining social equilibrium. Another strand of functionalist thinking emphasized how older people developed their own distinctive segregated subcultures, preferring to socialize with members of their own generation who shared their values and concerns (Rose, 1965).

Disengagement theory has been substantially criticized. It ignores the negative effects of such a process for older people themselves and implies that disengagement and segregation are voluntary. Moreover it can easily be established as empirically inaccurate. Even if older people are forced to give up paid employment, many of them remain active participants in other spheres of social life such as voluntary and community work, politics and leisure activities. Persistent government carping at the cost of the pensions bill casts doubt on the proposition that retirement is unproblematically functional for society. Critics such as Fennell et al. (1988) see retirement rather differently, linking it explicitly to the capitalist organization of production. This has become the dominant approach to old age and inequality in Britain.

Dependency theory and the political economy of age

The 'political economy' perspective was developed in Britain by Townsend (1981), Walker (1981) and Phillipson (1982), and in America by Minkler and Estes (1984). Critical of the functionalist presentation of older people as a homogeneous group, these authors emphasize social divisions among older people and locate their position firmly within the broader structure of inequalities of wealth and power. These are seen as deriving from capitalist relations and the disadvantages of age are linked to class. Within the field of gerontology, the political economy approach has opposed itself to biological and psychological understandings of ageing, arguing that the evils of old age are socially constructed rather than 'natural' (Phillipson, 1982; Fennell et al., 1988). Alan Walker summarizes the key concerns of the political economy approach as 'the social creation of dependent status, the structural relationship between the elderly and younger adults and between different groups of the elderly, and the socially constructed relationship between age, the division of labour and the labour market' (1981, p. 75).

The position of working-class older people who have formerly been dependent on wage labour for subsistence and who will rely heavily on the state security system after retirement is clearly very different from that of middle-class people or the capitalist elite. For middle-class people with good occupational pensions, backed by substantial savings, who own good quality housing, retirement may indeed be viewed as 'a successfully perpetuated holiday' (Blythe, 1979, p. 48). Manual workers are more likely to be forced into early retirement, either because of redundancy or ill health (often related to their work). They are also more likely to express negative views of retirement: as Phillipson states, 'while middle and upper-class people have resources of health and income to support a positive view of retirement, the working class has approached this period with considerable pessimism' (1982, p. 111).

A crucial part of the political economy approach to old age is the notion of structured dependency, which was elaborated by Townsend (1981). The institution of retirement forces people into dependency on the state for their subsistence needs. Since pension rates (especially in Britain) are characteristically set so low, at 'safety net' levels, low income becomes legitimated and seen as an inevitable concomitant of old age. Low incomes also mean that many older people who experience problems of health and mobility must turn to the state for further help. Institutional care for older people is organized in such a way as to deny them rights to self-determination, and agencies treat them as passive recipients of services. Older people become trapped in a cycle of helplessness and economic and psychological dependence.

The theory of dependency has been strongly attacked by Paul Johnson, who presents a more positive image of retirement. He argues (1989) that the political economy approach distorts the experience of retirement by equating work with independence and ignoring consumption. The important issue is whether older people have sufficient income to be active consumers. Johnson emphasizes that much early retirement is of a voluntary nature and that overall the financial situation of retired people has greatly improved since the early part of the century; they have greater command over resources and are less dependent on the goodwill of kin. He concludes: 'improved economic status now gives more elderly people the option of a fairly comfortable retirement which they may prefer to continued employment in unattractive work' (1989, p. 71). There is a real threat of 'rich pensioners' draining societal resources from 'poor parents' and children (Johnson et al., 1989, p. 15).

While it is useful to emphasize the potential benefits of retirement in this way, Johnson's account, based on an aggregated picture, glosses over the poverty and hardship endured by many working-class pensioners, especially women and ethnic minority members. Moreover his arguments, focusing specifically on economic issues, do not address the issues of ageism and status; these in turn are influenced by the specifically capitalist ethos which frames the experience of retirement. Under capitalism status is strongly linked to participation in the production process and its economic rewards. Dependency has a social aspect as well as an economic one and this is overlooked by Johnson.

Some of the criticisms of other perspectives made by those adopting the political economy approach are overstated. For example, it is not true that functionalists viewed age-groups as totally homogeneous; Parsons dealt with gender differences in his account of age-groups and Eisenstadt acknowledged that class background influenced the development of different types of youth groups. Indeed, the strong concern with class among the original proponents of the political economy perspective has led to criticisms that they in turn have neglected gender and ethnicity (Arber and Ginn, 1991a). But their major achievements are to have established age divisions firmly as a form of inequality; to have highlighted the problems associated with retirement; and to have linked the precise form of contemporary age inequality to capitalist production organization, which either excludes or exploits the labour of younger and older workers.

Postmodernist approaches to age

In contrast to the political economists, postmodernists reject the view of older people as victims and emphasize the variability of people's individual responses to ageing. Mike Featherstone and Mike Hepworth in their account of the 'postmodern life course' (1989) suggest that a more positive approach to old age may develop among the generation who grew up in post-war affluence, overturning prevailing definitions of age-appropriate behaviour. They argue that postmodern societies are characterized by processes of de-differentiation and de-institutionalization, which potentially free people from the compulsion to 'act their age'. Successful older people (they mention Ronald Reagan and Margaret Thatcher) may provide positive images of active, socially influential old age to offset negative stereotypes. Joan Collins might stand as an example of a woman who has managed to transcend the decline associated with the ageing female body. But it should be pointed out that it is only members of elite and wealthy groups who are normally in a position to transgress age-specific norms and afford the plastic surgery and lavish expenditure on what

Featherstone and Hepworth call 'body maintenance' (p. 146) which are necessary for those who want to avoid being described as 'mutton dressed as lamb'. There is little sign yet that the trends they describe have had much impact on the lives of the mass of older people.

Although postmodernism and post-structuralism have as yet had a rather limited impact in the study of old age, there is clearly a potential for the study of discourses on age; deconstruction of existing categories follows logically from the radical contention that old age is socially constructed. One such account is offered by Haim Hazan (1994). Hazan argues that academic discourses on age themselves contribute to setting apart old people from the rest of society as something less than human, though bureaucratic discourses are perhaps most influential in this process of segregation and dehumanization. Hazan believes that the real problem for old people is the search for meaning and identity. While academic and bureaucratic discourses present old age in terms of physical deterioration and the elderly as 'a mass of material exigencies' (p. 15), old people themselves may view their lives quite differently. Hazan suggests they respond to stigmatized meanings in a range of ways: internalizing and accepting them, becoming 'difficult' and cantankerous, or withdrawal into silence are three of them.

However, postmodernist approaches appear limited in relation to old age because of their failure to offer any substantial account of the poverty and material deprivation which afflict many older people (Arber, 1994). The postmodernist stress on identities as fluid, multiple and chosen appears less revealing when we are confronted with the stigmatized and non-negotiable social identities of the poor and frail elderly.

Explaining the experience of youth

While contemporary old age appears as a terminal stage marked by superannuation and redundancy, youth has been primarily studied as a transitional phase. The influential account of adolescence offered by G. Stanley Hall (1904) portrayed it as a time of stress and emotional turmoil as young people struggled towards discovery of their adult identities. Erikson (1965) subsequently reaffirmed this in his account of adolescence as a period of role confusion and identity crisis, a time for experimenting with possible future roles. Stage theories of this kind can be criticized for presenting an undifferentiated and universalistic view of youth as a time of crisis, ignoring the way in which youth is differently experienced and handled in different historical periods as well as variations of class, gender and ethnicity. Yet this psychological slant on youth has informed much subsequent research on youth within social science and social policy. The predominant view of young people has been one that emphasizes deviance, rebellion and problems of adjustment, despite repeated reminders from sociologists that the majority of young people are conformist, conservative and generally share their parents' values and get on well with them (Jenkins, 1983; Roberts, 1983; Coffield et al., 1986; M. Davis, 1990). Sociologists nonetheless share the psychologists' emphasis on youth as transition. If retirement is the key institution shaping contemporary lived relations of old age, the lengthened transition from childhood and dependency to adult status and independence marks out the contemporary experience of youth. Such a transition may last from the onset of puberty through into the early twenties.

The handling of this transition in other cultures and epochs has been highly variable, as Eisenstadt's work suggests (1956). In pre-industrial and early industrializing European societies the transition was often abrupt (though there were marked differences of class and gender). Aries (1962) argued that children in pre-industrial Europe were treated simply as small adults. In the nineteenth century most working-class children were sent out to work in their early teens or younger (some as young as seven or eight). While they did not achieve full independence from their parents until they married and established their own family, they gained some status from their contributions to the family budget, while having little time or resources to develop their own distinctive cultures. Although, as Pearson (1983) has shown, there is a long history of concern about younger people being out of control, this tendency has been heightened by twentieth-century circumstances. Now all young people spend a longer time in education before they are formally allowed to enter employment, extending the period of total economic dependency on parents. At the same time relative affluence has permitted the development of youth consumerism. This longer transition was pioneered among the bourgeois class in the nineteenth century, with the rise of the public school, to which many middle-class boys were sent. The development of mass schooling, and its consolidation after the war with a raised school-leaving age, meant that boys and girls of all classes spent much of their teenage stage out of the work-force. Increased parental affluence after the war meant both that dependent youth gained larger spending allowances from their parents and also that young people entering the labour market had access to unparalleled economic opportunities. Thus the 'teenage consumer' was born (M. Abrams, 1959).

The period of teenage affluence of the 1950s and 1960s was a crucial one for establishing the contemporary view of youth and saw the birth of youth subcultures and distinct youth styles. The booming economy meant that school leavers were able to pick jobs and move around till they found one that suited them. Mark Abrams's surveys of young people as consumers revealed that in the late 1950s they had an estimated £850 million in spending power, 5 per cent of national consumer spending. Since the necessities of life were provided for them by parents, most of this money was available for leisure consumer items: for example, records, clothes, magazines, cosmetics (Abrams, 1959). A rapidly expanding youth market fed off spontaneously developed youth styles, publicized them and ensured their further growth.

Davis (1990) argues that these decades witnessed the peaking of a 'cult of youth' which has evolved through the century. Young people are the object of adult envy and of fear. Publicity given to youth in this period reflected the academic view of generational change suggested by Mannheim: youth were seen as pioneers of a coming culture with new values and concerns, which transcended existing social division and youth cultures were seen as shared by all regardless of class: 'they will be cleverer than us . . . they're going to be classless. Their clothes already are. So are the things and places they like most – Wimpy Bars, bowling alleys, the M1' (quoted in Davis, 1990, p. 185).

This period, however, can be seen as exceptional. In the longer run, young people have been vulnerable within the capitalist labour market. In the nineteenth century young children were used as captive labour in factories and sweat shops. Apprenticeships were often a disguised form of cheap labour; in the 1930s young people regularly were laid off once they had qualified for an adult wage. Young people's relative lack of experience and skills expose them as a source of cheap labour. During the recessions of recent decades the experience of youth has hinged not round affluence but unemployment and restricted opportunities. While the 'classlessness' of 1960s youth culture was more apparent than real, it can be argued that class divergences in the experience of young people have become more marked (Roberts et al., 1990; Bates and Riseborough, 1993). Young working-class people have had to contend with mass unemployment. Jobs which are available are often low-paid and semi-permanent; such jobs in the service industry are often targeted specifically at youth, who are forced to accept low pay and poor conditions. There are reports of a rise in child labour, with children working at weekends and on six-hour evening shifts in factories, as families of the labour surplus class seek to maximize household income in whatever way is available. Government schemes such as YTS are resented by many young people as a disguised form of cheap labour (Coffield et al., 1986). It is suggested that one of their major functions is to discipline young people and channel their expectations into acceptance of low-status work (Hollands, 1990; Bates and Riseborough, 1993).

Such developments have seen a further lengthening of the transition period (Hollands, 1990). Working-class younger people are denied the chance to become independent, trapped in parental homes through unemployment or casualized work. More young people are spending longer in further and higher education, hoping to gain skills and qualifications which will allow them to escape from the trap of unemployment and limited opportunities. Youth homelessness is a growing problem in Britain and other countries. The London charity Centrepoint deals with an estimated 3000 young homeless a year. Heightened youth dependency and inequality is thus a feature of most post-industrial capitalist societies.

Recent research on youth has focused on these issues; but the major theme in the post-war sociology of youth has been the study of the distinctive subcultures which have evolved since the 1950s.

Functionalism and subculture theory

The notion of youth culture or subculture has been central to most functionalist accounts of youth. Parsons's account, discussed above, pointed to subculture as a means of bridging the transition as young people develop their own behavioural patterns which detach them from their parents and move them towards adult independence. As Rex (1982) points out, in the functionalist account of industrial society the problem is that children first must be socialized within the family and then out of it, as they learn to work within the impersonal achievement-orientated value-system of wider society rather than the particularistic ascribed values of the family.

This is the basis for Eisenstadt's extended account of youth stratification. Pointing to the ubiquity of youth-specific groupings in all types of society, he argues they act in various ways to bind young people into society. In modern societies, the institutionalized forms of age distinction (for example, the high degree of age segregation in schools) serve both to socialize young people into the universalistic values needed for successful integration into a complex social organization and to develop feelings of community and solidarity through identification with one's peer group. Homogeneous age-groups are also seen as an outlet for the tensions that arise between the generations in the family (for example, over young people's sexual maturation) and allow them to be resolved in a relatively harmless way (Eisenstadt, 1956).

Although Eisenstadt analyses age-groups primarily in terms of social integration, he does acknowledge the existence of deviant youth groups such as gangs which can be disruptive and disintegrative. He sees them as arising from the discrepancy between family aspirations and the opportunities for advancement which are realistically available in society. In this he follows Merton (1938), whose work has been the major influence in the American sociology of youth. Merton offered an explanation of deviancy in terms of anomie and the discrepancy between social goals (success, material prosperity) and the means available to gain them; where legitimate means are not available, illegitimate means such as crime and delinquency may be employed instead.

Most functionalist work on youth was focused on the explanation of deviancy and delinquency, and employed the notion of subculture. These theories and the critical responses to them from other perspectives have been thoroughly surveyed by Brake (1980; 1985). While there are many different strands, all emphasize the development of youth subcultures, with their own distinctive value systems. Sometimes these are said to mirror or exaggerate the 'focal concerns' of parent cultures (including criminal ones), sometimes to overturn them. Deviant behaviour is said to arise from blocked status aspirations, limited economic opportunities or the social disorganization associated with urban decline. Predominantly middle-class youth subcultural groups, such as beatniks and hippies, can be seen as examples of Merton's retreatist or innovatory mode of adaptation, where social goals themselves are challenged.

Functionalist approaches are standardly criticized for their neglect of class and inequality, but, with the exception of Parsons, these accounts of youth culture do take heed of class differences. While Merton's original theory of anomie and deviance was couched in terms of individual adaptations, the subcultural theorists of youth and deviance focus on collective responses to inequality and frustrated expectations. There are marked resemblances between these approaches and those influenced by Marxism. However, it can be argued that functionalists put more stress on shared values, while Marxists accentuate structured inequalities. Moreover, the functionalist stress on youth as transition implies that most deviant behaviour is only a transient phase, associated with the problems of achieving adult identity. While both age and class are involved in subcultural formation, arguably more weight is given to age.

Radical theories – youth and resistance

Radical theory of deviancy, strongly influenced by Marxism, developed in the 1960s and 1970s and became the dominant approach to the study of youth in Britain. Radical theorists ranged themselves against the psychological view of adolescence as a universal phase of emotional turmoil and criticized the notion of a 'classless' youth culture. Their concern was to show how youth and deviancy arose from the general structure of social inequality, particularly that of class. Youth subcultures were linked to the development of capitalism and were seen as class specific. Skinhead culture, for example, was analysed by Hebdige (1979) as a cultural style which derived from an exaggerated version of rough working-class masculinity, with its stress on sport and 'aggro' (violence and fighting) and its adoption of a parodic version of work clothing ('bovver' boots, rolled-up jeans and braces).

Mike Brake (1980) described youth cultures as 'magical' cultural solutions to the economic and social problems of class and ethnicity. They presented working-class youth with a moratorium, albeit brief, from the realities of their class-bound futures, analogous to the space for freedom and experimentation allowed to middle-class young people by their spell as university students: 'working-class cultures in particular infuse into the bleak world of the working-class adolescent a period of intense emotion, colour and excitement' (1980, p. 23). Middle-class forms of youth rebellion can also be interpreted in this way, as a (temporary) reaction against a future of conformism within the corporate cultures of capitalist bureaucracies.

A key feature of the radical approach was its view of deviancy and rebellion among young people as a form of 'resistance' to the capitalist system and to dominant social values (Hall and Jefferson, 1976). Rather than being understood as a social problem or the result of inadequate socialization, delinquency was considered a creative response to material inequality, a manifestation of incipient class awareness. In particular, the rioting among young people which has occurred sporadically in inner-city areas or deprived estates throughout the past decades was seen as a reaction to the crises of capitalism which had brought unemployment and urban decline, and to racist oppression resulting from the history of capitalist imperialism.

Radical approaches, in the same way as the political economy perspective in gerontology, were important in highlighting age as an aspect of social inequality and showing how the experience of age takes specific forms in capitalist societies. They can be criticized for an over-romantic view of youth culture and of deviancy in particular, underplaying the harm done to the victims of youth crime, the increased deterioration of environments associated with it. As Lea and Young (1984) argue, the victims of crime and delinquency are usually working-class themselves. This fact problematizes the notion of youth cultures as a form of class resistance, now viewed as a romanticized interpretation. Griffin (1993) suggests it has been replaced in recent radical texts by a stress on survival strategies and a defensive response to deprivation, especially by those studying ethnic minority youth.

The overriding concern with youth cultures and deviancy in both the subcultural and radical approaches and their neglect of 'ordinary kids' can also be criticized. Davis, in an incisive critical review of approaches to youth, suggests that the sensationalized presentation of young people in the media has been paralleled by an academic approach which presents 'over-theorized, over-generalized and generally exaggerated images of youth' (1990, p. 18). A more thorough account of youth inequality would need to study the experiences of the majority of youth who are broadly conformist. Recent accounts of youth employment and unemployment offer a more balanced view of young people (for example Coffield et al., 1986; Wallace and Cross, 1990; Bates and Riseborough, 1993).

New approaches: feminism, postmodernism and post-structuralism

Another criticism of radical theories was that in their preoccupation with class they ignored gender. McRobbie (1991) points to the near invisibility of young women in subcultural theories. This was rectified in the late 1970s and 1980s by a series of researches and texts which dealt with young women (for example, McRobbie, 1978, 1991; McRobbie and Nava, 1984; Griffin, 1985). These studies demonstrate that the experience of youth is gendered. Friendship groups and leisure activities are segregated by sex. Early youth subcultures enshrined sexist values and hinged around facets of masculine behaviour (fighting, motor bikes, football). Young women were relegated to the fringe (featuring as girlfriends, dolly birds, groupies and earth mothers). While recent cultural styles (punk, rave culture) are more sexually egalitarian, young women have tended to develop their own distinct forms of behaviour and 'focal concerns'.

The experience of youth is highly shaped by social definitions of masculinity and femininity. A preoccupation with romance and with appearance grooms young women towards conventional adult versions of femininity. Interactions between young women and men are often framed by the adoption of exaggeratedly sexist and macho behaviour among young men (Wood, 1984; Lees, 1993; Riseborough, 1993). Young women are treated differently by the various groups of adults with whom they come into contact. Parents, teachers, careers advisers and social workers steer young women towards traditional feminine roles. Sharp gender distinctions pressure many young women inexorably towards traditional 'women's work' with its lower rewards (Griffin, 1985).

More recent feminist approaches, reflecting the influence of postmodernism, trace the interaction between gender, ethnicity and class (Mirza, 1992; Griffin, 1993). The post-structuralist influence has also led to a move away from presenting young women as passive victims of gendered conditioning. Rather, studies emphasize how they creatively use and interpret the cultural forms available to them from both spontaneous youth cultures and commercial sources (Wolpe, 1988; McRobbie and Nava, 1984).

More generally some initial explorations have applied post-modern and post-structural insights to the study of youth. Willis et al. (1990) develop some aspects of postmodern views of culture in their account of young people as consumers of commercial culture, emphasizing the breakdown of hard and fast distinctions between 'high' and 'popular' cultural forms. Young consumers are able to subvert commercial cultural forms, imposing their own meanings on them and using tactics of bricolage to assemble their own versions of style. While Willis et al. emphasize the impact of unemployment, they suggest that consumption roles are more significant than productive ones in young people's lives: they utilize their cultural creativity to get by and develop individualized lifestyles even in the face of material constraints.

A different imput from post-structuralism is apparent in two books which investigate youth in terms of prevailing social and academic discourses. John Davis (1990), while not directly acknowledging a post-structural influence, traces the way youth as a social category has been presented in the media, by policy-makers and within academic theory, and argues that common to all is an exaggerated stress on youth as a problem stage and a preoccupation with spectacular subcultures. Such views reflect two contradictory tendencies, both the veneration and adulation of young people as innovators (the cult of youth) and the longstanding history of fears and anxieties about moral decline and delinquency. Taken together, Davis argues, youth is used as a symbol of 'the state of the nation'. Christine Griffin (1993) adopts an explicitly post-structural line, seeking to deconstruct key elements within discourses on youth to show how constructions about disaffection, deviance, adolescent disturbance and so on provide the framework for the analysis of youth in a way which may distort young people's experience. While not attempting to provide an alternative 'correct' approach, she suggests that more attention must be paid to the voices of young people themselves.

Featherstone and Hepworth (1989) have suggested that age differentiation may be eroding with the advent of postmodern societies, as adults adopt some facets of younger people's behaviour (for example, listening to popular music or adopting youth fashions) and younger people become more precocious in terms of sexual behaviour. But while this indicates that the boundaries between age-groups and social definitions of age-specific behaviour are constantly changing, it does not suggest a real breakdown of age barriers. Such a position neglects the differential access to power and resources which has been highlighted in the preceding discussion. In general postmodernist approaches, while commendably stressing the creativity of individual agents, may underestimate the power of ageist prescriptions and their effects on individuals' self-images.

Age and identity

As individuals we are apt to be very aware of our age. Young people face legal and social constraints on their actions and are often told they are 'too young' to do certain things. As people enter their forties they experience effects of physiological ageing which make them conscious that they are beginning to 'grow old'. Older people face the negative stereotypes of ageism and must adjust to the loss of friends and loved ones and the reality of their own approaching death. But age as a basis of collective social identity is more problematic. Historically, political activity based around age differences has been rare, although in the post-war period pressure groups have been formed in America and Britain to lobby for pensioners' rights (Phillipson, 1982). In general, political parties have not served as a vehicle for age-related interests and issues. Nor have age-based pressure groups attained the social and political prominence of feminism or anti-racist struggles. Age as an issue is very low on the political agenda. Thus while age is an important aspect of individual identity, the development of active or politicized identification with an age-group is less common.

This relates to two factors which have been already mentioned. First, the movement of individuals through the various age-groups prevents lasting age identification. It has frequently been remarked that today's young rebels may become tomorrow's respectable citizens. This works against the formation of long-lasting organizations promoting the interests of age. Secondly, in contrast to other forms of social hierarchy the powerful groups are the ones in the middle. The powerless groups, the old and the young, who might make common cause against the age elite, are so differentiated in terms of experience and attitudes that they may feel suspicion and hostility towards each other.

The existence of youth subcultures could be read as evidence of identification among young people, indicative of a propensity to share values and activities with others of the age-group. Some aspects of youth cultures express an active hostility to adult society and culture. Such views were displayed, for example, in The Who's classic song, *My Generation*:

> People try to put us down
> Just because we get around.
> Things they do look awful cold
> Hope I die before I get old!

In other songs the group lamented the powerlessness and lack of opportunities facing young people and the problem of 'teenage wastage': 'a young man ain't worth nothing in the world today.'

However, such topics are the exception rather than the rule in cultural expressions of youth cultures. More common themes are freedom, love and sexuality, pleasure and a generalized rebellion against the rules and repressions of society which is not necessarily age-specific. The more overtly political aspects of youth cultures, as emphasized in the radical accounts discussed above, are often linked to issues of class, gender or 'race' as in the denunciations of 'Babylon' (white society and power) which characterize much black popular music (Gilroy, 1987).

Where young people have become prominent in political movements it has often been as an aspect of class-based or other forms of politics. For example, young Asian men have played an active role in Britain in street demonstrations against racism or on behalf of Islamic movements. Youth wings within established parties, such as the Young Conservatives and Young Socialists, may work to promote new ideas and policies which in part are related to the broader concerns of their own age-groups, although they also reflect their own commitment to the different political ideologies, so that it is difficult to disentangle class and age interests. This tendency is best illustrated by the student movement of the 1960s in America, Britain and Europe. Many of its political objectives concerned class and ethnic issues: attacks on the capitalist system and on Western imperialism, support for socialism and the dominated people of Vietnam. At the same time it reflected many values which were specifically those of younger people: the attack on the materialist culture they identified with their parents, the demand for sexual liberation, calls for educational reform and student self-determination, hostility towards technology and bureaucracy with its rules and regulations ('who needs them?' sang Crosby, Stills, Nash and Young, one of the rock groups identified with student protest).

Arguably a more specifically age-based form of political activism may be emerging among young people today. In America the young people characterized as 'generation X' and the initiators of 'grunge' culture have voiced feelings of being denied opportunities and access to a good standard of living because of the selfishness and greed of their elders. While alienated attitudes among youth are nothing new, the decline in manufacturing industry has had a particularly severe impact on minority ethnic and working-class young males and the availability of 'Macjobs' has done little to remove the feeling that a ghetto of youth jobs is being created.

In Britain, the late 1970s and 1980s were marked by a relative absence of new youth subcultures; young people appeared to be conformist and materialistic, interested only in acquiring designer clothing and pursuing a consumerist 'yuppie' lifestyle. However, the 1990s have witnessed a more rebellious spirit among young people, with a coalition of various youth interests (New Age travellers, ravers, environmental groups and 'tribes') forming to fight against the Criminal Justice Bill. Although adults have been involved in this campaign, it is young people's lifestyles and practices which are particularly threatened by the legislation. While there are strong resemblances to the 'counter-culture' of the 1960s ('dropping out', drug-taking, communal living, bargain-basement clothing), the leaders of the movement have deliberately distanced themselves from existing political parties and show little interest in the ideals of socialism. The 'right to party' has never been high on any political party's agenda!

As we have seen, older people, too, have been victims of the recession, and there have been some signs in Britain of increasing militancy among pensioners' groups. Phillipson (1982) gives a useful survey of the various groups which have formed since the Second World War to work for the interests of the elderly, ranging from the philanthropic Age Concern to the radical British Pensioners' Trade Union Action Association, established in 1973 to organize demonstrations and petitions. However, only a tiny minority of older people are involved in such political activities.

One thing that may impede the development of a more general identification among older people is the stigmatization which arises from ageist attitudes. Younger and vigorous old people may not wish to identify with the 'elderly' because of the connotations of ill health, dependency and uselessness. Williams's study of attitudes among old people in Aberdeen confirms this point:

> Late age was certainly stigmatized by many older people themselves, in the sense that it was seen as a passive, pitied state, the outcome of living beyond the normal time to die . . . Late age was indeed viewed as the kind of discreditable identity which was regarded as abnormal and suitable for a degree of segregation. (1987, p. 99)

While Williams notes the variability of old people's circumstances, he comments on the evidence of solidarity among the younger old, in opposition to the young. This solidarity rested upon common values which were felt to be lacking among the 'younger generation': respect for neighbourliness, for authority, for perseverance and thrift. Fear and distrust of the young (including the fear of violence prevalent in deprived areas) may act as a spur to a heightened sense of generational identity. Mark Hudson's account of a deprived working-class community in the north-east also presents a state of mutual hostility and incomprehension between young and old:

> It sometimes seemed, talking to the older people in Horden, as though the younger generation had declared war on the old. They were said to be bent only on violence and destruction. They were the ones who were ruining everything with their vandalism, joy-riding and ram raiding. It was difficult to find anyone among the older generation with a good word to say about the young . . . They spoke of them as though they were of a species fundamentally different from themselves. (1994, p. 95)

While this kind of defensive identification among older people is probably quite common and is fostered by the various segregated institutions that have developed to cater for their needs (retirement homes, pensioners' clubs, SAGA holidays), the development of a more active political identity is rare. One reason why older people do not react more militantly to disadvantage and ageism may be that they grew up in a framework of lower expectations, as Blythe points out: 'Many of today's old people had such rough starts, such small scraps of education, wages and possessions generally, that they feel they are ending their days in clover' (1979, p. 11).

However, generational change may offset this. Many commentators have speculated that greater militancy may develop among older people, partly because of the greater numbers of early retired 'young old', partly because the newer cohorts of the elderly will contain many ex-activists from the 1960s or from the feminist movement who are experienced in political campaigning (Neugarten, 1970; Phillipson, 1982). The potential of such a movement is hinted at by the American Gray Panthers, a radical group with a much broader perspective on age inequality than those associated with the single-issue pensioners' groups. The Panthers' manifestos spoke specifically of the need to attack ageism and suggested that all disadvantaged age groups should work together:

> The Philadelphia Gray Panthers shall be a coalition of old and young people working together. We shall work for the liberation of older and younger people urging re-integration into the life of the community and enhancing and revitalizing the resources of both. We shall work also for the elimination of age discrimination that has isolated both the young and the old. (Quoted in Cain, 1975, p. 39)

The implication of the position developed in this book is that age for the age elite would be a default identity. However, a recent text has highlighted the potential clash of interests between the working sections of the populace and the retired elderly whose pensions must be funded from their tax payments. As the 'burden of dependency' of non-employed pensioners rises, it is argued, intergenerational conflict may break out along these lines (Johnson et al., 1989). This position has been endorsed by government policy-makers (Phillipson, 1982); and the American pressure group AGE (Americans for Generational Equity) explicitly blames the elderly for poverty among younger groupings. Sara Arber and Jay Ginn (1991b) refer to this scapegoating of the elderly as 'conflictual ageism' and point out that its main effect is to strengthen the hand of governments who want to squeeze back on pensions. Certainly, there is not much evidence that such attitudes are widespread. Survey data from Europe and Britain has indicated considerable sympathy for the plight of pensioners (Walker, 1993). What Arber and Ginn call 'compassionate ageism' (the view of old people as pathetic and pitiable and in need of looking after) is probably a great deal more common than conflictual ageism.

While age divisions hold the potential for intergenerational conflict, the relative rarity of political activities organized around age reflects the way in which age disadvantages are affected by other dynamics of stratification.

Interacting dynamics: age, ethnicity, gender and class

American researchers into old age coined the term 'double jeopardy' (or sometimes 'triple jeopardy') to describe the way in which disadvantages of age are compounded by those of ethnicity and/or gender or class. We might more aptly speak of quadruple jeopardy, for it is clear that these four factors come together to create the worst cases of poverty and misfortune.

Ethnicity

Markides and Mindel (1987) review debates about double jeopardy arising from racial discrimination, along with the counter-argument that age is a leveller, with people of all classes and ethnic groups experiencing a narrowing of income differentials. They state that the evidence is inconclusive: while ethnic minority members are more liable to poverty in old age because of the past experience of discrimination, they are often better integrated into community and neighbourhood networks and thus more psychologically braced to face old age. Moreover, ageist attitudes are less pronounced than among the majority population. They conclude that class is probably more significant than ethnicity.

Blakemore and Boneham (1994) draw somewhat similar conclusions on the basis of their research among Asians and Afro-Caribbeans in Britain; they challenge the view of all minority old people as poverty-stricken victims and cite the material success of some Asians in the east Midlands cities. They emphasize the variability of response to old age among different ethnic groups, commending the self-sufficiency of the pioneer immigrant groups who came to Britain after the war. Among Asians in particular, family and community support for the elderly is strong. An earlier study by Steve Fenton (1987) of Afro-Caribbeans in Bristol offers a more sombre view: many of his respondents suffered ill health and poverty and were deeply unhappy with their lives in Britain. The more optimistic accounts ignore the effect of racist stereotyping and prejudice which affect those who come into contact with the agencies catering for old age. In Fenton's words:

> They face the *common* hardships of old age which, for many, are characterized by dependency, and the *specific* indignities which are a consequence of racially defined ideas and practices, and are frequently concretized in transactions with public services and officials in dependency relations. (1987, p. 2)

Young people from racialized minorities face racism and discrimination. As we have seen in previous chapters, they are more vulnerable to unemployment; they experience racism at school from both teachers and fellow pupils and have more difficulty in gaining employment in line with their qualifications. Furthermore, 44 per cent of the young homeless in London are from ethnic minorities (Simmons, 1994). Although they may join in with white subcultural movements, the tendency among Afro-Caribbean and some working-class Asian youths has been to form their own gangs and groups. While black music and fashions are extremely popular among white young people, racial tension can lead to violence between gangs where ethnic and territorial loyalties are strong. Afro-Caribbean culture, with its emphasis on street life and on music, has been rich in spawning youth styles and cultural forms. Unfortunately, especially in the United States, such vibrant black cultures tend to become ghettoized and many young men slide from them into hard drug-taking and criminal activities.

Gender

There is little doubt that women suffer a double jeopardy of age and gender, although this is connected to one advantage they have over men: their greater longevity. As a result they are over-represented among the 'old old' who are more vulnerable to illness, especially Alzheimer's disease, loss of mobility and the necessity to receive residential or hospital care. They are twice as likely to be housebound. Living longer, women are more vulnerable to bereavement, widowhood and loneliness: half of all elderly women in Britain live on their own, as opposed to one fifth of elderly men (Arber and Ginn, 1991b).

There is a consensus that women are the greatest sufferers from poverty in old age (Walker, 1990; Fennell et al., 1988). This arises from the interrelated factors of women's responsibility for domestic labour and their inferior labour market situation. Time spent looking after children means they have lower entitlement to pensions; women's earnings are generally low so that they have less money for savings and investment; fewer women than men have access to occupational pensions. Taken together these factors mean that women are more likely to depend on inadequate state pensions for their income. Arber and Ginn argue that the relative disadvantage of women persists across all classes, although single women from higher occupational groupings can achieve a better standard of living. There is no doubt that motherhood is a cause of disadvantage for women in later life. As Arber and Ginn put it, for women 'personal poverty is the price of fertility' (1991b, p. 100).

In addition, women are likely to suffer more from the stigmatization and ageist attitudes. There is a double standard in ageing. While it is allowed that some men age with dignity and even gain in attractiveness to women (certainly elderly millionaires seem to have no difficulty in finding a succession of young women to be their brides!), the bodies of ageing women have long been viewed with special disgust. The loss of sexual attractiveness is particularly significant as it is so crucially bound up with social definitions of femininity and womanhood. As Arber and Ginn (1991b) point out, women suffer a double social exclusion in old age; they share with men the loss of their role in the capitalist production system, while also losing their reproductive capacities. Since women are valued for their feminine bodily attractions, many older women suffer deeply from feelings of low esteem.

Younger women's position, too, is affected by prevailing definitions of femininity and the association with domesticity and motherhood. While boys' leisure lives revolve around sport and drinking and take place to a large degree outside, in the street, girls' leisure has been more constrained, partly because of parental anxiety about young women's sexuality and personal safety. McRobbie (1978) described what she called the 'bedroom culture' of working-class teenage girls which revolved around make-up, fashion, pop music and idols and gossip about boys. This preoccupation with romance and appearance channelled girls towards marriage and motherhood, while their male compeers' culture involved 'learning to labour' (Willis, 1977). Within schools and YTS schemes young working-class women are steered towards traditional women's work, which offers them unenticing alternatives to motherhood.

Recently it has been claimed that young women are catching up. Their educational achievements are equal to if not surpassing those of young men and the labour market appears more favourable to them. Girls are said to be breaking free of traditional restraints and engaging in forms of activity similar to boys', including delinquent behaviour such as membership of 'girl gangs'. Although there is dispute as to how new these forms of female behaviour are, and whether they merely reflect a general rise in levels of violence in society, it can be argued that feminism has encouraged a loosening of the internal controls which used to inhibit women's behaviour (Heidensohn, 1985). However, for working-class girls prospects remain restricted. Recent research on youth unemployment suggests that it results in greater pressure for young working-class women to take up domestic roles (Presdee, 1982; Coffield et al., 1986). Here the effect of class is strongly registered.

Class

> From birth until death . . . the influence of class continues to exert a disproportionate effect both on the quality of life and on the quantity of resources which people receive. (Phillipson, 1982, p. 159)

Working-class people experience the greatest risks of poverty, isolation and ill health and are most dependent on the state. A recent study of 300,000 people carried out by the London School of Hygiene showed that poorer people are much more likely to die before the age of seventy (Sloggett and Joshi, 1994). By contrast middle-class people enjoy many advantages in facing up to old age:

> For those in the middle classes with the prospect of generous pension incomes and who have planned for retirement, old age holds out the prospect of a prolongation of the plateau-like phase of adult life, with continued relatively high consumption and the pursuit of consumer culture lifestyles, body maintenance and styles of presentation. (Featherstone and Hepworth, 1989, pp. 145–6)

Members of the capitalist elite may not be affected by retirement policies at all, but retain the pre-industrial practice of continuing in their occupation until they no longer are able to or wish to.

Class differences are equally sharp among young people, with working-class youth encountering limited opportunities and risks of unemployment. Involvement in deviant cultures purveying anti-school values only heightens the chance of ending in dead-end jobs (Willis, 1977; Mac an Ghaill, 1988). Education is a crucial factor. Research has persistently shown how the education system processes young people through class-specific channels. Upper- and middle-class parents can afford to send children to private schools which offer a more academically orientated and disciplined environment, or get them accepted by comprehensive schools with better academic records. Working-class children habitually attend less successful comprehensives and go on to YTS schemes which are themselves stratified in terms of 'rough' and 'respectable' segments of lower-class occupations (Bates and Riseborough, 1993). There is evidence that the educational system is becoming more class-segregated; grammar schools used to provide a route for academically orientated working-class children to enter a middle-class world, while comprehensive schools have arguably been less successful. The introduction of student loans will deter working-class recruits from entering universities.

The current economic climate might serve to unite young people through their experience of diminishing opportunities. Even middle-class young people are finding it more difficult to find jobs for which they consider themselves qualified. There has been a considerable degree of graduate unemployment in Britain throughout the 1980s and 1990s. While it has been emphasized that youth cultures are class specific, researchers have found that young people register little sense of class identification (Willis et al., 1990; McRobbie, 1991). A shared interest in music, dancing and other youth-related cultural forms might serve to strengthen young people's sense that they, as well as the old, are victims of ageism.

Summary and conclusions

'A life form in which chronological age was much less relevant was replaced by an increasingly age-relevant one' (Featherstone and Hepworth, 1989, pp. 143–4). Almost all the perspectives discussed in this chapter share this view, that the development of modern industrial capitalist societies brought increased awareness of age as a basis of social distinctions and greater segregation of age-groups. While most societies have elements of age stratification, capitalism has promoted a distinct form of age inequality which rests upon the socially dependent status of the young and the old.

Economic rewards and status are linked to participation in the productive system. The institution of retirement has promoted the withdrawal of many older people from paid work at an increasingly early age; financial hardship linked to dependency on inadequate state pensions is augmented by ageist attitudes, although middle-class affluence acts as a cushion against some of the more damaging aspects of ageing. Younger people, especially those of the working class or from ethnic minority communities, are also experiencing increasingly longer periods of dependency on their parents or on the state because of youth unemployment.

While it is acknowledged that age is a key aspect of stratification in post-industrial capitalist societies, theories of age are relatively underdeveloped. The theory of age stratification, developing from the functionalist framework, and Mannheim's analysis of generations and generation units, were a promising start, but their potential has not been fully explored. Rather, the investigation of inequalities of age has evolved within sociological subspecialisms, although there have been recent attempts to integrate those through a sociology of the life course.

Within the sociology of youth and social gerontology radical perspectives broadly derived from Marxism have become dominant in the past decades. Since these are, in relative terms, fairly new areas of sociological investigation, it is perhaps not surprising that the modernist framework has not yet received a major challenge from sociologists employing postmodernist and post-structuralist premises. In fact, the political economy approach with its emphasis on the social construction of old age seems to have led logically into a postmodernist concern with deconstructing prevailing attitudes to age. In the study of youth, a new interest in studying discourses of age has not necessarily been at odds with radical accounts of youth subcultures and inequality.

The radical perspectives stressed that the experience of age was differentiated by class, and more recent research has highlighted the interaction of disadvantages of age with gender and ethnicity. Such divisions impede the development of coherent or long-lasting political movements based on age divisions. Nonetheless, age is both an important aspect of individual identity and of more transient but recurrent generational conflicts. With the development of global capitalism, younger and older people in the societies of the West have suffered disproportionately from the effects of unemployment and limited opportunities consequent upon economic restructuring. The next few decades may witness an outbreak of 'age warfare' as the disadvantaged groups take a more militant stance against ageism and the age elite.

Further reading

Mike O'Donnell, *Age and Generation* (Tavistock, 1985) offers a general introduction to the sociology of age-groups. An excellent textbook on older people is Graham Fennell, Chris Phillipson and Helen Evers, *The Sociology of Old Age* (Open University, 1988), while Ken Blakemore and Margaret Boneham, *Age, Race and Ethnicity* (Open University, 1994) is a highly readable account of 'race' and age. Mike Brake, *Sociology of Youth Culture and Youth Subcultures* (Routledge, 1980) provides a classic introduction to subcultural theories, while a thorough overview of past and contemporary perspectives is offered by Christine Griffin, *Representations of Youth* (Polity, 1993). John Davis, *Youth and the Condition of Britain: images of adolescent conflict* (Athlone, 1990) is a lively social history of ideas about youth, and Inge Bates and George Riseborough (eds.), *Youth and Inequality* (Open University Press, 1993) is a stimulating study of youth inequalities in education.

7

Some International Comparisons

So far the discussion in this book has dealt primarily with Britain, although some examples from other European countries and from North America have been used. How far are the theories and concepts developed to explain inequalities in Britain applicable to other countries? Are the dynamics of inequality similar in all highly industrialized societies?

There are two broad positions on this question. Those espousing modernist and structuralist positions (that is, those employing the frameworks of classical sociology or modified versions of them) would answer yes. The structures of capitalism, patriarchy, of racial exclusion, of the heightened dependency of old and young which their theories identify will operate in a broadly similar fashion in all societies. This does not mean that dynamics of class, gender, ethnicity and age will be *identical* in each society. Each will have its own unique trajectory of development, influenced by specific historical, cultural and political circumstances (Bradley, 1992). The pre-industrial organization of society and its traditions will have a strong influence; late industrializers will differ from early industrializers; the trajectory of each economy and its specialisms (differing resources, balances between economic sectors, degree of concentration) will affect the patterns of inequality; cultural factors such as religion may influence processes of social differentiation; and the state has played a crucial role in moderating or maintaining social inequality. Nonetheless, the logic of class, gender, 'race' and age dynamics is such that we should expect to discern similar trends in each society.

By contrast, those espousing postmodern and post-structuralist perspectives challenge the idea of an underlying logic of development. Following Lyotard, they argue that grand narratives must be replaced by local ones. Relations of class, gender, 'race' and age are influenced by the specific context in which they are at play; they derive from discursive formations which shape their development and which are fluid and variable. Any discussion of general trends and tendencies only obscures differences within social experiences, and acts to impose a false unity on that which is diverse. Randomness, chance and historical contingency shape developments rather than any logical working-out of structural tendencies. In place of formulating any kind of general theory, we should explore particular historical examples and we should expect marked divergences between different societies.

The aim of this chapter is to explore these two propositions by looking at some examples of social divisions in different countries. There is no attempt to develop a systematic account of the dynamics of class, gender, 'race' and age in a sample of highly industrialized societies, which would be a massive task. Here I simply review some literature which has drawn international comparisons in order to highlight the differences and similarities between societies.

Class

There are many apparent differences in class dynamics between nations. Britain, for example, is generally viewed as an exceptionally hierarchical and class-bound society (Edgell, 1993). In common with other older European societies, it is said to have been influenced by its feudal past, which had habituated the population to accept hierarchy and inequality. In contrast, newer societies such as Australia and North America started out with a greater commitment to equality, as de Tocqueville showed in *Democracy in America*. Class relations may be affected by the presence of the remnants of the peasantry (France, Italy) or by a large petite bourgeoisie (Australia, Japan). The greater egalitarianism of the Scandinavian societies is linked to the strength of their welfare systems. Sweden in particular exemplifies a social democratic alternative to free market capitalism.

Two countries considered to demonstrate 'exceptionalism' in their class relations are America and Japan. America is often proclaimed to be a 'classless' society by its citizens: 'we don't have classes in our town' (Fussell, 1983, p. 3). Japan is portrayed contradictorily as a society marked by deference and respect for status, while simultaneously lacking class boundaries, with a working population viewed by Western observers as 'notoriously hard-working, loyal to its employers and lacking in class consciousness' (Steven, 1983, p. 155). Yet, despite these apparent differences, cross-cultural comparison of the advanced industrial societies has highlighted common patterns of class formation and development, leading one commentator to conclude:

> There is a family resemblance between the systems of social stratification in the European countries because they have in common the same, and increasingly internationalized, capitalist production and market

system. They also have in common the features of state welfare. (Davis, 1992, p. 32)

Howard Davis discerns what he calls a typical European class structure, consisting of a capitalist class, a service class (subdivided into two groups: one of managers and professionals, the other lower grade professionals, technicians, supervisors and so forth), a (shrinking) working class and a 'lower working class' made up of casualized and unemployed workers (he rejects the term underclass). Across the European Community there has been a switch to service-sector employment. Between 1960 and 1987 employment in agriculture declined from 23 to 8 per cent, in manufacturing from 40 to 33 per cent, while services rose from 37 to 59 per cent (Commission of the European Communities, 1989). If we employ 'post-industrial' in a purely descriptive sense in terms of the predominant type of employment, it is clear that during these three decades Europe as a whole, in the footsteps of America, has made the switch from an industrial to a post-industrial form of capitalism, although some member states, such as Greece and Portugal, lag behind.

A number of recent comparative studies have considered class in the context of these changes. Lash and Urry (1987) based their account of 'disorganized capitalism' upon case studies of five countries (Britain, France, Germany, Sweden and the USA). While emphasizing that these were at different stages along the road to disorganization, they spoke of similar developments in all five. All had experienced a decline in manufacturing since the 1960s, with a shrinking of the traditional working class. These tendencies were less marked in Germany, which remained closest to the 'organized' model of capitalism (see chapter 2). In all countries service-sector employment, particularly in the private sector, was expanding and the power of the service class had been enhanced. Traditional forms of class consciousness and action were in decline, eroded by a growing spirit of consumerist individualism, with new social movements substituting for class-based political activities.

Esping-Andersen and colleagues, in their survey of six countries (1993), also noted common trends, while placing more stress on variations. For example, they point to the greater degree of social openness and mobility in Sweden and the persistence of skilled male manual work in Germany. They saw the United States as furthest along the route to a post-industrial economy, with Germany and Britain in the rear. But like Lash and Urry, and Davis, they note the decline of the manual working class and the rise of the service class in all the countries in the study. Moreover, they suggest a common pattern of class interaction with dynamics of age and gender, arguing that the evolving post-industrial economies are broadly 'sexually democratic' with increases in jobs for women; while many of the new unskilled service jobs are being filled by older workers, on their way out of traditional manual work, or by young people.

While Esping-Andersen et al. suggest some variability in mobility between countries, Robert Erikson and John Goldthorpe argue in their study of ten industrial societies (1992) that there is a common 'core' pattern of mobility in these societies. They concede that absolute rates of mobility are highly variable, and suggest that this cannot be explained systematically, for example in terms of different patterns or 'routes' to industrialization (B. Moore, 1966; Kemp, 1978). Instead they link variations to specific historical contingencies. However, the societies exhibit common patterns of relative mobility (the differential chances of mobility for each class grouping). Erikson and Goldthorpe impute this to the ability of privileged groups to use the resources they have to maintain the class position of themselves and their families. For example, they make use of the education system as a hedge against downward mobility. This contrasts with the optimistic view of Esping-Andersen, who cites the growing importance of education and qualifications as a common feature and implies that this contributes to the relative openness of these evolving post-industrial societies.

Erikson's and Goldthorpe's view of the persistence of class structures is shared by Bottomore and Brym (1989), although the latter write from a Marxist perspective. They reject accounts featuring the notion of class decline, stating that these concentrate on occupational change affecting the middle and working class but ignore the capitalist class. Bottomore and Brym suggest that the continued existence and increasing power of the capitalist elite is the most important feature of modern capitalist societies, a view also expressed by Westergaard (1994). On the basis of case studies of seven countries they argue that 'the capitalist class in the leading capitalist countries has effectively maintained its position as a ruling class and in some cases has enhanced its power, notably during the past decade' (Bottomore and Brym, 1989, p. 12).

The contributors to their collection of case studies for the most part endorse this view, although national variations in the power and composition of the capitalist class are indicated. In France and Italy, control of capital is still exercised by powerful individuals and families, forming a socially and politically coherent group, which Marceau (1989) refers to as an 'elite familiale'. In Japan, the USA and Canada capital takes a more corporate form, with Britain half-way between the two. The capitalist class is said to be weakest in Germany, where the power of the old economic elite was dismantled after the war. The imposition on West Germany of a corporate structure of industrial relations by America during post-war reconstruction is seen to have impaired the cohesiveness of the capitalist group (Spohn and Bodemann, 1989). In contrast, Martinelli and Chiesi (1989) describe how in Italy the social authority and legitimacy of the business elite greatly increased in the 1980s. Capitalist values have been widely adopted (especially in the booming northern regions), with the influence of two rival ideologies, those of the Catholic church and the Marxist bloc, on the wane. This account seems especially pertinent, if not prophetic, in view of the subsequent extraordinary rise to power of the businessman Silvio Berlusconi, a media tycoon with no previous experience of political office. Van der Pijl (1989) suggests that the 1980s are witnessing the slow formation of a world bourgeoisie, generated by the globalization of capital and the de-regulation of the world money market. This group is united by an international network of interlocking directorships.

America and Japan have received attention for their reputed lack of class awareness and antagonism. In neither of these countries is the category of class employed to the same extent as in Europe to explain social divisions and inequalities of wealth. There is no longer any working-class-based political movement in the USA comparable to those in Britain, France and Italy, despite a long, if submerged, history of industrial struggle and socialist activism in the nineteenth and early twentieth centuries (Pelling, 1960; Guerin, 1979). Lash (1984), in comparative research into French and American manual workers, found that among his French sample 68 per cent described themselves as being in the lowest class, while a full 90 per cent of the Americans considered themselves middle class.

Many theories have been put forward to explain American exceptionalism. Particularly renowned is Sombart's explanation of *Why is there no Socialism in the United States?* (1976) which built on de Tocqueville's arguments that the 'new world' countries were spared the heritage of traditional social hierarchies. Sombart also stressed the relative affluence of American workers, declaring that socialist ideals had foundered on 'roast beef and apple pie'; in comparison to German working people, he said, the American worker doesn't eat, he dines! Other explanations have focused on the existence of the frontier and expansionism as a kind of safety valve; the incorporation of organized labour into the political system through the New Deal and its industrial legislation; the conservatism of the well-paid labour aristocracy of skilled craftsmen; and the adoption by the American Federation of Labor of an economistic sectionalist form of 'business unionism' (Lash, 1984; M. Davis, 1980). Mike Davis argues that burgeoning class-based movements in the USA have persistently been crushed out of existence by the formidable power of American capital.

Class identification may be less developed in the United States than in Europe; but according to the Rowntree Report America has the greatest degree of inequality of any industrial society. The concentration of wealth at the top end of society is as marked as in Britain (Edgell, 1993). Studies have identified the existence of a powerful self-recruiting and socially exclusive capitalist class (Useem, 1984). Fussell (1983) states that despite the lack of apparent class awareness there exists an intricate and pervasive system of signs and cultural markers which distinguishes the various class groupings from one another and prevents them from mixing socially.

Recent processes of industrial restructuring and change have begun to highlight class interests more sharply. During Bill Clinton's presidency there has been considerable talk of the 'squeezed middle', leading to consideration of tax changes which would benefit middle-class groupings. However, it has been the ethnic minority groups and the industrial manual workers who have suffered most from three decades of de-industrialization and globalization. A case study by Weis (1990) of a Midwest steel town revealed that from 1960 to 1980 there had been a fall of 26 per cent in craft and maintenance work and 20 per cent in operative and labouring jobs, while female employment in service work rose. Although displaced manual males may find employment in unskilled service work (for example as janitors and security guards), Weis argues that such changes constitute a radical redrawing of class and gender lines, with working-class males the losers. One response may be an assertion of agressive and brutal machismo against women and heightened racial hostility. These new lines of conflict are seen by Weis as replacing 'the historical conflict between capital and labour' in America (p. 198).

Certainly, conflicts around gender and race are more overt in contemporary America than those surrounding class. Three factors appear relevant in explaining the relative lack of class awareness of American workers. First, as Lash (1984) argues, consciousness does not arise automatically from the experience of material inequalities. If class is to become an active or politicized identity there is need of a radical political vehicle such as a party or trade union movement to articulate class demands. Such a vehicle is currently lacking in America, where parties and labour unions have followed different paths. Secondly, deep ethnic cleavages have diverted attention from class inequalities. The existence from the pre-industrial phase onward of a racialized and extremely disadvantaged black community has allowed white working-class people to view themselves, quite correctly, as relatively privileged. It is noteworthy that many of Lash's respondents placed black people along with 'the poor' as being in a class beneath them. Thirdly, Sennett's and Cobb's powerful study of *The Hidden Injuries of Class* (1977) considers cultural factors that have transposed the experience of class from a material to a psychic level. They suggest that the strength of the individualistic values and the egalitarian image of America as the 'land of opportunity' have led working-class people to see their low position in the social hierarchy as the result of personal failures and inadequacies. They pin their hopes on the education system as a means of upward mobility for their children to vindicate the hardships of their own lives.

Education operates similarly in Japan. The traditional explanation for Japan's uniqueness has been in terms of its distinctive culture and the persistence into the industrial era of features from traditional Japanese society (Fukutake, 1967; Dore, 1973; Nakane, 1973). These include the prevalence of vertical ties which breed a sense of loyalty and deference in subordinates; established procedures for achieving consensus and glossing over sources of conflict; the Japanese traditional ethic of subordination of individual interests to the 'ie' (the household/family grouping). These customary procedures are incorporated in the paternalist management practices used by successful Japanese corporations which offer their employees lifetime employment and a range of benefits (Dore, 1973). Nakane suggests that status considerations (the importance of being an employee of a successful company) are more significant to the Japanese than class.

However, these culturalist arguments have been criticized. Erikson and Goldthorpe (1992) suggest that Japan, although exhibiting differences in class groupings still conformed to the common pattern of relative mobility chances. Chalmers (1989) points out that the culturalist perspective ignores the position of powerless and vulnerable workers in the secondary small-firm sector. This point is also made by Rob Steven (1983), who applies Marxist class categories to Japan and finds that they fit well. Wealth is highly concentrated with 1 per cent of the population holding three quarters of shares. Steven speaks of the extraordinary power of the core element within the capitalist class, the large combines or 'keiretsu', each of which 'has more financial and industrial clout than the entire capitalist classes of many countries' (p. 47).

Steven points to several features of the class dynamic which may account for the lack of class identification. First, the capitalist class is very large (he calculates that one tenth of the population belong to it). There is an extensive petite bourgeoisie, who, although hostile to the large companies, espouse capitalist values. The middle class also identify themselves as having a stake in the system. The working class is internally divided into the aristocracy of core workers in the successful companies who are also beneficiaries of Japan's economic success; the mass workers; and the labour reserve. The latter bear the brunt of insecurity, poverty, hard labour and conditions, but are mainly old people and women. In this way divisions of gender and age serve to obscure the realities of class. And, like Sennett and Cobb, Steven stresses the important legitimating role of education: 'upper-class life has been made to look like a reward for educational success and working-class life a punishment for laziness and a lack of ability' (1983, p. 291).

Comparative study of class reveals both differences and similarities. There are variations in the precise composition of class groupings, the power they command and, most especially, in degrees of class identification, political mobilization and class-based activity. But there are also common patterns, especially in relation to the dynamic of globalization and economic restructuring. All advanced industrial societies show a move to a post-industrial pattern of class relations, a decline in the traditional working class and its institutions, a numerically increasing middle class, the growth of low-paid service employment. Most are marked by the increasing power and wealth of the capitalist class and polarization between the rich and poor; and all display complex patterns of interrelation between class inequalities and those of age and gender.

Gender

It has been stressed that gender relations are diffuse. We should expect to find considerable diversity between societies, particularly in the way masculinity and femininity are defined in different cultural contexts. On the other hand, comparative studies reveal that gender inequalities persist in all advanced industrial societies, despite the influence of feminism and the politics of gender equity. As I have argued elsewhere, the precise form of the sexual division of labour may vary, but all societies display a sexual division of labour and once established it is hard to overturn (Bradley, 1989).

Material from the Commission for the European Communities (CEC) provides a useful base for comparison between Western European countries. A survey of 11,651 people carried out in 1987 found that in all twelve member-states there was increased support for gender equality: 41 per cent believed in husbands and wives equally sharing domestic labour and undertaking paid employment (as opposed to 36 per cent in 1983); 25 per cent clung to the traditional family model of male breadwinner and female housewife; and 29 per cent believed that women should do more of the domestic work and have a less demanding job outside the home. There is still a majority, therefore, in favour of traditional roles, but a growing minority endorse complete equality. Egalitarian attitudes were strongest in Denmark, followed by Britain and Spain; and traditional views were most marked in Luxembourg, Germany and Ireland (CEC, 1987).

Despite support for equality, data issued in 1992 from the twelve EC states showed inequalities between women and men in most areas (CEC, 1992a). This accords with evidence from Britain which has demonstrated the gulf between theory and practice as far as gender equality is concerned. The British Social Attitudes Survey has revealed gaps between the proportions of people who believe that household tasks *should* be shared and those reporting that this *actually occurs*. It has also shown rising support for egalitarian relations in marriage and the right of married women to work (British Social Attitudes, 1985; 1990; 1992). Yet a study carried out in the late 1980s by Brannen and Moss (1991) of couples where the women were employed full-time found that, while these women were pioneering a new model of motherhood, this was not a model in which husbands took an equal share of housework and child-care. This is reaffirmed in Hochschild's (1989) account of the 'second shift' or 'double day' undertaken by American women. Her longitudinal study of Californian couples found women undertook the main burden of domestic work, even where couples actually imagined that they were sharing!

In all the EC countries women were under-represented in government. Denmark had the highest proportion of women among its members of Parliament (33 per cent), Greece the lowest (4.3 per cent) with France and Britain also trailing at 5.7 and 9 per cent respectively. In all countries there was an increase in women's share in the labour market; Denmark had the highest rate with women constituting 46 per cent of the work-force. Lowest proportions were in those countries with a sizeable agrarian or peasant community, such as Ireland (33 per cent) and Greece (35 per cent), though it should be noted that in such countries women's contribution to family concerns (businesses and farms) is often excluded from official statistics. Germany also has a lower participation rate. This can be linked to the relative wealth of the German Federal Republic in the post-war period (less need for both partners to earn), and to a socially conservative culture with a stress on women's domestic role which is supported by state social policy. Also, as we have seen, the male-dominated skilled manual sector is still strong (Erler, 1988; Glasner, 1992). The incorporation of East Germany, which shared the communist bloc policy of commitment to full-time employment for women, into the Republic has merely resulted in increasing levels of unemployment among former East German women.

While the proportion of women in part-time work varies greatly between countries, women are always more likely to work part-time than men. Everywhere women earn less than men and are concentrated in the lowest-paid jobs. Across the OEDC countries women earn on average 20–40 per cent less than men (Bakker, 1988). In all countries but Britain women were more likely to be unemployed than men (in Germany 61 per cent of the unemployed were women). The deviant position of Britain may be in part due to the fact that countries use different methods of counting who is unemployed. In all countries women bore a heavier burden of domestic labour (CEC, 1992a). For example, a study of families in Turin and Milan showed that women spent on average 45 hours a week in work for the family, with 75 per cent of women reporting they got no help from their partners (Del Boca, 1988). An earlier EC survey (CEC, 1988) highlighted the prevalence of domestic violence and sexual harassment in all member-states, along with widespread prostitution, which 'degrades the concept of women as dignified human beings' (CEC, 1992a, p. 91).

Gender segregation has not disappeared with the rise in female employment. Women are clustered in a limited range of occupations. In France, for example, 45 per cent of women are concentrated in twenty traditionally female occupations, in which only 5 per cent of male employees are located. Across Europe, around 70 per cent of women work in the service sector (CEC, 1992a; Glasner, 1992). Both horizontal and vertical segregation appear widespread. For example, in Denmark, which has a good record on women's rights and the provision of childcare, 36 per cent of the labour force work in highly segregated jobs where 90–100 per cent of employees were of the same sex, and another 52 per cent where the concentration is 60–90 per cent. In the Danish Civil Service only 10 per cent of middle executive and 3.3 per cent of top executive posts are held by women; and in the universities, while 44.5 per cent of students are now female, women make up only 17 per cent of teaching and research staff and 5 per cent of professors (CEC, 1992a). A familiar picture!

An earlier study indicated that segregation was most pronounced in countries where the move of women into the labour market was most advanced (Glasner, 1992). Women's employment is highest in the most industrially developed countries where the sexual division of labour was established at a period when traditional doctrines of gender differences were dominant (Bradley, 1989). Later industrializers may not display such marked stereotyping if women enter the labour market in a more liberal era. On the other hand, in some of the later developers, such as Ireland and Greece, religion and traditional values may retard women's progress.

Educational data from Portugal give support to this hypothesis. A heartening fact for supporters of gender equality is that in all EC states the proportion of women undergraduates has risen; in some countries they now outnumber men (for example, in France and Britain). However, in most countries women students pursue traditionally feminine disciplines, predominating in arts and social sciences, rather than in the scientific and technical areas which hold better career prospects. But this is not true in Portugal where women students are distributed more equitably across the disciplines, constituting 54 per cent of students in industrial engineering and in maths and computer science (CEC, 1992a). This is a sharp contrast with the older generation of women, working mainly in the agricultural sector; 4.4 per cent of the female labour force perform unpaid labour in family concerns and 18 per cent of women are illiterate.

The response to these gender inequalities has been the development of feminist movements in all the advanced capitalist societies. Feminism has been particularly powerful in the United States and Australia, but has made its presence felt in all European societies to some degree. Where feminism has been strong it has succeeded in influencing state policies in areas such as employment, social security arrangements and reproductive rights (especially abortion, a key rallying issue for feminists).

In general, the state has a very important influence upon patterns of gender inequality. Early feminist analysis of the state portrayed it rather unquestioningly as serving patriarchal and capitalist interests, for example through its support for the traditional family of male breadwinner and female carer and its backing for familial ideology which retained women in dependency (E. Wilson, 1977; McIntosh, 1979). However, more recent approaches have enshrined a more pluralist view of the state, seen as an arena of struggle, a site of competing interests or of a 'plurality of discursive forums' (Sassoon, 1987; Pringle and Watson, 1992, p. 63). Borchorst and Sim (1987) argue, in reference to Scandinavia, that a form of state feminism which sponsors feminist policies has emerged. Sweden, for example, has the highest proportion of women in employment (80 per cent), and in 1980 they were earning 90 per cent of male pay levels (Ruggie, 1988). Sweden is renowned for its generous system of state-supported childcare, with the provision of pre-school nurseries and ample maternity and paternity leave. Ruggie imputes this to the corporatist nature of Swedish society and a longstanding integration of feminist demands into the socialist agenda which has shaped the Swedish brand of social democracy. Nevertheless, gender segregation in employment is as marked in Sweden as everywhere else.

Women's influence in state politics has been crucial in promoting gender equity in both the USA and Australia. Legal commitment to equal pay and to outlawing of sexual discrimination came a decade earlier in America than in Britain, and the feminist movement paid particular attention to utilizing and monitoring these legal provisions and developing an effective system of political lobbying (Gelb and Palley, 1982; Dex and Shaw, 1986). In the 1970s, Congress passed seventy-one laws which arose from the feminist political agenda (Steinberg, 1988). Women have manoeuvred themselves into positions of political influence and decision-making at both state and federal level. The election of President Clinton on a liberal democratic programme, which included endorsement for gender equality and rights for homosexuals, was followed by the promotion of many women to prominent public posts, although it can be argued that this was followed by a backlash from disgruntled male conservatives. Steinberg suggests that 'women have become an institutionalized force in American politics and, because of this, there is a shift in expectations' (Steinberg, 1988, p. 191). Key issues have included reproductive rights, along with a commitment to getting women into top posts and to achieving pay equity, hinging around the notion of 'comparable worth' in re-evaluating women's jobs in comparison to men's (Acker, 1989). In Australia, too, women have worked within the state, which plays a more interventionist role than in Britain and America. The liberal tendency in feminism has utilized the electoral system to influence the political parties, especially the Labour party. This has promoted the rise of a group of women labelled by Australian commentators 'femocrats', who have been involved in policy-making, and campaigns for equal opportunities (Curthoys, 1993).

Despite these political advances, however, the same patterns of gender inequality are observable in the USA and Australia as in Europe. American women's participation rates are the highest in any industrial society apart from Sweden. Women constitute 50 per cent of the work force and 50 per cent of mothers return to work within a year of birth (Goldin, 1990). In the 1970s and 1980s women made some headway in pushing into traditional male areas, especially in the managerial and professional sectors (Reskin and Roos, 1990). However, Goldin points to the 'tenacity of gender differences' (1992, p. vii). Reskin and Roos suggested that the breakdown in gender segregation revealed in aggregate statistics masked processes of re-segregation in which women were relegated to lower-paid and lower-status sub-specialisms within an occupation. Bergmann provides a breakdown of 335 major occupational categories: in 130 of these women constituted 20 per cent or less of the work-force and in another 44 they were 80 per cent or more. Segregation remains strong in blue-collar occupations.

Pay differences persist, with women earning about 70 per cent of male earnings. In 1982, 27 per cent of men earned over 500 dollars a week as opposed to only 6 per cent of women, while 33 per cent of women and only 13 per cent of men earned below 200 dollars (Ciancanelli and Berch, 1987). The instability of marriage in the USA combined with lower pay rates for women means that many women are at risk of falling into poverty. In 1987, women constituted 63 per cent of poor adults and 68 per cent of poor adults of colour (Goldin, 1990). In 1983, 41 per cent of white single mothers and 63 per cent of black single mothers were living below the poverty line (Bergmann, 1986). As in other countries, sexual harassment and violence directed at women are prevalent (Sheffield, 1987).

In Australia full-time women employees earn 83 per cent of male earnings, suggesting that state support for equal opportunities has been effective. But Connell claims that when women's different working patterns are brought into the picture the equality disappears: the average yearly income for women is only 45 per cent of men's (Connell, 1987). Williams's survey of women's employment points to the persistence of gender segregation and the association of women with 'emotional labour'. Studies indicate that women undertake about 70 per cent of domestic labour (Williams and Thorpe, 1992). In the remote rural areas of Australia which are highly conservative, the persistence of the patriarchal division of labour is even more pronounced (Poiner, 1990).

In Australia 85 per cent of part-time employees are women, and 40 per cent of women employees are part-timers, a similar figure to Britain (42 per cent). This contrasts with France and Belgium where only 25 per cent are part-timers (Williams and Thorpe, 1992; CEC, 1992a). The particularly high level of part-time work in Britain is seen by Glasner to explain why British women are less disadvantaged in unemployment. Economic restructuring in Britain has involved the loss of full-time male jobs in manufacturing, while growth has been in part-time service work. This in turn relates to the lack of protection given by the British state to part-time employees, while in other European countries they have pro-rata rights to pensions, benefits, holidays and so forth. There is less incentive for French and Belgian employers to utilize women as part-timers, whereas in Australia, like Britain, part-time employment is used to cut labour costs. An additional factor in Britain is the lack of state childcare and nursery provision, which makes it more difficult for women with small children to undertake full-time employment: in 1990 in Denmark there was provision for 44 per cent of children under two and 87 per cent aged three to five, as opposed to 2 per cent of under-twos and 38 per cent of three-to-five-year-olds in Britain (Glasner, 1992). However, this cannot be the whole story, since in Denmark, with its excellent childcare record, women's part-time employment is also high. It may be that in more affluent societies women are exercising a genuine preference to lighten the double burden.

The case of part-time employment illuminates the role of economic development and state policy in influencing patterns of gendered inequality. If we were to look in more detail at the gender relations beneath the broad tendencies outlined here, there is no doubt that many political and cultural differences would be revealed. Nonetheless, overall we can discern broad patterns of similar gender inequalities between societies. These operate cross-societally in several of the areas identified by Walby as key sites of patriarchal domination: here I have considered domestic labour, paid employment and sexual violence. In particular, the domestic division of labour is remarkably constant across industrial societies. As Goldin argues, 'as long as women bear a disproportionate burden in rearing children, the labour market will reflect these differences' (1990, p. 213). The Dutch women's movement demand for a drastically shorter working week of 25 hours reflects the belief among feminists that a major challenge to the male norms which shape work relations is the only way to achieve real equality in the division of labour. But in the cut-throat competitive world of the globalizing economy such a development appears a Utopian dream.

'Race' and ethnicity

Relationships of 'race' and ethnicity are of necessity highly varied, as was emphasized in chapter 5. They depend upon the original disposition across territories of ethnic groups and specific patterns of migration. Variations relate to when and in what circumstances migrants arrived, whether they are settled or retain migrant status, what jobs they filled when they arrived and what jobs they subsequently occupy.

For example, Husbands (1991), discussing the situation of migrant workers in Europe with special reference to France, distinguishes five different groups: rotational and short-term migrants, such as the 'guest-workers' employed in Germany and Switzerland; guest-workers who have subsequently become permanent settlers (numerous in France where immigration was until the 1980s handled in a relatively liberal fashion); patrial repatriates (colonialists subsequently returning home either voluntarily or because they have been expelled, such as the French 'pieds-noirs' from Algeria); non-patrial repatriates, who may have served a colonial power and subsequently become *personae non gratae*, such as the 'harkis' (Muslim soldiers who served on the French side in the Algerian war of liberation); and refugees. The latter constitute a growing group in Europe, many of them, such as the Kurds, Tamils and various groups from Yugoslavia, fleeing from bitter civil wars or ethnic conflicts. In France, the number of refugees tripled between 1981 and 1989 to around 60,000 (Husbands, 1991). However, the majority of refugees in the European Community are found in Germany, which received 256,100 requests for asylum in 1991 (CEC, 1992b). Many are from the former Soviet bloc and some of them constituted German-speaking minorities in the various countries of Eastern Europe. All these different groups are treated differently, enjoy different rights and are likely to encounter different economic fortunes.

A quick survey around the EC countries affirms the complexity of relations arising from migration. In 1992, 16 million of the 320 million residents in the EC countries (5 per cent) originated from outside. Of these, 8 million are non-white (CEC, 1992b). In Britain, the Netherlands, Belgium and France many migrants have come from former colonies and protectorates. Germany, Switzerland and Sweden have employed temporary migrant workers from the peripheral parts of Europe (Portugal, Italy and Turkey) as well as from the Far East (Allen and Macey, 1990). Spain and Italy have large gypsy minorities. Luxembourg, which has a continued shortage of labour, has the highest proportion of foreign-born workers (27 per cent), many of whom are Portuguese (CEC, 1992b). By contrast, the Mediterranean countries such as Greece, Spain and Portugal are still countries of net emigration. Newer phenomena include the rising number of refugees and also of illegal immigrants. It is reported that increasing numbers of these are young, female and headed for jobs in the expanding service and informal sectors, for example finding work as maids or in the booming sex industries (Miles, 1993; Campani, 1993). Many of these jobs are semi-legal and others offer very poor pay and conditions.

The treatment accorded immigrants varies considerably between countries. In Britain, though immigration of non-patrials is now virtually at a standstill, settled ex-colonial populations have achieved citizen rights, including the right to vote. Such rights are not granted to the guest-workers in Germany and Switzerland, nor to the immigrants to France from the ex-protectorates of the Maghreb, Morocco and Tunisia. The latter, classified as 'étrangers' are denied voting rights along with rights to political organization. The situation in France is very complicated, with some second-generation 'beurs' (the slang name for North African Arabs) gaining citizenship by virtue of having been born in France (Wihtol de Wenden, 1991). France also has taken a tough line in requiring immigrant groups to assimilate into the national culture and refusing to recognize the rights of groups to maintain their own cultural and religious practices. This has led, for example, to conflict over the rights of young Muslim women to wear headscarves in school. After a number of incidents, the French government passed legislation in 1994 forbidding this practice within the strictly secular education system. By contrast, other European societies, such as Belgium and Holland, espouse a deliberately pluralist and multicultural line. Portugal appears to be the EC country which is most tolerant and liberal with very little control over immigration, while Campani notes that in Italy there has been 'a progressive shift from a sort of "social tolerance" to a culture of hostility and xenophobia' (1993, p. 511).

Despite these different approaches, Allen and Macey argue that while 'the pattern of recruitment and the conditions attached to migrant workers varied between countries . . . each developed its own form of state racism' (1990, p. 380). They point to 'a clear European convergence towards increasing limitation on immigration' (p. 378). During the 1980s there has been a virtual shut-off of legal immigration of non-European people, apart from the concessions made to political refugees. Germany has developed a new system of short-term contracts for 'guest-workers' but this is aimed at incomers from Eastern Europe (Carter et al., 1993). The French tightened up their rather flexible immigration policy in the mid-1980s, partly as a result of government fears of far-right electoral appeal. Between 1983 and 1987 the number of expulsions doubled (Husbands, 1991). Even previously liberal countries such as Spain and Sweden are beginning to tighten barriers to entry. Commentators have noted the emergence of a growing 'Fortress Europe' mentality as the boundaries between European states are dismantled (Rex, 1992; Brah, 1993).

The political restriction of immigration has taken place within a growing climate of racism among sections of the indigenous community, linked in many cases to the growth of ultra-right and neo-Nazi parties, such as Le Pen's Front Nationale in France. Across Europe, attacks on members of racialized minorities are on the increase. For example, in Germany in 1991 there were 2368 reported incidents of racially motivated attacks, a tenfold increase over previous yearly averages of 200–250 (CEC, 1992b).

Whatever their political status, ethnic minority immigrants across Europe find themselves in a common economic position. The majority of minority workers fill jobs at the bottom of the hierarchy, typically in badly paid unskilled jobs refused by majority members (CEC, 1992a, p. 9). Such jobs include hotel and catering work; personal domestic service; contract cleaning and hospital domestic work; construction; seasonal agricultural work and, at the bottom rung of all, street selling. Minority workers are also vulnerable to unemployment. For example, in Belgium in 1988 unemployment was 6 per cent among the male population, but 15 per cent among Italians, 20 per cent among Turks and 25 per cent among Moroccans (Martiniello, 1993); while in Holland 40–50 per cent of Moroccans and Turks are unemployed, three times the rate for the indigenous population, (Forbes and Mead, 1992). Minority and migrant workers are also at risk of poverty and are concentrated in large urban areas, often facing discrimination in housing and confinement to ghetto localities. In Portugal many migrants from Africa live in slum conditions, run-down areas or shanty towns, 'barrios de lata' – literally tin towns (Eaton, 1993). While in some of the longstanding ethnic communities economic elites have formed, such as among Italians in Belgium, or the evolving '*beur*geoisie' of younger more educated North Africans in France, such groups have little power to improve the condition of their fellows (Hargreaves, 1991; Martiniello, 1993).

There is particular cause for concern about the newest immigrant groups, the refugees and clandestine immigrants. Trapped in the informal or the black economy, their chances of finding stable employment and thence attaining housing and a secure livelihood are minimal. Rex (1992) suggests that a new racial hierarchy is evolving in Europe. At the top are EC nationals, and beneath them settled groups of African and Asians who have attained citizenship. Next come migrants and refugees from the eastern European states. Less secure than them are the guest-workers and contract workers, on short-term residence schemes. Finally at the bottom is a residuum or underclass of illegal immigrants and Third World refugees. Miles (1993), however, strikes a slightly more positive note, pointing out that there is a managerial and professional stratum among the newer migrants. In each country migrant groups are arranged in hierarchies in which 'white' groups tend to be more privileged than racialized 'black' groups; thus in Belgium, Italians – although themselves disadvantaged as compared to the indigenous population – fare better than Turks, with Moroccans at the bottom.

Ethnic and racial relations in the 'new Europe' are in a state of flux which contrasts with the more evolved structures of the 'new world' countries, such as America and Australia. As Allen and Macey (1990) point out, it is to America (and South Africa) that British race relations analysts have primarily looked for comparative study, because of the presence in Britain of numbers of people of African descent. This accounts for the British tendency to analyse migration in terms of 'race', as opposed to the concepts of 'aliens', 'foreigners' or 'strangers' more commonly employed in the other European states (Rex, 1992). America and Britain, despite the multi-ethnic nature of both societies, have been preoccupied with handling the relationship with black Africans, perhaps because that relationship has been so adversely marked by the terrible history of slavery (Van den Berghe, 1978).

Yet one crucial and significant difference between Europe and the 'new world' societies is the presence in the latter of dispossessed indigenous groups who form the lowest tier of the racial hierarchy, to such a degree that until very recently they hardly figured in accounts of 'race'. The invisibility of these groups, such as the Australasian aboriginals and the Indians and Inuit of North America, was a reflection of their social marginalization. Dispossessed of their ancestral territories, their cultures and religions ignored, some indigenous groups were exterminated, others decimated and the survivors condemned to poverty and social exclusion. Attempts to handle the 'problem' of native peoples by setting up reservations and government payment systems only served to emphasize their 'otherness' and to confirm their social dependency.

Thorpe argues (Williams and Thorpe, 1992) that what distinguished Australian aboriginals from all later immigrant groups was the view of their labour as superfluous. What white settlers desired from the native peoples was their land; they themselves were seen as an irritant. This was so even though the aboriginals had many skills, arising from their knowledge of their land, to offer the colonists; they could act as guides, as prospectors, and had knowledge of how to survive in the harsh and dangerous conditions of the bush. Both women and men, working as farm labourers, helped to overcome those conditions and foster successful agricultural developments. Yet such labour was often unacknowledged by those who employed it, to the extent that it was frequently rewarded in kind, sometimes with alcohol, with subsequent stigmatization of aboriginals as prone to drunkenness.

Similarly, Brodie (1986) describes how the subsistence economies of the Canadian native tribes, though highly successful and adaptable, are viewed by the white populace as untenable and doomed; he notes 'the white man's inability or refusal even to see the existence of Indian economic systems' (p. 273). Native skills in hunting, fishing and trapping have been developed in ways which husband rather than exhaust natural resources and animal populations. The native economies are threatened by the wasteful and polluting activities of white Canadians: for example, by pointless killing of wildlife under the guise of 'leisure hunting', and by industrial developments involving roads, dams, oil-lines, hydro-electric power and forestry which destroy habitats, disrupt traplines and pollute the environment. This devaluation of indigenous people's culture and labour has contributed to their stigmatization and confinement to unskilled, low-status and often casual jobs in the mainstream economy. In 1986, 35 per cent of Australian aboriginal people were unemployed as opposed to 9 per cent of the non-aboriginal population (Williams and Thorpe, 1992). Native Americans, too, suffer disproportionately from unemployment, from homelessness, and have lower life expectancy (Markides and Mindel, 1987; Rossi and Wright, 1993). In recent years, political movements have evolved among Australian, American and Canadian native peoples with the aim of regenerating indigenous cultures and claiming citizen rights, especially in relation to tribal territories. While governments have become much more sensitive to such claims, the context of recession means that progress to equal opportunities has been limited.

Recession in the USA has likewise adversely affected the racialized African American population, which has received the most attention in the literature. Mike Davis's account of post-industrial Los Angeles in *City of Quartz* (1990) presents a bleak future for the racialized minority groups. He describes a form of 'spatial apartheid' where the white middle-class population is increasingly protected from contact with the urban poor, barricaded away within walled and guarded private housing estates. Davis argues that the affluent postmodern lifestyle of the privileged classes rests upon 'the social imprisonment of the third-world service proletariat who live in increasingly repressive ghettoes and barrios' (p. 227). Although Davis employs a class analysis here, it is clear that African Americans and Latinos make up the bulk of the Los Angeles poor. Unemployment among black youth in the late 1980s was 45 per cent; many young blacks and Latinos, seeing no realistic future of employment, joined in the self-destructive gang warfare of the Bloods and Crips.

As in Britain, black people are under-represented in professional and managerial jobs and concentrated in manual work and low-paid service jobs (Bergmann, 1986). They are unlikely to benefit from the move to a post-industrial economy. Davis's pessimistic account is mirrored by the more conventional academic studies of William Julius Wilson, who has described the development of a 'ghetto underclass' in the northern cities, drawing on data from Chicago and elsewhere (Wilson, 1987; 1993). He uses the term in a specific way in relation to a combination of economic deprivation and social isolation which he argues is characteristic of inner-city blacks. The key issue is growing unemployment among African Americans (and also Hispanics) which is linked to de-industrialization; working-class black males were heavily concentrated in blue-collar employment, which is now in decline. The plight of the unemployed is worsened by the movement of whites, middle-class blacks and even employed working-class blacks out of the inner cities, which leaves the ghetto communities deprived of leadership and of positive role-models for the young. The resulting demoralization precipitates a drift into crime, violence, drug-taking and other anti-social behaviour. One in three young black males aged 14–35 is in prison, awaiting trial or on probation (Walker, 1995). Wilson suggests that young black males, unable to present themselves as breadwinners to young women, affirm their masculinity through sexual conquest and fathering children, which in turn pushes young black women into dependence on welfare. In contrast to Murray's account of the underclass, Wilson emphasizes that all these symptoms spring from forced (not voluntary) joblessness, rather than from an autonomous culture of poverty.

Whether defined as a ghetto underclass or a service proletariat, it is clear that African Americans from working-class backgrounds who lack educational qualifications are at risk of economic deprivation. But not all African Americans fall into this category. There appears to be less class homogeneity among America's racialized minorities than in Britain. There is a developed 'black bourgeoisie' of educationists, professionals and entrepreneurs (Marable, 1983). The number of black households with incomes of above $50,000 per year doubled in the last ten years (Walker, 1995). African Americans are better represented in the structures of government than in Britain. Young African American women, though unfortunately not their brothers, have been taking advantage of higher education to gain qualifications.

In many ways, the USA appears to be a more successful example of ethnic pluralism than Britain. This may be linked to the larger size of its minority populations (African Americans, for example, are 15 per cent of the population), its long history as a nation of immigration, its espousal of the rights of local communities to self-determination, and the struggles for civil rights and political representation among the descendants of the freed slaves, which forced the issue of 'race' and equal opportunities on to the political agenda. Against this must be set the history of racial degradation arising from slavery and the devastating treatment of native Americans (from genocide to social marginalization). Advances towards racial equality are currently in danger of being vitiated by the operation of the class dynamic of the free market, which pushes racialized minority members into the labour surplus class. Moreover, in 1995 the Republican party is putting its weight behind a 'whitelash' which aims to demolish the structures of affirmative action designed to help ethnic minority members, despite the clear evidence of racial disadvantage.

As Campani states, 'the wind of xenophobia, racism and a new fascism, which is blowing through Europe, assumes specific characteristics in each country, depending upon the historical context' (1993, p. 532). The pattern of race and ethnic relations in each country differs, for example, in the way specific ethnic groups are ordered in the hierarchy, the extent and form of discrimination, the state response and degree of immigration control, and also the level of mobilization among disadvantaged ethnic groups and the extent to which they have succeeded in breaking out of ethnic ghettoes and gaining access to better opportunities. Yet ethnic groups, particularly racialized minorities of African and Asian origin, face similar problems; xenophobic nationalism, racial hostility and attacks are common experiences, along with relegation to the lowest slots in the economic hierarchy. In particular, global restructuring brings unemployment to racialized minorities.

Age

If race relations are deteriorating with the development of global capitalism, the same can be claimed for relations between age-groups. While the comparative study of age inequalities is still little developed, what information is available suggests common trends in many advanced capitalist societies.

As was stated in chapter 6 the phenomenon of the 'ageing population' is characteristic of all advanced industrial societies. Across Europe, the dependency ratio is calculated at 20 per cent (Simons, 1992) and is set to rise over the next decades. There is an allied trend in most societies for men to withdraw from the labour market at an earlier age. As Townsend (1981) points out, in the 1930s in all advanced societies, between 40 to 70 per cent of men over sixty-five were economically active. Not only are there now very few men working over the official retirement age (8 per cent in Britain in 1994), but activity rates among younger men have fallen substantially in the past decades. Guillemard (1989) provides figures for the period 1975–85: in the United States the labour force participation rate for men aged fifty-five to sixty-four fell from 75 to 60 per cent, in the UK from 88 to 66 per cent and in France from 69 to 50 per cent. Only Sweden and Japan departed from the trend. In Japan the rate fell only from 86 to 83 per cent.

As we saw in chapter 6, there is debate as to whether the trend to early retirement is voluntary or coerced. Thomson (1989), using data for New Zealand, suggests that the current generation of older people are benefiting from the over-generous provisions of post-war welfare states at the expense of young people, especially families. The elderly choose to enjoy a 'golden age' of affluent retirement. However, for the British case, Walker (1989) and Phillipson (1982) both contend that much early retirement is forced (a position shared by Guillemard) and that working-class people in particular would prefer to go on working. There is agreement that in most societies people in their fifties who are made redundant will have difficulty in finding new employment (CEC, 1989). It is impossible to deduce from purely statistical data what people's motivations are, but it is likely that such decisions will vary according to state provision for retirement and to the financial resources available to the retired.

Here there is evidence of considerable variation between societies. Walker's review of the position across Europe (1993) suggests that poverty among older people is most severe in Portugal and least in Germany; in Denmark, the Netherlands and Luxembourg there is also less financial hardship. Everywhere older people are more likely to be in the lower income groups. However, the gap between the income of the retired and the working populace is most pronounced in Britain, least in the Scandinavian countries where pensions and benefits are higher. The basic pension rate in Britain is the lowest in Europe (Walker, 1990). While age differentials appear less marked in America, an earlier piece by Walker (1981) suggested that one-fifth of old people in the USA had incomes below federal minimum level.

Aggregate data conceal variations among the elderly. Old people with ample private pensions enjoy substantial material comfort. Where state pensions are more generous, hardship will be reduced for everybody. Some European states, such as Denmark and Sweden, are trying to cope with the problems posed by the trend to early retirement by developing schemes for partial retirement, whereby older people are allowed to work part-time and draw a partial pension (CEC, 1989). Where state provision is being cut back and there are no schemes to cushion the effect of early retirement, the effect may be to increase hardship. In all societies the older old and women are more vulnerable to poverty and low income. In Germany the average pension paid to women was 42 per cent of the male average (Walker, 1993). Again Denmark is the exception, which reaffirms the point that welfare policies have an important effect in modifying inequality.

Even affluent old people suffer from ageist prejudice. One country, Japan, is said to depart from the common pattern of diminished respect for old people. In Japan old people are supposed to enjoy the status associated with age in pre-industrial societies: they have an important place in the family carrying out various formal duties linked to religious and social ritual (Markides and Mindel, 1987). Seniority is a major basis for social ranking (Nakane, 1973). As we have seen, older Japanese men have not withdrawn from employment to the same extent as elsewhere. This can be linked to consideration for the elderly which is also reflected in the employment conditions in Japanese core firms. The practice of 'nenko seido' (lifetime employment) rewards seniority and long service, even where it may be necessary to move older people sideways from more strenuous jobs. However, against this it must be noted that older people are over-represented in the insecure and poorly paid secondary sector (Steven, 1983; Chalmers, 1989); one way of honouring the obligation to maintain employment is to demote older men from the core enterprise to one of the small firms connected to it through the sub-contracting system. According to Walker (1981), as many as nine-tenths of older Japanese people may be living on low incomes.

Some evidence supports Thomson's (1989) contention that some older people are now enjoying an unparalleled level of affluence. Data from the EC confirm that there is movement of poverty away from older to younger groups (CEC, 1989). However, the affluence of the newest generation of retirees arises from the exceptional circumstances of post-war economic expansion (full employment and secure career paths) along with welfare state provisions which are now being eroded in many countries (Denmark as usual is an exception!). A more characteristic feature of the deployment of older workers within capitalist economies has been their confinement to secondary jobs; the return to free market principles along with the institution of flexible employment practices bodes ill for retired people in the future, unless generous state pension levels are maintained.

At the moment younger people are the more obvious victims of change. The past decades have seen a deterioration of the youth labour market in many industrial societies, along with a rise in youth unemployment. Junankar (1987) provides data for a number of OECD countries. Between 1980 and 1985 youth unemployment rose in most countries apart from the United States (where it was already quite high at 13 per cent), and Japan, where it remained steady at 5 per cent, reflecting Japan's phenomenal economic success. We have already noted the higher incidence of unemployment in America among young blacks and Hispanics. Marsden (1987) speculates that the long-term decline in levels of pay for young workers relative to adults may have prevented further rises in youth unemployment. There is a tradition in the United States of young people taking low-paid, temporary and part-time jobs, often to finance higher education.

In 1985 the youth unemployment rate (for those aged between fifteen and twenty-five) was 26 per cent in France, 22 per cent in the UK and 16 per cent in Canada. Young people were disproportionately represented among the long-term unemployed. In eleven European countries the average youth share of long-term unemployment rose from 32 per cent in 1979 to 38 per cent in 1984, with young males especially affected; the United States figure for 1984 was 30 per cent (Junankar, 1987). In 1987 across Europe nearly a quarter of all those aged twenty to twenty-four were unemployed, a level twice that of other age-groups, with the position particularly bad in Portugal, Spain and Italy (CEC, 1989).

The shake-up in the youth labour market has hit young men more drastically than young women because of the decline in manufacturing industry. An industrial apprenticeship was the traditional way for many young working-class men to enter the labour market. This route is rapidly disappearing, except in West Germany, which has one of the lowest levels of youth unemployment in Europe. One sign of the impact of post-industrial change on young men is that in all the EC countries except Germany and Portugal they are much more likely than older men to undertake part-time work. The move into part-time work is particularly marked in Denmark and Holland (CEC, 1989). However, youth unemployment has also affected young women. Indeed Eurostat data for 1981, cited by Marsden (1987), show higher levels of unemployment among young women than men in Belgium, France and Italy.

Public concern over youth has surrounded delinquency rather than unemployment. In chapter 6 the rise of youth subcultures was linked to post-war affluence. But Brake's analysis of youth subcultures as solutions to problems arising from class implies they will appear where social divisions are most apparent. This is confirmed by his own comparative analysis of Britain, the United States and Canada (1985); youth culture is less developed in Canada, with young people tending to conform and rebellion being individualistic. Styles are borrowed from the vibrant American and British subcultures. Brake relates this to the relative affluence of Canada and the lack of overt class and ethnic conflict. Although most countries have experienced deviant and rebellious youth behaviour in the post-war epoch, it is hard to explain why youth cultures have appeared most spontaneously in Britain and America. Following the functionalist argument it might be hypothesized that they are likely to develop where age segregation is sharpest, which in turn is linked to the degree of urbanization and industrialization. Certainly youth protest seems less marked in rural areas where young people are still more integrated into the community through heterogeneous age-group activity; in rural France and Italy, for example, people of all ages can be observed dancing at village fiestas, in sharp contrast to the age-segregated discotheques and clubs which are so central to the experience of urban youth.

Recently international concern has been growing about the impact of economic change on young people. Youth unemployment has been linked to an increase in crime, as well as to homelessness and a general slide into demoralization (Liddiard and Hutson, 1990; Wilson, 1993). Davis speaks of a 'juvenation of poverty' among America's urban poor: in Los Angeles county during the 1980s, 40 per cent of children lived below or around the official poverty line (1990, p. 306). West (1994) states that approximately one in five children are in poverty (one in two among blacks, two in five among Hispanics). Presdee's study (1990) of young unemployed homeless people in Australia, among whom aboriginal youth were particularly numerous, showed how many slip into crime and prostitution purely to survive. For those who see little hope of employment in 'straight society', involvement in criminal subculture, with its promise of status, wealth and glamour, is an attractive option. Drugs are a particular focus for generational conflict. Surveys have revealed high levels of drug-taking among schoolchildren and students in Britain and America (up to 50 per cent among older schoolchildren), fostered by the cultures of 'rave' and 'rap' music. Countries which keep soft drugs such as cannabis illegal in effect criminalize a high proportion of the young generation.

We should not forget that the majority of young people are conformist, as is shown, for example, by Chang's ethnographic study of typical high school students in 'Middle America' (1992). These young people are integrated into community activities, largely endorsing their parents' values. Those who succeed in higher education can gain access to well-paid professional and managerial jobs (Roberts et al., 1990; Bates and Riseborough, 1993). Nonetheless the potential for heightened generational inequality and conflict is exposed in David Thomson's account of current changes which will affect all young people, not only those at the base of class and ethnic hierarchies.

Thomson (1989) argues that long-term social investment in youth is on the wane: an insecure financial future looms for many young people. Drawing on data for New Zealand, Australia and America, he points to the decline in full-time employment among young men, in contrast to the experience of youth in the 1940s, 1950s and 1960s. Young people can no longer expect a secure career or lifetime employment. The drive for flexibility is leading to short-term contract work even for professionals and managers. This inevitably affects benefits especially pensions. Finally, young people now characteristically have to pay through taxation and loan schemes for higher education which their parents obtained free. The erosion of welfare states and the switch from public to private forms of social insurance may bring insecurity for many. Thomson concludes this amounts to 'a crushing of youthful expectations' (1990, p. 53).

The sense of disillusion and anger among the young, which we should predict if Thomson is correct, seems most noticeable in America, where Kurt Cobain and Bret Easton Ellis have represented a sense of frustration and despair even among young people from relatively privileged backgrounds. Indeed, it appears to be in America that age interests have received their clearest articulation (Neugarten, 1970; Achenbaum, 1989). The American Association of Retired Persons is said by Achenbaum to be the largest voluntary organization in the USA apart from the Roman Catholic church. Against that, Americans for Generational Equity argue for justice for young adults and families.

In most industrial societies both young and old are increasingly excluded or marginalized in the labour market. Many are consequently forced into dependency, either on their families or the state. The degree to which this is happening varies considerably between nations. Such variations are partly to do with the direction taken by the national economy, but the most significant factor is social policy, with the old faring best in countries with highly developed welfare states. Yet trends indicate increasing degrees of age inequality with the middle groups retaining a position of privilege.

Summary and conclusion

This chapter has discussed research into inequalities of class, gender, ethnicity and age in a number of post-industrial capitalist economies. Japan has featured as a society claimed to demonstrate some distinctive traits, although these claims have been qualified here. This brief survey has revealed many national differences but also highlighted common tendencies between societies, particularly in terms of the impact on class, gender, ethnic and age relations of the development of global capitalism and the characteristic changes it brings to national economies and to employment practices. Clearly there are many local divergences, some of which may be explained in terms of factors such as state policies, political responses and differing cultural values, some of which are hard to explain and may appear random and contingent. The state has a particularly crucial role. But there are striking cross-societal resemblances in terms of economic inequalities; the persistence of the sexual division of labour; racial hostilities and the exclusion of racialized minorities; and the social dependency of the old and the young. Hierarchies of class, gender, race and age are remarkably similar in all advanced industrial societies.

Conclusion
Fractured Identities: Processes of Fragmentation and Polarization in Post-industrial Capitalist Societies

---

Everything fleeting, and nothing stable, everything shifting and changing and nothing substantial.

George Lippard, *The Quaker City*, 1845

It was impossible, situated as we were, not to imbibe the idea that everything in nature and human existence was fluid, or fastly becoming so.

Nathaniel Hawthorne, *The Blithedale Romance*, 1852

These fragments I have shored against my ruins

T. S. Eliot, *The Waste Land*, 1992

London's my city, Jamaica's my country, Africa's my history . . .
I know who I am, I'm not who you think I am . . .
I'm Marcus Garvey, I'm Harvey Keitel . . .

Earthling, 1994

In this book I have considered class, gender, 'race' and age both as social categories, constructs we employ to think about processes of social differentiation, and as lived relations to which they refer. Such lived relations are real sociological phenomena in the Durkheimian sense: they exist outside of us as individuals, they put constraints upon us, they affect our life-chances. Each can be viewed as a different type of social location (Mannheim, 1952) or different set of social arrangements. Although they are all highly involved with each other, I have suggested that we can distinguish for each a distinct 'existential location'. Class refers to relations arising from the organization of production, distribution and consumption. Gender refers to the varied and complex arrangements between women and men, encompassing the organization of reproduction, the sexual division of labour and cultural definitions of femininity and masculinity. 'Race' and ethnicity refer to arrangements surrounding the possession of territories and processes of migration arising from them. Age refers to the way we organize the progress of individuals and cohorts through the life course. All these lived relations involve differential access to power and resources and are therefore not only aspects of social differentiation but also of social inequality. They merge together to form the complex hierarchies which are characteristic of contemporary societies.

In this book, I have attempted both to give some indication of the nature of each dynamic of inequality and how it is changing, and also to sketch the history of the concepts and theories developed by sociologists to explain each form of inequality. Throughout, I have contrasted modernist approaches with postmodern and post-structural perspectives. Modernist approaches, deriving from the classical sociological theories of industrial and capitalist development, or from modified versions or adaptations of them, present class, gender, 'race' and age as persisting materially based structures of inequality which are integral features of the construction of society. Post-structuralists view them as discursive constructs, contingent upon the particular sets of discourses in which they are embedded, and upon specific cultural and historical events which form their context. Consequently they are fluid and variable. Some postmodernists take this line, others retain some kind of idea of structure; but they point to the way recent processes of cultural change have eroded and destabilized long-standing relationships to create a more fragmented and individualized society. A major theme which runs through all varieties of postmodernist thinking is the stress on difference and diversity. Divisions within categories (either individual or group differences) preoccupy postmodernists as much as differences between categories.

In response to these postmodern critiques of modernism, three broad strategies for the future study of social inequalities appear to be on offer:

(1) Acceptance of Lyotard's dictum that local narratives must replace grand narratives. Totalizing and general theories of inequality are rejected as essentialist and distortive. This leads to study of particular manifestations of inequality in very specific contexts, to the tracing of the history of such manifestations in these contexts, or to the study of particular discourses or language games which are implicated in inequalities. This strategy is employed by many postmodernists and has become particularly popular among feminists and some analysts of race relations.

(2) While accepting local variations and internal divisions, an affirmation that these exist within the framework of powerful and controlling unitary tendencies, notably that of the globalization of capital. This strategy

is adopted by those postmodernists such as Harvey and Jameson who emphasize the globalization process. Arif Dirlik mounts a powerful critique of post-colonialist theories from such a stance, arguing that the stress on heterogeneity and difference serves to disguise 'the power relations that shape a seemingly shapeless world' and the way in which 'totalizing structures persist in the midst of apparent disintegration and fluidity' (1994, pp. 355–6). Dirlik asserts that, despite the complexity of current social and international relations, 'global capitalism . . . however fragmented in appearance, serves as the structuring principle of global relations' (p. 331).

(3) A suggestion that previous modernist theories were flawed because of the failure to appreciate the way that different dynamics of inequality intersect. Thus, rather than abandoning modernist theories the aim should be to provide better versions of them (Holmwood, 1994; B. Marshall, 1994). Walby (1992) has argued that most existing accounts have been able to accommodate only two at the most of the dimensions of 'race', class and gender: future analysis should combine the three. Anthias and Yuval-Davis (1993) have also proceeded along these lines, and this is broadly the position endorsed in this book.

Which of these three options offers the best understanding of social inequalities? Although it is clear that there is much to be gained from studying aspects of variability and difference, the analysis offered in the last chapter suggests that global as well as local tendencies are at play and it is thus a mistake to abandon all attempts at general analysis. As Maynard argues, 'it is not necessary to abandon categories such as woman . . . in order to recognize that they are internally differentiated' (Maynard, 1994, p. 22). The local strategy, then, will not do on its own. It needs to be supplemented by some account of general and unifying tendencies as in the second strategic option. The problem is that such accounts often slip back towards the traditional 'one-sided story' (Marshall, 1994, p. 6) of social development, in which the power of global capital seems so formidable that other aspects of inequality become subordinated to it. In this sense, the third option seems preferable. But it may be that even this approach does not quite go far enough in tackling the issue of fragmentation.

In this final chapter I want to review the discussion of fragmentation and juxtapose it with an account of countervailing tendencies to polarization which have also been commented on. I argue that both fragmentation and polarization are notable features of contemporary societies: as Giddens states: 'It has become commonplace to claim that modernity fragments, dissociates . . . Yet the unifying features of modern institutions are just as central to modernity . . . as the disaggregating ones' (1991, p. 27). To conclude, I consider the implications for processes of social identification. Finally, we need to consider whether these contradictory processes constitute a real change in society in what is increasingly being referred to as a 'postmodern' era. Or is it just the way we view society that has changed?

Fragmentation

'If the seventies were dominated by the exhilaration of discovering and naming ourselves as women, bound together in sisterhood, the eighties have been dominated by the discovery and definition of our differences as women' (Musil, quoted in Yuval-Davis, 1993, p. 4). Musil's comment epitomizes the shift in feminist analysis in the past two decades and can be linked to the general tendency in sociology to put increasing stress on diversity and fragmentation. As was indicated in chapter 1, the notion of fragmentation is not new. Indeed, the quotations at the top of this chapter suggest it has been a continual theme ever since humans conceived the idea of 'modern society'. But in the 1980s and 1990s it has become a veritable leitmotif in stratification theory. However, the term is used in a loose and non-specific way. It is possible to distinguish at least four senses in which it is currently being employed:

1 Internal fragmentation, or fragmentation occurring within a collectivity as a result of tendencies inherent within it. For example, if classes are seen to be groups sharing a common relationship to processes of production, consumption and distribution, such as occupational groups, it is possible to subdivide these internally on the basis of more minutely specified shared characteristics: the working class can be split into unskilled, semi-skilled and skilled sections, and so on.

Many examples of internal fragmentation have been touched on in preceding chapters. Weberian class analysis has always made the issue of fragmentation central, as opposed to the Marxist stress on unifying tendencies (see p. 53). In contemporary class analysis both the working- and middle-class groupings are presented as fragmenting. Racial and ethnic categories, too, are subject to splitting. We have seen how the original formulation of 'black' as a way of characterizing race relations has given way to a recognition of the different social locations of different ethnic groups. Newer categories such as 'Afro-Caribbean' are themselves liable to fragmentation, where the primary identification is made to a specific island of origin. The former Soviet Union provides another prime example of ethnic fragmentation. The arbitrary nature of age-group boundaries means that new internal boundaries could easily be drawn. For example, we have noted the division between the 'old old' and 'young old' which is made by gerontologists and also by elderly people themselves. Other broad age-groups could be divided in a similar fashion. Finally, less attention has been paid here to internal fragmentation of the genders. However, the logic of relations of sexuality and reproduction, crucial aspects of gender differentiation, allows for fragmentation of genders on the basis of heterosexual, homosexual or bisexual affiliation and also by reproduction status: whether people are married, single, have children or not. These distinctions bring divergences of preoccupations and interests.

2 *External fragmentation,* which arises from the interaction of the various dynamics. For example, classes are divided by gender, age, ethnicity, region and so forth.

Processes of external fragmentation have been highlighted constantly through this study and have been presented as of crucial importance. My strategy has been to look at the way any two of the four dynamics under discussion interact with each other. Of course, in any given concrete situation all four dynamics (along with others) are at play. We may take as a good example Wilson's account of the ghetto underclass, discussed in chapter 7. Not only are forces of class and 'race' combining to push African Americans into unemployment and social disorganization, age and gender are also centrally involved as young black men demonstrate their virility through sexual predation and street violence.

It is still an issue whether we should seek to uncover systematic ways in which dynamics of stratification interact, to search for a 'unified' system, or whether we should follow Brah's prescription that relations between them are best viewed as 'historically contingent and context-specific' (1993, p. 14). Knowles and Mercer (1993) contend there is no general relationship between 'race' and gender and that we should approach particular instances through case studies. In this book, while arguing that each dynamic has a logic derived from its existential base, I have presented their interaction within particular contexts. My own view is that the search for a unified system is not fruitful; but I believe we can uncover *characteristic* patterns in the way the elements interrelate, enough to merit the formulation of sociological generalizations. Indeed, I consider this a central task for stratification theorists in the future.

3 *Fragmentation as a result of general processes of social change.* Classes can be said to be fragmenting when a particular class formation goes through processes of decomposition as a result of economic change.

The use of the term fragmentation to describe broad processes of social change has been particularly associated with class. For example, Esping-Andersen (1993) is implicitly employing such a framework in his account of how old classes are collapsing and new ones coming to replace them with the shift to a post-industrial economy. This form of fragmentation should be a temporary one, as decomposition will eventually be followed by recomposition: new classes are formed. But since processes of social change are habitually slow, piecemeal and uneven, the period of fragmentation may be prolonged.

The notions of decomposition and recomposition have been less explicitly employed in relation to ethnicity, gender and age. However, the upheavals in Europe in the 1980s and 1990s (caused partly by the break-up of the Soviet Union, partly by the formation of the EC and partly by the influx of refugees because of famine and warfare around the globe) could be seen as an example of the decomposition and recomposition of established racial and ethnic hierarchies. New migrant groups may form the basis of new settler communities, while older groups face expulsion. Rex's (1992) account of the emerging racial hierarchy, outlined in chapter 7, illustrates this. Age and gender relations, having more link to biological factors, are perhaps less susceptible to processes of decomposition. But postmodern writers have certainly hinted that such events are on the cards, for example, the collapsing of age distinctions or the overturning of conventional categories of sex and gender. My own view is that there is as yet no evidence of sufficient change to support such claims.

4 Fragmentation as a synonym for individuation. In this scenario collective and communal ties and identities in society are seen to be dissolving with the rise of individualism and consumer culture.

'There is no such thing as society,' declared Margaret Thatcher, famously. Of course no sociologist could accept such a statement! But there are many different ways of conceptualizing society, one of which is that it is made up of self-interested, atomized individuals. The view that the progress of industrial development fosters greater individualization and breaks up social collectivities is a longstanding one. It lay behind many modernist theories, such as Tonnies's account of the switch from *Gemeinschaft* to *Gesellschaft* or Durkheim's characterization of industrial societies as based on organic rather than mechanical solidarity. The theme has now been taken up by postmodernists who emphasize the importance of consumer choices and the cult of individualized lifestyles. However, such views rest on extrapolation from individual definitions of personal identity. In this way they misrepresent the complex and fluctuating relationship between processes of social identification and the lived relationships which surround them. As Marshall et al. (1988) suggest in reference to class consciousness, individualistic and collectivistic meanings and impulses coexist. This applies to gender, ethnicity and age as well.

The combined effect of these various forms of fragmentation is to produce complex and fluid patterns of inequality. Sensitive accounts of class, gender and ethnicity have always taken account of this. As Hollands has argued,

> Class is never a homogeneous category, nor is class formation the same for every generation. Instead it is understood here as a changing and dynamic set of conditions and identities which are formed in specific historical circumstances and historical sites. (1990, p. 5)

Polarization

Class analysis in the 1980s has been preoccupied with issues of fragmentation when considering both the working and middle classes. But when the capitalist class is brought into consideration, a contrary theme, that of polarization, emerges. Polarization is a term used by Marxists to indicate a concentration of individuals at both ends (poles) of the class spectrum, accompanied by widening differences in the fate of those at the top and bottom. Such 'immiseration' implies increased inequality between the dominant and subordinate classes. As the subordinate class is forced into hardship and poverty it becomes increasingly homogenized, and so polarization also implies a greater potential for political unity. I am arguing here that tendencies towards polarization, and consequent unifying impulses, coexist with the tendencies to fragmentation described above.

Two forms of economic polarization have been manifest in the past decades. First, at least in Britain and America, there has been persistent evidence over the past decades of a steadily widening gap between the rich and poor within the nation, as discussed in chapter 3; the economic share of the labour surplus class has steadily worsened, while elite groups have prospered through government policies and the freeing of the market from restrictions – factors which jointly have resulted in 'capital doing extremely well at the expense of labour' (Elliott, 1995). In 1994 this trend was symbolically proclaimed to the British nation when Cedric Brown, chief executive of British Gas, received a pay rise of 75 per cent, while showroom staff were threatened with pay cuts and redundancies.

The other form of economic polarization has been between the 'North' and the 'South', the growing gap between the rich and poor nations, which is perhaps the most striking feature of the late twentieth-century world order. The less developed societies of Africa, and to a lesser extent those of South America and some parts of Asia, have struggled to keep going in the face of famine, natural disasters, internal conflicts and debt, a situation starkly exemplified by the horrors of the civil war in Rwanda. The UNICEF Annual Report for 1994 estimated that the poorest forty or fifty countries have experienced a substantial decline in their share of world income; one-fifth of the world's people share less than 1.5 per cent of world income (Brittain, 1994). Some one billion people survive on less than a dollar a day. At the same time, there is a dramatic discrepancy within those countries between the relative affluence of the economic and political elites who share in the lifestyle of the West, and the condition of the peasantry and the industrial poor.

These tendencies must be seen in the context of a feature which has been emphasized throughout this book: the ever-increasing power and reach of globalizing capital. The economic as well as the cultural dimensions of this power are encapsulated in a chilling comment from young postmodernist

Japanese writer, Harumi Murakami, when he describes 'the massive capital web' in his novel *Dance, Dance, Dance*:

> Everything before is nothing compared to the exacting detail and sheer power and invulnerability of today's web of capitalism. And it's mega-computers that have made it all possible, with their inhuman capacity to pull together every last factor and condition on the face of the earth into their net calculations. Advanced capitalism has transcended itself. Not to overstate things, financial dealings have practically become a religious activity . . . People worship capital, adore its aura, genuflect before Porsches and Tokyo land values. It's the only stuff of myth that's left in the world. (p. 55)

It is easy to become hypnotized by this phenomenon and overlook the contribution of other aspects of inequality to deepening social divisions. While the term polarization comes from class analysis, it can also be applied to ethnicity, age and gender. At the same time, the interaction of the four dynamics is displayed in concomitant tendencies for class polarization, arising from capital globalization, to display itself within ethnic and age-groups and among women.

Two forms of ethnic polarization can be discerned. We have seen that ethnic divisions often coincide with the class divisions characteristic of post-industrial change, so that members of the groups at the bottom of each national ethnic hierarchy are over-represented among the poor and the labour surplus class. This has a specifically racial dimension, as people of African, Asian and Arabic origin, racialized on the basis of colour, are particularly affected in this way. A more broadly ethnic form of polarization can be seen emerging with the renaissance of nationalist and neo-fascist movements which set a mythologized 'native' population against all 'aliens' in the society. At the same time we noted in earlier chapters that in America and some European countries ethnic elites employed in entrepreneurial and professional roles were increasingly being distanced from their own communities.

Age polarization also seems to be an emergent trend. We have noted the potential for increased suspicion between young and old as age-groups are more explicitly drawn into competition for scarce national resources, especially as globalization and economic restructuring are curbing economic opportunities for both young and old. A growing polarization among the elderly can also be discerned, as the experience of those affluent pensioners experiencing a 'golden age' of retirement diverges from that of the aged poor. Blakemore and Boneham comment:

> Social divisions among older people as a whole are widening . . . The uneven spread of occupational pension schemes and other changes are leading to increasing fragmentation and inequality. The frontiers of old

age faced by black and Asian people involve possibilities of widening gaps between winners and losers. (1994, p. 141)

It may seem strange to talk about polarization between the sexes, as some progress towards equality has been achieved. However, the very gains made by women have provoked confrontation. It may not be too much of an exaggeration to speak of a 'sex war' (especially in America) as women prepare to defend their new privileges and men fight back to restore waning patriarchal dominance. Issues such as the legal and definitional struggles around sexual harassment and 'date rape'; the divorced fathers' campaigns against the Child Support Act; and the men's 'backlash' in the workplace against equal opportunities programmes which they see as bias towards women are signs that both women and men are acting under the spur of heightened awareness of gender interests. At the same time, there is evidence of growing inequalities among women, as equal opportunities promise to smash the 'glass ceiling' for middle- and elite-class women in professional and managerial careers, but do little to improve the prospects of low-paid women workers from working-class backgrounds. A report from Europe confirms that 'the price to be paid for a minority of women to achieve equality with men could be greater inequalities for those at the bottom of the ladder' (CEC, 1992a, p. 52).

I have suggested that the economic changes which spring from the global restructuring of the economy have effects on all four dynamics of stratification. These combine to produce growing disparities between privileged and underprivileged groups.

Contradictory tendencies

At the beginning of this book, I suggested that a 'both/and' approach would be more fruitful than an 'either/or' one. I re-emphasize this now. The discussion above confirms the view that contemporary societies are both fragmented *and* subject to polarizing and unifying tendencies. This is reflected in the insight of Musil, who characterizes the 1970s as a period where unity among women was identified and the 1980s as marked by the recognition of diversity and differences of interest. But, she concludes, 'the challenge of the nineties is to hold on simultaneously to these two contradictory truths: as women, we are the same and we are different' (quoted in Yuval-Davis, 1993, p. 4).

With this in mind, we can now reassess the contributions of modernist and postmodernist thought to the study of inequality. While the theorists of modernism were not unaware of internal divisions and diversities, their bias was always towards uncovering underlying potentialities for unity and exposing continuities of development. In stratification theory this led to an excessive preoccupation with class at the expense of other aspects of inequality and of social identification. Theorists of postmodernism quite rightly criticized the one-sidedness of many modernist accounts. They drew our attention to the other aspect of social reality, its centrifugal as opposed to its centripetal nature, and focused our attention on fluidity, diversity and individual difference. However, some postmodernists fall into the contrary error of overlooking the homogenizing and unifying features of social organization. Preoccupied with the specific and contingent, they underplay regularities and general patterns.

We should not underestimate the impact of postmodernism and post-structuralism; they have certainly made a significant contribution to the major shift in the sociological analysis of social inequalities, discerned, for example, by Griffin in her account of youth studies: 'by the end of the 1980s many radical analyses were considering the intersections of "race", sex/gender, age, class and (less fully) dis/ability rather than the overwhelming focus on class relations which had characterized the radical texts of the 1970s' (1993, p. 55). But perhaps now we need to move beyond the critical deconstruction of classic stratification theories offered by postmodernism, returning to some of the key issues and themes of modernism, acknowledging their limitations and trying to refine them, in the way suggested as the third option set out at the start of this chapter. In this way we may reach a better understanding of the *double and contradictory* nature of the dynamics of inequality, at once unifying and dividing.

This possibility appears to be recognized by Dirlik. While highly critical of the post-colonial neglect of the totalizing forces of global capitalism which, he argues, is in fact the very condition for the emergence of postmodern and post-colonial sensibilities, he also acknowledges the complexity of current relationships of class, 'race' and 'ethnicity':

> The globe has become as jumbled up spatially as the ideology of progress has temporally. Third Worlds have appeared in the First World and First Worlds in the Third. New diasporas have relocated the Self there and the Other here, and consequently borders and boundaries have been confounded. And the flow of culture has been at once homogenizing and heterogenizing; some groups share in a common global culture regardless of location even as they are alienated from the culture of their hinterlands, while others are driven back into cultural legacies long thought to be residual. (1994, pp. 352–3)

If we accept these changes, it is not surprising that we are now all more fully aware that the issue of identifying oneself in terms of loyalties of class, gender, ethnicity and age is a highly complex business.

Fractured identities

As individuals we stand at the points of intersection between all these processes of fragmentation and polarization. We are all exposed to the dynamics of class, gender, ethnicity and age, all of which are potential elements in our individual identities. But it has been argued in this book that there is no necessary relation between social location and identification; only in certain circumstances will passive identities become active or politicized. It is not surprising that postmodernists have stressed the fractured and multiple nature of social identities in modern society.

Postmodernists rightly emphasize that we function as active agents in the construction of our identities, rather than responding automatically to the dynamics that act upon us. But this is not exactly a matter of choice, as is sometimes implied. Few of us can, as yet, *choose* to be English, male and middle class if we were born Indian, female and working class, even though technologies of the future may make some of these changes possible. Identities are *not* free-floating. The lived relations in which each of us is located put constraints and limits upon the possible range of identifications, though within those limits we can work creatively with the potentialities at hand. Above all, as has been emphasized in preceding chapters, the construction of identity is a *political* process. It is framed by changing political movements, practices and discourses which promote awareness. If class as a source of social identification is currently in decline it is because class has been de-politicized.

Haraway (1990) has used the image of the 'cyborg', half organism, half machine, as a metaphor to challenge essentialist views of gender and to point to the impossibility of separating what is 'natural' and what is 'social' in our make-up. The cyborg is the latest in a line of mythological hybrids, from mermaids and gorgons to Frankenstein's monster, which express society's concern with categorization and anxiety about phenomena that do not fit neatly into the existing sets of categories. Nationalist claims about the need for ethnic purity are a recent manifestation of this prevalent way of thinking. Haraway is right to challenge this kind of thinking with its tendency to reduce identity to one single element rather than recognize its inevitable complexity. As the new theorists of ethnicity have stressed (Bhabha, 1990a; Gilroy, 1993) we are all hybrids and monsters now.

But how new is this? Can we speak of a new postmodern phase which has caused this fracturing of identities? Or is it the way we comprehend social reality that has changed? Are we dealing, in Bauman's terms, with a sociology of postmodernism or a postmodern sociology?

The answers must be tentative. People have always been subject to processes of economic differentiation together with differences of ethnicity, gender and age. The potential for fracturing of identities has long existed. There is, however, a sense that fragmentation has increased in the past decades. Certainly we are living in a period of rapid change. On the other hand, as has been argued in this book, there are many continuities with the past. Capitalist industrialism has always been a dynamic and fluid system. Like Pollert (1988) and Thompson (1993), I am sceptical as to whether current changes constitute a radical rupture with the past. As Davis points out, each generation of sociologists is inclined to consider itself as 'astride some major historical watershed':

> Sociological theory has indeed tended to conceptualize social change in terms of more or less clear-cut breaks of a fundamental nature . . . whereas the trend of change, whilst extensive and rapid enough in many senses, has nonetheless been essentially uneven, embodying leads, lags and continuities. (1990, p. 217)

The change, then, may be more in our perceptions of society. Giddens (1991) has found one way to explain this in his assertion that a period he describes as 'late modernity' is characterized by a much higher degree of 'reflexivity' about ourselves and our place in society. This is superficially persuasive. It is eloquently exemplified in the anthem by British Afro-Caribbean band, *Earthling*, from which the quotation at the beginning of this chapter was taken. The lyric playfully and with irony celebrates the elasticity of identity, proclaiming the singer's right to multiple self-definitions while resisting others' attempts to label him. However, the problem with Giddens's approach is that it makes some unsubstantiated assumptions about the behaviour of people in the past. Any study of history will cast doubt on the view that our forebears were simpler and less sophisticated than ourselves. Study of the Victorians reveals their awareness of complexities and ambiguities (Houghton, 1957). Indeed, Barbara Marshall (1994) suggests that the postmodern preoccupation with fragmentation and social decomposition is a manifestation of just such a *fin-de-siècle* malaise as characterized the end of the eighteenth and nineteenth centuries.

Perhaps it is not so much that our perceptions have changed but that new analytic and narrative frameworks are on offer which we may draw on to make sense of our selves and our place in society. Sociologists bear some responsibility for this, in helping publicize the notion of postmodernity and change. The greater politicization of ethnic and gender issues has also made us more aware of these aspects of our circumstances as opposed to earlier preoccupations with class. The collapse of the Soviet Union and the challenge to socialism has turned the thoughts of radicals away from Marxism and encouraged an interest in other types of critical explanation of social relations. We should be grateful that such developments have heightened our sensibility to the multi-dimensional nature of social inequality. But that multi-dimensionality is not new.

Commenting on the effects of postmodern cultural change, Bryan Turner has speculated on the possibility that current sociological theories of inequality, as set out in this book, may become quite inadequate to analyse a new type of social differentiation. In his words, 'social differentiation and social evaluation will not be eroded by these developments, but we may well move towards a social system based upon somewhat different principles of stratification, which will render much contemporary sociology redundant' (1988, p. 76). In this book I have argued against this position. Existing theories do need to be refined and modified, in order to capture the complex nature of the dynamics of inequality. But the tendencies noted by the theorists of modernism are far from played out. A reworked version of modernist analysis, benefiting from the critical insights of postmodern and post-structuralist thought, offers the best hope for an adequate understanding of the double and contradictory nature of contemporary society, both fragmenting and polarizing. Such an approach must grasp the persisting nature of social hierarchies as well as exploring the interplay of relationships which gives rise to the fractured identities characteristic of post-industrial capitalist societies.

Bibliography and Sources

Abercrombie, N. and Turner, B. 1978: The dominant ideology thesis. *British Journal of Sociology*, 29(2), 149–70.

Abercrombie, N. and Urry, J. 1983: *Capital, Labour and the Middle Classes*. London: Allen & Unwin.

Abrams, M. 1959: *The Teenage Consumer*. London Press Exchange Papers, 5.

Abrams, P. 1970: Rites de passage: the conflict of generations in industrial society. *Journal of Contemporary History*, 5(1), 175–90.

Abu Odeh, L. 1993: Post-colonial feminism and the veil: thinking the difference. *Feminist Review*, 43, 26–37.

Achenbaum, W. A. 1989: Public pensions as intergenerational transfers in the United States. In P. Johnson, C. Conrad and D. Thomson (eds), *Workers Versus Pensioners: intergenerational justice in a changing world*. Manchester: Manchester University Press, 113–36.

Acker, J. 1989: *Doing Comparable Worth: gender, class and pay equity*. Philadelphia: Temple University Press.

Afshar, H. 1994: Muslim women in West Yorkshire. In H. Afshar and M. Maynard (eds), *The Dynamics of 'Race' and Gender*. London: Taylor & Francis, 127–47.

Afshar, H. and Maynard, M. (eds) 1994: *The Dynamics of 'Race' and Gender*. London: Taylor & Francis.

Allatt, P., Keil, T., Bryman, A. and Bytheway, B. (eds) 1987: *Women and the Life Cycle*. London: Macmillan.

Allen, S. 1994: Race, ethnicity and nationality: some questions of identity. In H. Afshar and M. Maynard (eds), *The Dynamics of 'Race' and Gender*. London: Taylor & Francis, 85–105.

Allen, S. and Macey, M. 1990: Race and ethnicity in the European context. *British Journal of Sociology*, 41(3), 375–93.

Allen, S. and Wolkowitz, C. 1987: *Homeworking: myths and realities*. London: Macmillan.

Amos, V. and Parmar, P. 1984: Challenging imperial feminism. *Feminist Review*, 17, 3–18.

Anderson, B. 1991: *Imagined Communities* (2nd edn). London: Verso.

Anderson, B. 1994: Exodus. *Critical Enquiry*, 20, 314–27.

Anderson, P. 1964: Origins of the present crisis. *New Left Review*, 23, 26–53.

Anthias, F. and Yuval-Davis, N. 1983: Contextualizing feminism: gender, ethnic and class divisions. *Feminist Review*, 15, 62–75.

Anthias, F. and Yuval-Davis, N. 1993: *Racialized Boundaries*. London: Routledge.

Arber, S. 1994: Wrinkles in the fabric of society. *The Higher*, 18 Nov.

Arber, S. and Ginn, J. 1991a: The invisibility of age: gender and class in later life. *Sociological Review*, 39(2), 260–90.

Arber, S. and Ginn, J. 1991b: *Gender and Later Life*. London: Sage.

Aries, P. 1962: *Centuries of Childhood*. Harmondsworth: Penguin.

Bagguley, P. and Mann, K. 1992: Idle thieving bastards? Scholarly representations of the 'underclass'. *Work Employment and Society*, 6(1), 113–26.

Bakker, I. 1988: Women's employment in comparative perspective. In J. Jenson, E. Hagen and C. Reddy (eds), *Feminization of the Labour Force*. Cambridge: Polity, 17–44.

Banks, O. 1981: *Faces of Feminism*. Oxford: Martin Robertson.

Barker, M. 1981: *The New Racism*. London: Junction Books.

Barrett, M. 1980: *Women's Oppression Today: problems in Marxist feminist analysis*. London: Verso.

Barrett, M. 1992: Words and things: materialism and method in contemporary feminist analysis. In M. Barrett and A. Phillips (eds), *Destabilizing Theory*. Cambridge: Polity, 201–19.

Barrett, M. and Phillips, A. 1992: *Destabilizing Theory*. Cambridge: Polity.

Bartky, S. 1990: *Femininity and Domination*. New York: Routledge.

Bates, I. 1993: 'A job which is right for me'? Social class, gender and individualization. In I. Bates and G. Riseborough (eds), *Youth and Inequality*. Milton Keynes: Open University Press, 14–41.

Bates, I. and Riseborough, G. (eds) 1993: *Youth and Inequality*. Milton Keynes: Open University Press.

Bauman, Z. 1988: Sociology and postmodernity. *Sociological Review*, 36(4), 790–813.

Bauman, Z. 1992: *Intimations of Postmodernity*. London: Routledge.

Beauvoir, S. de 1949: *Le Deuxième Sex* (trans. as *The Second Sex*). Paris: Gallimard.

Beck, U. 1992: *Risk Society*. London: Sage.

Beechey, V. 1977: Some notes on female wage labour in capitalist production. *Capital and Class*, 3, 45–66.

Bell, D. 1973: *The Coming of Post-industrial Society*. New York: Basic Books.

Bergmann, B. 1986: *The Economic Emergence of Women*. New York: Basic Books.

Berman, M. 1983: *All that is Solid Melts into Air: the experience of modernity*. London: Verso.

Bernard, J. 1976: *The Future of Marriage*. Harmondsworth: Penguin.

Berry, D. and O'Dwyer, N. 1987: Is racism driving blacks out of their minds? *Guardian*, 30 October.

Bhabha, H. 1990a: The third space. In J. Rutherford (ed.), *Identity*. London: Lawrence & Wishart, 207–21.

Bhabha, H. (ed.) 1990b: *Nation and Narration*. London: Routledge.

Bhavnani, K. 1993: Towards a multi-cultural Europe? 'Race', nation and identity in 1992 and beyond. *Feminist Review*, 45, 30–45.

Blackwell, T. and Seabrook, J. 1985: *A World Still to Win*. London: Faber and Faber.

Blakemore, K. and Boneham, M. 1994: *Age, Race and Ethnicity*. Milton Keynes: Open University Press.

Blau, P. and Duncan, O. 1967: *The American Occupational Structure*. New York: Wiley.

Blauner, R. 1969: Internal colonialism and ghetto revolt. *Social Problems*, 16(4), 393–408.

Blythe, R. 1979: *The View in Winter*. London: Allen Lane.

Bocock, R. 1992: Consumption and lifestyles. In Bocock, R. and Thompson, K. (eds), *Social and Cultural Forms of Modernity*. Cambridge: Polity, 119–68.

Bocock, R. 1993: *Consumption*. London: Routledge.

Bodily, C. 1994: Ageism and the deployment of 'age': a constructionist view. In T. Sarbin and J. Kitsuse (eds), *Constructing the Social*. London: Sage, 174–94.

Borchorst, A. and Sim, B. 1987: Women and the advanced welfare state: a new kind of patriarchal power? In A. S. Sassoon (ed.), *Women and the State*. London: Hutchinson, 128–51.

Bottomore, T. and Brym, R. (eds) 1989: *The Capitalist Class*. Hemel Hempstead: Harvester Wheatsheaf.

Bourdieu, P. 1986: *Distinction*. London: Routledge.

Bradley, H. 1989: *Men's Work, Women's Work*. Cambridge: Polity.

Bradley, H. 1992: Changing social divisions: class, gender and race. In R. Bocock and K. Thompson (eds), *Social and Cultural Forms of Modernity*. Cambridge: Polity, 11–56.

Bradley, H. 1994: Class and class consciousness in a northern conurbation. In R. Blackburn (ed.), *Social Inequality in a Changing World* [papers presented to Cambridge Social Stratification Seminar, September 1993], 151–68.

Brah, A. 1986: Unemployment and racism: Asian youth on the dole. In S. Allen, A. Waton, K. Purcell and S. Wood (eds), *The Experience of Unemployment*, London: Macmillan, 61–78.

Brah, A. 1992: Difference, diversity and differentiation. In J. Donald and A. Rattansi (eds), *'Race', Culture and Difference*. Milton Keynes: Open University Press, 126–45.

Brah, A. 1993: Re-framing Europe: engendered racisms, ethnicities and nationalisms in contemporary western Europe. *Feminist Review*, 45, 9–28.

Brah, A. 1994: 'Race' and 'culture' in the gendering of labour markets. In H. Afshar and M. Maynard (eds), *The Dynamics of 'Race' and Gender*. London: Taylor & Francis, 151–71.

Brake, M. 1980: *Sociology of Youth Culture and Youth Subcultures*. London: Routledge & Kegan Paul.

Brake, M. 1985: *Comparative Youth Culture*. London: Routledge & Kegan Paul.

Brannen, J. and Moss, P. 1991: *Managing Mothers*. London: Unwin Hyman.

Braverman, H. 1974: *Labor and Monopoly Capital*. New York: Basic Books.

Briggs, A. 1974: The language of 'class' in early nineteenth-century England. In M. Flinn and T. Smout (eds), *Essays in Social History*. Oxford: Oxford University Press, 154–78.

Briskin, L. and McDermott, P. (eds) 1993: *Women Challenging Unions*. Toronto: University of Toronto Press.

Brittain, V. 1994: Millions of children 'traumatised by war'. *Guardian*, 16 December.

Brodie, H. 1986: *Maps and Dreams*. London: Faber and Faber.

Brown, C. 1984: *Black and White Britain*. London: Heinemann.
Brownmiller, S. 1976: *Against Our Will: men, women and rape*. Harmondsworth: Penguin.
Bruegel, I. 1989: Sex and race in the labour market. *Feminist Review*, 32, 49–68.
Bryan, B., Dadzie, S. and Scafe, S. 1985: *The Heart of the Race*. London: Virago.
Bryman, A., Bytheway, B., Allatt, P. and Keil, T. (eds): *Rethinking the Life Cycle*. London: Macmillan.
Butler, J. 1990: *Gender Trouble*. New York: Routledge.
Cain, L. 1975: The young and the old: coalition or conflict ahead? In A. Foner (ed.), *Age in Society*. London: Sage, 35–45.
Calvert, P. 1982: *The Concept of Class*. London: Hutchinson.
Campani, G. 1993: Immigration and racism in southern Europe: the Italian case. *Ethnic and Racial Studies*, 16(3), 507–35.
Campbell, B. 1993: *Goliath*. London: Methuen.
Carby, H. 1982: White woman listen! Black feminism and the boundaries of sisterhood. In Centre for Contemporary Cultural Studies (eds), *The Empire Strikes Back*. London: Hutchinson, 212–36.
Carchedi, G. 1977: *On the Economic Identification of Social Classes*. London: Routledge.
Carter, F., French, R. and Salt, J. 1993: International migration between East and West in Europe. *Ethnic and Racial Studies*, 16(3), 467–91.
Cashmore, E. and Troyna, B. (eds) 1982: *Black Youth in Crisis*. London: George Allen & Unwin.
Cashmore, E. and Troyna, B. 1983: *Introduction to Race Relations*. London: Routledge & Kegan Paul.
Castles, S. 1984: *Here for Good*. London: Pluto.
Castles, S. and Kosack, G. 1973: *Immigrant Workers and Class Structure in Western Europe*. Oxford: Oxford University Press.
Cavendish, R. 1982: *Women on the Line*. London: Routledge.
Centre for Contemporary Cultural Studies (eds) 1982: *The Empire Strikes Back*. London: Hutchinson.
Chalmers, N. 1989: *Industrial Relations in Japan*. London: Routledge.
Chang, H. 1992: *Adolescent Life and Ethos*. London: Falmer.
Charvet, J. 1982: *Feminism*. London: Dent.
Chaudhuri, A. 1994: *Afternoon Raag*. London: Minerva.
Chodorow, N. 1978: *The Reproduction of Mothering: psychoanalysis and the sociology of gender*. Berkeley: University of California Press.
Ciancanelli, P. and Berch, B. 1987: Gender and the GNP. In B. Hess and M. Ferree (eds), *Analyzing Gender*. London: Sage, 244–66.
Clark, A. 1982: *Working Life of Women in the Seventeenth Century* (1st edn 1919). London: Routledge.
Clarke, J. 1993: The demography of ageing in Europe. In P. Kaim-Caudle, J. Keithley and A. Mullender (eds), *Aspects of Ageing*. London: Whiting & Birch, 71–80.
Clarke, J. and Critcher, C. 1985: *The Devil Makes Work*. London: Macmillan.
Coates, D. 1989: Britain. In T. Bottomore and R. Brym (eds), *The Capitalist Class*. Hemel Hempstead: Harvester Wheatsheaf, 19–45.
Cockburn, C. 1983: *Brothers*. London: Pluto.

Cockburn, C. 1985: *Machinery of Dominance*. London: Pluto.
Cockburn, C. 1991: *In the Way of Women*. London: Macmillan.
Coffield, F., Borrill, C. and Marshall, S. 1986: *Growing up at the Margins*. Milton Keynes: Open University Press.
Cohen, P. 1988: The perversions of inheritance: studies in the making of multi-racist Britain. In P. Cohen and H. Bains (eds), *Multi-racist Britain*. London: Macmillan, 9–118.
Cohen, S. 1972: *Folk Devils and Moral Panics*. London: MacGibbon & Kee.
Collins, P. H. 1990: *Black Feminist Thought*. London: HarperCollins.
Comer, L. 1974: *Wedlocked Women*. Leeds: Feminist Books.
Commission of the European Communities (CEC) 1987: *Men and Women of Europe in 1987* (Supplement to *Women of Europe*, 26).
Commission of the European Communities 1988: *Women of Europe: Ten Years* (*Women of Europe*, 27).
Commission of the European Communities 1989: *Employment in Europe*.
Commission of the European Communities 1992a: *Women of Europe*, 70.
Commission of the European Communities 1992b: *Legal Instruments to Combat Racism and Xenophobia*.
Connell, R. 1987: *Gender and Power*. Cambridge: Polity.
Cowgill, D. and Holmes, L. 1972: *Aging and Modernization*. New York: Appleton-Century-Crofts.
Cox, O. 1970: *Caste, Class and Race*. New York: Monthly Review Books.
Crompton, R. 1993: *Class and Stratification*. Cambridge: Polity.
Crompton. R. and Gubbay, J. 1977: *Economy and Class Structure*. London: Macmillan.
Crompton, R. and Jones, G. 1984: *White-Collar Proletariat*. London: Macmillan.
Crompton, R. and Mann, M. (eds) 1986: *Gender and Stratification*. Cambridge: Polity.
Crompton, R. and Sanderson, K. 1990: *Gendered Jobs and Social Change*. London: Unwin Hyman.
Crook, S., Pakulski, J. and Waters, M. 1992: *Postmodernization*. London: Sage.
Crowley, H. 1992: Women and the domestic sphere. In R. Bocock and K. Thompson (eds), *Social and Cultural Forms of Modernity*. Cambridge: Polity, 69–118.
Cumming, E. and Henry, W. 1961: *Growing Old: The Process of Disengagement*. New York: Basic Books.
Curran, J., Stanworth, J. and Watkins, D. (eds) 1986: *The Survival of the Small Firm*. Aldershot: Gower.
Curthoys, A. 1993: Feminism, citizenship and national identity. *Feminist Review*, 44, 19–38.
Dahrendorf, R. 1959: *Class and Class Conflict in Industrial Society*. London: Routledge.
Dahrendorf, R. 1987: The erosion of citizenship and its consequences for us all. *New Statesman*, 12 June, 12–15.
Dale, A. 1986: Social class and the self-employed. *Sociology*, 20(3), 430–4.
Daniel, W. W. 1968: *Racial Discrimination in Britain*. Harmondsworth: Penguin.
Davies, B. 1989: *Frogs and Snails and Feminist Tales*. Sydney: Allen & Unwin.
Davis, H. 1992: Social stratification in Europe. In J. Bailey (ed.), *Social Europe*. London: Longman, 17–35.
Davis, J. 1990: *Youth and the Condition of Britain: images of adolescent conflict*. London: Athlone Press.

Davis, K., Leijenaar, M. and Oldersma, J. 1991: *The Gender of Power*. London: Sage.
Davis, K. and Moore, W. 1945: Some principles of stratification. *American Sociological Review*, 10, 242–9.
Davis, M. 1980: Why the US working class is different. *New Left Review*, 123, 3–44.
Davis, M. 1990: *City of Quartz*. London: Vintage Books.
Dawe, A. 1970: The two sociologies. *British Journal of Sociology*, 21(2), 207–18.
Dean, H. 1991: In search of the underclass. In P. Brown and R. Scase (eds), *Poor Work*. Milton Keynes: Open University Press, 23–39.
Del Boca, D. 1988: Women in a changing workplace: the case of Italy. In J. Jenson, E. Hagen and C. Reddy (eds), *Feminization of the Labour Force*. Cambridge: Polity, 120–36.
Delphy, C. 1977: *The Main Enemy*. London: Women's Research and Resources Centre.
Dennis, N., Henriques, F. and Slaughter, C. 1956: *Coal Is Our Life*. London: Eyre & Spottiswoode.
Devine, F. 1992: *Affluent Workers Revisited*. Edinburgh: Edinburgh University Press.
Dex, S. and Shaw, L. 1986: *British and American Women at Work*. London: Macmillan.
Dirlik, A. 1994: The postcolonial aura: third world criticism in the age of global capitalism. *Critical Inquiry*. 20. 328–56.
Donald, J. and Rattansi, A. (eds) 1992: *'Race', Culture and Difference*. Milton Keynes: Open University Press.
Dore, R. 1973: *British Factory, Japanese Factory*. London: Allen & Unwin.
Duchen, C. 1987: *French Connections*. London: Hutchinson.
Durkheim, E. 1952: *Suicide*. London: Routledge.
Durkheim, E. 1964: *The Division of Labour in Society*. New York: Free Press.
Dworkin, A. 1981: *Pornography: men possessing women*. London: Women's Press.
Eaton, M. 1993: Foreign residents and illegal immigrants: os negroes em Portugal. *Ethnic and Racial Studies*, 16(3), 536–62.
Edgell, S. 1993: *Class*. London: Routledge.
Ehrenreich, B. and English, D. 1979: *For Her Own Good*. London: Pluto.
Eisenstadt, S. 1956: *From Generation to Generation; age groups and social structure*. New York: Free Press.
Elliott, L. 1995: Capital times if you're rich. *Guardian*, 11 January.
Elshtain, J. B. 1987: Feminist political rhetoric and women's studies. In J. Nelson, A. Megill and D. Mclosky (eds), *The Rhetoric of the Human Sciences*. Madison: Wisconsin University Press, 319–40.
Employment Gazette, March 1990: 'Ethnic origins and the labour market', pp. 125–37, London: Department of Employment.
Erikson, E. 1965: *Childhood and Society*. Harmondsworth: Penguin.
Erikson, R. and Goldthorpe, J. 1992: *The Constant Flux: a study of class mobility in industrial societies*. Oxford: Clarendon Press.
Erler, G. 1988: The German paradox. In J. Jenson, E. Hagen and C. Reddy (eds), *Feminization of the Labour Force*. Cambridge: Polity, 231–42.
Esping-Andersen, G. (ed.) 1993: *Changing Classes*. London: Sage.
Faludi, S. 1992: *Backlash*. London: Chatto & Windus.
Featherstone, M. 1991: *Consumer Culture and Postmodernism*. London: Sage.
Featherstone, M. and Hepworth, M. 1989: Ageing and old age: reflections on the postmodern life course. In B. Bytheway, T. Keil, P. Allatt and A. Bryman (eds), *Becoming and Being Old*. London: Sage, 143–57.

Featherstone, M. and Hepworth, M. 1990: Images of ageing. In J. Bond and P. Coleman (eds), *Ageing in Society: an introduction to social gerontology*. London: Sage, 250–76.

Fennell, G., Phillipson, C. and Evers, H. 1988: *The Sociology of Old Age*. Milton Keynes: Open University Press.

Fenton, S. 1987: Black elderly people in Britain. Department of Sociology, University of Bristol.

Feuer, L. 1969: *The Conflict of Generations: the character and significance of student movements*. New York: Basic Books.

Field, F. 1989: *Losing Out: the emergence of Britain's underclass*. Oxford: Blackwell.

Firestone, S. 1971: *The Dialectic of Sex*. London: Jonathan Cape.

Fleming, S. 1991: Sport, schooling and Asian male youth culture. In G. Jarvie (ed.), *Sport, Racism and Ethnicity*. London: Falmer, 30–57.

Foner, A. 1975: Age in society: structure and change. In A. Foner (ed.), *Age in Society*. London: Sage, 13–34.

Forbes, I. and Mead, G. 1992: Measure for measure, Department of Employment, Research Series, 1.

Ford, J. and Sinclair, R. 1987: *Sixty Years On: women talk about old age*. London: Women's Press.

Foucault, M. 1972: *The Archaeology of Knowledge*. London: Tavistock.

Foucault, M. 1979: *The History of Sexuality (Vol. I)*. London: Allen Lane.

Frankenberg, R. 1993: Growing up white: feminism, racism and the social geography of childhood. *Feminist Review*, 45, 51–84.

Fraser, N. and Nicholson, L. 1988: Social criticism without philosophy: an encounter between feminism and postmodernism. *Theory Culture and Society*, 5, 373–94.

Friedan, B. 1965: *The Feminine Mystique*. Harmondsworth: Penguin.

Friedmann, G. 1955: *Industrial Society*. New York: Free Press.

Frisby, D. 1985: *Fragments of Modernity*. Cambridge: Polity.

Fukutake, T. 1967: *Japanese Rural Society*. Ithaca, NY: Cornell University Press.

Fukuyama, F. 1989: The end of history? *The National Interest*, 16 (summer), 3–18.

Fuller, M. 1982: Young, female and black. In E. Cashmore and B. Troyna (eds), *Black Youth in Crisis*. London: Allen & Unwin, 87–99.

Fussell, P. 1983: *Class*. New York: Ballantine Books.

Gabriel, J. and Ben-Tovim, G. 1979: The conceptualization of race relations in sociological theory. *Ethnic and Racial Studies*, 2(2), 190–212.

Gelb, J. and Palley, M. L. 1982: *Women and Public Policies*. Princeton: Princeton University Press.

Gellner, E. 1983: *Nations and Nationalism*. Oxford: Basil Blackwell.

Gerth, H. and Mills, C. 1970: *From Max Weber*. London: Routledge.

Ghosh, A. 1994: *In an Antique Land*. London: Granta Books/Penguin.

Giddens, A. 1973: *The Class Structure of the Advanced Societies*. London: Hutchinson.

Giddens, A. 1976: *New Rules of Sociological Method*. London: Hutchinson.

Giddens, A. 1984: *The Constitution of Society: outline of a theory of structuration*. Cambridge: Polity.

Giddens, A. 1990: *The Consequences of Modernity*. Cambridge: Polity.

Giddens, A. 1991: *Modernity and Self Identity*. Cambridge: Polity.

Gifford Inquiry 1989: *Loosen the Shackles*. Liverpool 8 Law Centre.

Gilbert, N., Dale, A., Arber, S., Evandrou, M. and Laczko, F. 1989: Resources in old age: ageing and the life course. In M. Jefferys (ed.), *Growing Old in the Twentieth Century*. London: Routledge, 93–114.
Gilroy, P. 1987: *There Ain't no Black in the Union Jack*. London: Routledge.
Gilroy, P. 1993: *The Black Atlantic*. London: Verso.
Glasgow, D. 1981: *The Black Underclass*. New York: Vintage Books.
Glasner, A. 1992: Gender and Europe: cultural and structural impediments to change. In J. Bailey (ed.), *Social Europe*. London: Longman, 70–105.
Glass, D. (ed.) 1954: *Social Mobility in Britain*. London: Routledge.
Glendinning, C. and Millar, J. (eds) 1992: *Women and Poverty in Britain: the 1990s*. London: Harvester Wheatsheaf.
Glucksmann, M. 1990: *Women Assemble*. London: Routledge.
Goldin, C. 1990: *Understanding the Gender Gap*. Oxford: Oxford University Press.
Goldthorpe, J. 1980: *Social Mobility and Class Structure in Modern Britain*. Oxford: Clarendon Press.
Goldthorpe, J., Lockwood, D., Bechhofer, F. and Platt, J. 1969: *The Affluent Worker in the Class Structure*. Cambridge: Cambridge University Press.
Goldthorpe, J. and Heath, A. 1992: Revised class schema. *Joint Unit for the Study of Social Trends*, working paper 13.
Goodman, A. and Webb, S. 1994: For richer for poorer. Institute of Fiscal Studies.
Gorz, A. 1982: *Farewell to the Working Class*. London: Pluto.
Gorz, A. 1989: *Critique of Economic Reason*. London: Verso.
Greer, G. 1971: *The Female Eunuch*. London: Paladin.
Griffin, C. 1985: *Typical Girls*. London: Routledge.
Griffin, C. 1993: *Representations of Youth*. Cambridge: Polity.
Griffin, S. 1981: *Pornography and Silence*. New York: Harper & Row.
Groves, D. 1992: Occupational pension provision and women's poverty in old age. In C. Glendinning and J. Millar (eds), *Women and Poverty in Britain: the 1990s*. London: Harvester Wheatsheaf, 193–206.
Guerin, D. 1979: *One Hundred Years of Labor in the USA*. London: Ink Links.
Guillemard, A.-M. 1989: The trend towards early labour force withdrawal and the reorganization of the life course: a cross-national analysis. In P. Johnson, C. Conrad and D. Thomson (eds), *Workers Versus Pensioners: intergenerational justice in an ageing world*. Manchester: Manchester University Press, 163–81.
Hall, G. S. 1904: *Adolescence*. New York: D. Appleton & Co.
Hall, S. 1980: Race, articulation and societies structured in dominance. In UNESCO, *Sociological Theories: race and colonialism*. Paris: UNESCO, 305–46.
Hall, S. 1990: Cultural identity and diaspora. In J. Rutherford (ed.), *Identity*. London: Lawrence & Wishart, 222–37.
Hall, S. 1992a: The west and the rest: discourse and power. In S. Hall and B. Gieben (eds), *Formations of Modernity*. Cambridge: Polity, 177–228.
Hall, S. 1992b: The question of cultural identity. In S. Hall, D. Held and A. McGrew (eds), *Modernity and Its Futures*. Cambridge: Polity, 277–326.
Hall, S. 1992c: New ethnicities. In J. Donald and A. Rattansi (eds), *'Race', Culture and Difference*. London: Sage, 252–99.
Hall, S., Critcher, C., Jefferson, T., Clarke, J. and Roberts, B. 1978: *Policing the Crisis*. London: Macmillan.
Hall, S. and Jacques, M. (eds) 1989: *New Times*. London: Lawrence & Wishart.

Hall, S. and Jefferson, J. (eds) 1976: *Resistance through Rituals: youth subculture in postwar Britain*. London: Hutchinson.
Halsey, A., Heath, A. and Ridge, J. 1980: *Origins and Destinations*. Oxford: Clarendon Press.
Halson, J. 1991: Young women, sexual harassment and heterosexuality: violence, power relations and mixed-sex schooling. In P. Abbott and C. Wallace (eds), *Gender, Power and Sexuality*. London: Macmillan, 97–114.
Haraway, D. 1990: A manifesto for cyborgs: science technology and socialist feminism in the 1980s. In L. Nicholson (ed.), *Feminism/Postmodernism*. London: Routledge, 190–233.
Harding, S. 1986: *The Science Question in Feminism*. Ithaca, NY: Cornell University Press.
Harding, S. (ed.) 1987: *Feminism and Methodology*. Milton Keynes: Open University Press.
Hargreaves, A. 1991: The political mobilization of the North African immigrant community in France. *Ethnic and Racial Studies*, 14(3), 350–67.
Harper, S. and Thane, P. 1989: The consolidation of 'old age' as a phase of life, 1945–65. In M. Jefferys (ed.), *Growing Old in the Twentieth Century*. London: Routledge. 43–61.
Harris, C. 1987: The individual and society: a processual approach. In A. Bryman, B. Bytheway, P. Allatt and T. Keil (eds), *Rethinking the Life Cycle*. London: Macmillan, 17–29.
Harris, C. 1991: Recession, redundancy and old age. In P. Brown and R. Scase (eds), *Poor Work*. Milton Keynes: Open University Press, 103–15.
Hartmann, H. 1976: Patriarchy, capitalism and job segregation by sex. *Signs*, 1(3), 137–68.
Hartmann, H. 1981: The unhappy marriage of marxism and feminism: towards a more progressive union. In L. Sargent (ed.), *Women and Revolution: the unhappy marriage of feminism and marxism*. London: Pluto, 1–41.
Hartsock, N. 1987: The feminist standpoint: developing the ground for a specifically feminist historical materialism. In S. Harding (ed.), *Feminism and Methodology*. Milton Keynes: Open University Press, 157–80.
Harvey, D. 1989: *The Condition of Postmodernity*. Oxford: Blackwell.
Hazan, H. 1994: *Old Age: constructions and deconstructions*. Cambridge: Cambridge University Press.
Hearn, J. and Parkin, W. 1993: Organizations, multiple oppressions and postmodernism. In J. Hassard and M. Parker (eds), *Postmodernism and organizations*. London: Sage, 148–61.
Hebdige, D. 1979: *Subcultures: the meaning of style*. London: Methuen.
Heidensohn, H. 1985: *Women and Crime*. London: Macmillan.
Herrnstein, R. and Murray, C. 1994: *The Bell Curve: intelligence and class structure in American life*. New York: Free Press.
Hiro, D. 1992 (2nd edn): *Black British, White British*. London: Paladin.
Hobsbawm, E. 1968: *Industry and Empire*. Harmondsworth: Penguin.
Hochschild, A. 1989: *The Second Shift*. New York: Viking.
Hollands, R. 1990: *The Long Transition: class, culture and youth training*. Basingstoke: Macmillan.
Holmwood, J. 1994: Postmodernity, citizenship and inequality. In R. Blackburn (ed.),

Social Inequality in a Changing World. Papers presented to Cambridge Social Stratification Seminar, 7–27.
hooks, b. 1982: *Ain't I a Woman? Black women and feminism*. London: Pluto.
Houghton, W. 1957: *The Victorian Frame of Mind*. New Haven: Yale University Press.
Hudson, M. 1994: *Coming Back Brockens*. London: Jonathan Cape.
Hudson, R. and Williams, A. 1989: *Divided Britain*. London: Belhaven Press.
Humphries, J. 1983: The emancipation of women in the 1970s and 1980s. *Capital and Class*, 20, 6–27.
Hunt, P. 1980: *Gender and Class Consciousness*. London: Macmillan.
Husbands, C. 1991: The mainstream right and the politics of immigration in France: major developments in the 1980s. *Ethnic and Racial Studies*, 14(2), 170–98.
Jackson, S. 1993: Love and romance as objects of feminist knowledge. In M. Kennedy, C. Lubelska and V. Walsh (eds), *Making Connections*. London: Taylor & Francis, 39–50.
Jacobs, J. 1993: Careers in the US service economy. In G. Esping-Andersen (ed.), *Changing Classes*. London: Sage, 195–224.
Jameson, F. 1991: *Postmodernism or, the cultural logic of late capitalism*. London: Verso.
Jefferys, M. (ed.) 1989: *Growing Old in the Twentieth Century*. London: Routledge.
Jencks, C. 1986: *What is Post-Modernism?* London: Academy Editions.
Jenkins, R. 1983: *Lads, Citizens and Ordinary Kids*. London: Routledge.
Jenkins, R. 1986: *Racism and Recruitment*. Cambridge: Cambridge University Press.
Jenson, J., Hagen, E. and Reddy, C. (eds) 1988: *Feminization of the Labour Force*. Polity: Cambridge.
Johnson, P. 1989: The structured dependency of the elderly: a critical note. In M. Jefferys (ed.), *Growing Old in the Twentieth Century*. London: Routledge, 62–71.
Johnson, P., Conrad, C. and Thomson, D. (eds) 1989: *Workers Versus Pensioners: intergenerational justice in an ageing world*. Manchester: Manchester University Press.
Jones, T. and McEvoy, D. 1986: Ethnic enterprise: the popular image. In J. Curran, J. Stanworth and D. Watkins (eds), *The Survival of the Small Firm*. Aldershot: Gower, 197–219.
Jowell, R., Brook, L., Prior, G. and Taylor, B. (eds) 1992: *British Social Attitudes: the ninth report*. Aldershot: Dartmouth Publishing.
Junankar, P. (ed.) 1987: *From School to Unemployment*. London: Macmillan.
Kaim-Caudle, P., Keithley, J. and Mullender, A. (eds) 1993: *Aspects of Ageing*. London: Whiting & Birch.
Kemp, T. 1978: *Historical Patterns of Industrialization*. London: Longman.
Kennedy, M., Lubelska, C. and Walsh, V. (eds) 1993: *Making Connections*. London: Taylor & Francis.
Kerr, C., Dunlop, J., Harbison, F. and Myers, C. 1962: *Industrialism and Industrial Man*. London: Heinemann.
Kimmel, M. 1987: The contemporary crisis of masculinity in historical perspective. In H. Brod (ed.), *The Making of Masculinities*. London: Allen & Unwin, 121–53.
Kitzinger, C. and Wilkinson, S. 1993: The precariousness of heterosexual feminist identities. In M. Kennedy, C. Lubelska and V. Walsh (eds), *Making Connections*. London: Taylor & Francis, 24–36.

Klingender, F. 1935: *The Condition of Clerical Labour in Britain*. London: Martin Lawrence.
Knowles, C. and Mercer, S. 1992: Feminism and antiracism: an exploration of the political possibilities. In J. Donald and A. Rattansi (eds), *'Race', Culture and Difference*. London: Sage, 104–25.
Kumar, K. 1978: *Prophecy and Progress*. Harmondsworth: Penguin.
Labour Force Survey, 1994–5. London: HMSO.
Lasch, C. 1977: *Haven in a Heartless World*. New York: Basic Books.
Lash, S. 1984: *The Militant Worker: class and radicalism in France and America*. Heinemann: London.
Lash, S. 1990: *The Sociology of Postmodernism*. London: Routledge.
Lash, S. and Urry, J. 1987: *The End of Organized Capitalism*. Cambridge: Polity.
Lash, S. and Friedman, J. 1992: *Modernity and Identity*. Oxford: Blackwell.
Laslett, P. 1977: *Family Life and Illicit Love in Earlier Generations*. Cambridge: Cambridge University Press.
Lea, J. and Young, J. 1984: *What is to be Done about Law and Order?* Harmondsworth: Penguin.
Lees, S. 1993: *Sugar and Spice: sexuality and adolescent girls*. Harmondsworth: Penguin.
Liddiard, M. and Hutson, S. 1990: Youth homelessness in Wales. In C. Wallace and M. Cross (eds), *Youth in Transition*. London: Falmer, 164–80.
Lockwood, D. 1958: *The Black-Coated Worker*. London: Allen & Unwin.
Lockwood, D. 1975: Sources of variation in working-class images of society. In M. Bulmer (ed.), *Working-class Images of Society*, London: RKP, 16–31.
Lockwood, D. 1988: The weakest link in the chain? In D. Rose (ed.), *Social Stratification and Economic Change*, London: Unwin Hyman, 57–97.
Lovenduski, J. 1986: *Women and European Politics*. Brighton: Harvester.
Luckmann, B. 1978: The small lifeworlds of modern man. In T. Luckmann (ed.), *Phenomenology and Sociology*. Harmondsworth: Penguin.
Lyon, D. 1994: *Postmodernity*. Milton Keynes: Open University Press.
Lyotard, J.-F. 1984: *The Postmodern Condition*. Manchester: Manchester University Press.
Mac an Ghaill, M. 1988: *Young, Gifted and Black*. Milton Keynes: Open University Press.
Macdonald, R. and Coffield, F. 1991: *Risky Business*. London: Falmer.
Mallet, S. 1975: *The New Working Class*. Nottingham: Spokesman.
Mama, A. 1984: Black women, the economic crisis and the British state. *Feminist Review*, 17, 21–36.
Mandel, E. 1975: *Late Capitalism*. London: New Left Books.
Mann, M. 1970: The social cohesion of liberal democracy. *American Sociological Review*, 35, 423–39.
Mann, M. 1986: A crisis in stratification theory? In R. Crompton and M. Mann (eds), *Gender and Stratification*. Cambridge: Polity, 40–56.
Mannheim, K. 1952: *Essays in the Sociology of Knowledge*. London: Routledge.
Marable, M. 1983: *How Capitalism Underdeveloped Black America*. London: Pluto.
Marceau, J. 1989: France. In T. Bottomore and R. Brym (eds), *The Capitalist Class*. Hemel Hempstead: Harvester Wheatsheaf, 46–72.

Markides, K. and Mindel, C. 1987: *Aging and Ethnicity*. Beverly Hills: Sage.
Marsden, D. 1987: Youth pay in some OECD countries since 1966. In P. Junankar (ed.), *From School to Unemployment*. London: Macmillan, 15–50.
Marshall, B. 1994: *Engendering Modernity*. Cambridge, Polity.
Marshall, G. 1988: Some remarks on the study of working-class consciousness. In D. Rose (ed.), *Social Stratification and Economic Change*. London: Hutchinson, 98–126.
Marshall, G. 1990: *In Praise of Sociology*. London: Unwin Hyman.
Marshall, G., Rose, D., Newby, H. and Vogler, C. 1988: *Social Class in Modern Britain*. London: Unwin Hyman.
Martin, H. and Roberts, C. 1984: *Women and Employment: a lifetime perspective*. London: HMSO.
Martinelli, A. and Chiesi, A. 1989: Italy. In T. Bottomore and R. Brym (eds), *The Capitalist Class*. Hemel Hempstead: Harvester Wheatsheaf, 109–39.
Martiniello, E. 1993: Ethnic leadership, ethnic communities' political powerlessness and the state in Belgium. *Ethnic and Racial Studies*, 16(2), 236–55.
Marx, K. and Engels, F. 1934: *Manifesto of the Communist Party*. London: Lawrence & Wishart.
Marx, K. 1976: *Capital*, vol. I. Harmondsworth: Penguin.
Mason, D. 1992: Some Problems with the Concepts of Race and Racism (Discussion Papers in Sociology, S92/5). University of Leicester.
Maynard, M. 1994: 'Race', gender and the concept of difference in feminist thought. In H. Afshar and M. Maynard (eds), *The Dynamics of 'Race' and Gender*. London: Taylor & Francis, 9–25.
McGrew, A. 1992: A global society? In S. Hall, D. Held and A. McGrew (eds), *Modernity and its Futures*. Cambridge: Polity, 61–116.
McIntosh, M. 1979: The welfare state and the needs of the dependent family. In S. Burman (ed.), *Fit Work for Women*. London: Croom Helm, 153–72.
Mckee, L. and Bell, C. 1986: His unemployment, her problem: the domestic and marital consequences of male unemployment. In S. Allen, A. Waton, K. Purcell and S. Woods (eds), *The Experience of Unemployment*, 134–49.
McNay, L. 1992: *Foucault and Feminism*. Cambridge: Polity.
McRobbie, A. 1978: Working class girls and the culture of femininity. In Women's Studies Group (eds), *Women Take Issue*. London: Hutchinson, 96–108.
McRobbie, A. 1991: *Feminism and Youth Culture*. London: Macmillan.
McRobbie, A. and Nava, M. (eds) 1984: *Gender and Generation*. London: Macmillan.
Meacham, S. 1977: *A Life Apart*. London: Thames & Hudson.
Mercer, K. 1990: Welcome to the jungle: identity and diversity in postmodern politics. In J. Rutherford (ed.), *Identity*. London: Lawrence & Wishart, 43–71.
Merton, R. 1938: Social structure and anomie, *American Sociological Review*, 3, 672–82.
Middlemas, K. 1979: *Politics in Industrial Society*. London: Deutsch.
Middleton, C. 1988: The familiar fate of the famulae: gender divisions in the history of wage labour. In R. Pahl, *On Work*. Oxford: Basil Blackwell.
Miles, R. 1982: *Racism and Migrant Labour*. London: Routledge.
Miles, R. 1989: *Racism*. Milton Keynes: Open University Press.
Miles, R. 1993: Europe 1993: the significance of changing patterns of migration. *Ethnic and Racial Studies*, 16(3), 459–66.

Millett, K. 1971: *Sexual Politics*. London: Sphere.
Minkler, M. and Estes, C. (eds) 1984: *Readings in the Political Economy of Old Age*. New York: Baywood Publishing.
Mirza, H. 1992: *Young, Female and Black*. London: Routledge.
Mitchell, J. 1975: *Psychoanalysis and Feminism*. Harmondsworth: Penguin.
Mitter, S. 1986: *Common Fate, Common Bond: women in the global economy*. London: Pluto.
Modood, T. 1992: *Not Easy Being British*. Stoke-on-Trent: Trentham Books.
Mohanty, C. 1992: Feminist encounters: locating the politics of experience. In M. Barrett and A. Phillips (eds), *Destabilizing Theory*. Cambridge: Polity, 74–92.
Moore, B. 1966: *Social Origins of Dictatorship and Democracy*. Harmondsworth: Penguin.
Moore, S. 1988: Getting a bit of the other: the pimps of postmodernism. In R. Chapman and J. Rutherford (eds), *Male Order*. London: Lawrence & Wishart.
Morris, L. 1990: *The Workings of the Household*. Cambridge: Polity.
Morris, L. 1994: *Dangerous Classes*. London: Routledge.
Mukta, P. (forthcoming): New Indian historiography and the politics of Hindu nationalism.
Mungham, G. and Pearson, G. 1975: *Working-Class Youth Culture*. London: Routledge & Kegan Paul.
Murakami, H. 1994: *Dance, Dance, Dance*. London: Hamish Hamilton.
Murphy, M. 1987: Measuring the family life cycle: concepts, data and methods. In A. Bryman, B. Bytheway, P. Allatt and T. Keil (eds), *Rethinking the Life Cycle*. London: Macmillan, 30–50.
Murray, C. 1984: *Losing Ground*. New York: Basic Books.
Murray, C. 1990: *The Emerging British Underclass*. London: Institute of Economic Affairs.
Myles, J., Picott, G. and Wannell, T. 1993: Does post-industrialism matter? the Canadian experience. In G. Esping-Andersen (ed.), *Changing Classes*. London: Sage, 171–94.
Naipaul, V. S. 1994: *A Way in the World*. London: Heinemann.
Nakane, C. 1973: *Japanese Society*. Harmondsworth: Pelican.
Neugarten, B. 1970: The old and the young in modern societies. In E. Shanas (ed.), *Aging in Contemporary Society*. London: Sage, 13–24.
Nicholson, L. (ed.) 1990: *Feminism/Postmodernism*. London: Routledge.
Nicolaus, M. 1967: Proletariat and middle class in Marx: Hegelian choreography and the capitalist dialectics. *Studies on the Left*, 11.
Oakley, A. 1974: *The Sociology of Housework*. Oxford: Martin Robertson.
Oakley, A. 1981: *Subject Woman*. Harmondsworth: Penguin.
O'Donnell, M. 1985: *Age and Generation*. London: Tavistock.
Offe, C. 1985: *Disorganized Capitalism*. Cambridge: Polity.
O'Neill, J. 1995: *The Poverty of Postmodernism*. London: Routledge.
Ortner, S. 1974: Is female to male as nature is to culture? In M. Rosaldo and L. Lamphere (eds), *Woman, Culture and Society*. Stanford: Stanford University Press, 67–88.
Pahl, R. 1984: *Divisions of Labour*. Oxford: Blackwell.
Parkin, F. 1972: *Class Inequality and Political Order*. London: Paladin.
Parkin, F. 1979: *Marxism and Class Theory: a bourgeois critique*. London: Tavistock.

Parmar, P. 1990: Black feminism: the politics of articulation. In J. Rutherford (ed.), *Identity*. London: Lawrence & Wishart, 101–26.
Parsons, T. 1954: *Essays in Sociological Theory*. Glencoe, Ill.: Free Press.
Pearson, G. 1983: *Hooligan: a history of respectable fears*. London: Macmillan.
Pelling, H. 1960: *American Labor*. Chicago: University of Chicago Press.
Phillips, A. 1987: *Divided Loyalties*. London: Virago.
Phillips, A. 1992: Universal pretensions in political thought. In M. Barrett and A. Phillips (eds), *Destabilizing Theory*. Cambridge: Polity, 10–30.
Phillipson, C. 1982: *Capitalism and the Construction of Old Age*. London: Macmillan.
Phillipson, C. 1990: The sociology of retirement. In J. Bond and P. Coleman (eds), *Ageing in Society: an Introduction to Social Gerontology*. London: Sage, 144–60.
Phillipson, C. 1993: Understanding old age: social and policy issues. In P. Kaim-Caudle, J. Keithley and A. Mullender (eds), *Aspects of Ageing*. London: Whiting & Birch, 42–58.
Phizacklea, A. 1990: *Unpacking the Fashion Industry: gender, racism and class in production*. London: Routledge.
Phizacklea, A. and Miles, R. 1980: *Labour and Racism*. London: Routledge.
Pilkington, A. 1984: *Race Relations in Britain*. Slough: University Tutorial Press.
Pilkington, A. 1992: The underclass thesis and 'race'. Unpublished paper, British Sociological Association Annual Conference, University of Kent.
Poiner, G. 1990: *The Good Old Rule*. Sydney: Sydney University Press.
Pollert, A. 1981: *Girls, Wives, Factory Lives*. London: Macmillan.
Pollert, A. 1988: Dismantling flexibility. *Capital and Class*, 3(4), 42–75.
Porter, M. 1983: *Home and Work Consciousness*. Manchester: Manchester University Press.
Presdee, M. 1982: Invisible girls – a study of unemployed young women. Paper presented at Tenth World Congress of Sociology, Mexico City.
Presdee, M. 1990: Creating poverty and creating crime: Australian youth policy in the eighties. In C. Wallace and M. Cross (eds), *Youth in Transition*. London: Falmer, 146–63.
Pringle, R. 1989: *Secretaries Talk*. London: Verso.
Pringle, R. and Watson, S. 1992: 'Women's interests' and the post-structuralist state. In M. Barrett and A. Phillips (eds), *Destabilizing Theory*. Cambridge: Polity, 53–73.
Randall, V. 1982: *Women and Politics*. London: Macmillan.
Rapoport, R. and Rapoport, R. 1975: *Leisure and the Family Life Cycle*. London: Routledge.
Rattansi, A. 1992: Changing the subject? Racism, culture and education. In J. Donald and A. Rattansi (eds), *'Race', Culture and Difference*. Milton Keynes: Open University Press, 11–48.
Reskin, B. and Roos, P. 1990: *Job Queues, Gender Queues*. Philadelphia: Temple University Press.
Rex, J. 1970: *Race Relations in Sociological Theory*. London: Weidenfeld and Nicolson.
Rex, J. 1982: West Indian and Asian youth. In E. Cashmore and B. Troyna (eds), *Black Youth in Crisis*. London: Routledge & Kegan Paul.
Rex, J. 1986a. The role of class analysis in the study of race relations – a Weberian perspective. In J. Rex and D. Mason (eds), *Theories of Race and Ethnic Relations*. Cambridge: Cambridge University Press, 64–83.

Rex, J. 1986b: *Race and Ethnicity*. Milton Keynes: Open University Press.
Rex, J. 1992: Race and ethnicity in Europe. In J. Bailey (ed.), *Social Europe*. London: Longman, 106–20.
Rex, J. and Moore, R. 1967: *Race, Community and Conflict*. London: Oxford University Press.
Rex, J. and Tomlinson, S. 1979: *Colonial Immigrants in a British City: a class analysis*. London: Routledge & Kegan Paul.
Rich, A. 1980: Compulsory heterosexuality and lesbian existence. *Signs*, 5(4), 631–90.
Richards, W. 1994: Are you too old at forty? *AUT Woman*, 33.
Richardson, J. and Lambert, J. 1985: *The Sociology of Race*. Ormskirk: Causeway Books.
Riley, D. 1988: *Am I That Name?* London: Macmillan.
Riley, M. W., Johnson, M. and Foner, A. 1972: *Aging and Society: a sociology of age stratification*. New York: Sage.
Riseborough, G. 1993: GBH – the gobbo barmy harmy: one day in the life of the YTS boys. In I. Bates and G. Riseborough (eds), *Youth and Inequality*. Milton Keynes: Open University Press, 160–228.
Roberts, K. 1983: *Youth and Leisure*. London: Allen & Unwin.
Roberts, K., Campbell, R. and Furlong, A. 1990: Class and gender divisions among young adults at leisure. In C. Wallace and M. Cross (eds), *Youth in Transition*. London: Falmer, 129–45.
Roberts, K., Cook, F., Clark, S. and Semeonoff, E. 1977: *The Fragmentary Class Structure*. London: Heinemann.
Rohrlich-Leavitt, R. (ed.) 1975: *Women Cross Culturally: continuity and change*. The Hague: Mouton.
Rosaldo, M. and Lamphere, L. (eds) 1974: *Women, Culture and Society*. Stanford: Stanford University Press.
Rose, A. 1965: The subculture of aging: a framework in social gerontology. In A. Rose and W. Peterson (eds), *Older People in Their Social World*. Philadelphia: Davis, 3–16.
Rossi, P. H. and Wright, J. D. 1993: The urban homeless: a portrait of urban dislocation. In W. J. Wilson (ed.), *The Ghetto Underclass*. London: Sage, 149–59.
Rowbotham, S. 1981: The trouble with 'patriarchy'. In Feminist Anthology Collective (eds), *No Turning Back*. London: Women's Press, 72–8.
Rowntree Report 1995: *Joseph Rowntree Inquiry into Income and Wealth*.
Ruggie, M. 1988: Gender, work and social progress. In J. Jenson, E. Hagen and C. Reddy (eds), *Feminization of the Labour Force*. Cambridge: Polity, 173–88.
Rutherford, J. 1990: *Identity*. London: Lawrence & Wishart.
Said, E. 1985: *Orientalism*. Harmondsworth: Penguin.
Sarre, P. 1989: Race and the class structure. In C. Hamnett, L. McDowell and P. Sarre (eds), *The Changing Social Structure*. London: Sage, 124–57.
Sassoon, A. S. (ed.) 1987: *Women and the State*. London: Hutchinson.
Saunders, P. 1984: Beyond housing classes: the sociological significance of private property rights in means of consumption. *International Journal of Urban and Regional Research*, 8(2), 202–27.
Saunders, P. 1990: *Social Class and Stratification*. London: Routledge.
Saunders, P. 1994: Is Britain a meritocracy? In R. Blackburn (ed.), *Social Inequality*

in a Changing World. Papers presented to Cambridge Social Stratification Seminar, 85–111.
Savage, M., Barlow, J., Dickens, A. and Fielding, T. 1992: *Property, Bureaucracy and Culture: middle-class formation in contemporary Britain*. London: Routledge.
Scase, R. 1992: *Class*. Buckingham: Open University Press.
Scase, R. and Goffee, R. 1989: *Reluctant Managers*. London: Unwin Hyman.
Schreiner, O. 1911: *Women and Labor*. New York: Frederick A. Stoles.
Scott, J. 1979: *Corporations, Classes and Capitalism*. London: Hutchinson.
Scott, J. 1982: *The Upper Classes*. London: Macmillan.
Scott, J. 1991: *Who Rules Britain?* Cambridge: Polity.
Scott, J. W. 1988: *Gender and the Politics of History*. New York: Columbia University Press.
Seabrook, J. 1988: *The Leisure Society*. Oxford: Blackwell.
Sennett, R. and Cobb, J. 1977: *The Hidden Injuries of Class*. Cambridge: Cambridge University Press.
Sharpe, S. 1976: *Just Like a Girl*. Harmondsworth: Penguin.
Sheffield, C. 1987: Sexual terrorism. In B. Hess and M. Ferree (eds), *Analyzing Gender*. London: Sage, 171–89.
Showalter, E. 1987: *A Female Malady*. London: Virago.
Simmons, M. 1994: Big rise in sleeping rough. *Guardian*, 12 December.
Simons, J. 1992: Europe's ageing poulation – demographic trends. In J. Bailey (ed.), *Social Europe*. London: Longman, 50–69.
Sivanandan, A. 1982: *A Different Hunger*. London: Pluto.
Sivanandan, A. 1990: All that melts into air is solid: the hokum of New Times. *Race and Class*, 31, 1–31.
Skellington, R. and Morris, P. 1992: *'Race' in Britain Today*. London: Sage.
Sloggett, A. and Joshi, H. 1994: Higher mortality in deprived areas: community or personal disadvantage, *British Medical Journal*, 309, 1470–74.
Smart, B. 1990: Modernity, postmodernity and the present. In B. Turner (ed.), *Theories of Modernity and Postmodernity*. London: Sage, 14–30.
Smith, D. 1977: *Racial Disadvantage in Britain*. Harmondsworth: Penguin.
Social Trends. London: HMSO.
Sombart, W. 1976: *Why Is there No Socialism in the United States?* London: Macmillan.
Spencer, A. and Podmore, D. 1987: *In a Man's World*. London: Tavistock.
Spohn, W. and Bodemann, Y. M. 1989: Federal Republic of Germany. In T. Bottomore and R. Brym (eds), *The Capitalist Class*. Hemel Hempstead: Harvester Wheatsheaf, 73–108.
Stacey, J. 1993: Untangling feminist theory. In D. Richardson and V. Robinson (eds), *Introducing Women's Studies*. London: Macmillan, 49–73.
Stanfield, J. (ed.) 1993: *A History of Race Relations Research*. London: Sage.
Stanley, L. and Wise, S. 1983: *Breaking Out*. London: Routledge.
Steedman, C., Urwin, C. and Walkerdine, V. (eds) 1985: *Language, Gender and Childhood*. London: Routledge & Kegan Paul.
Steinberg, R. 1988: The unsubtle revolution: women, the state and equal employment. In J. Jenson, E. Hagen and C. Reddy (eds), *Feminization of the Labour Force*. Cambridge: Polity, 189–213.
Steven, R. 1983: *Classes in Contemporary Japan*. Cambridge: Cambridge University Press.

Still, J. 1994: 'What Foucault fails to acknowledge . . .': feminists and *The History of Sexuality*. *History of the Human Sciences*, 7(2), 150–7.
Strathern, M. 1993: *After Nature: English kinship in the late twentieth century*. Cambridge: Cambridge University Press.
Stuart, A. 1990: Feminism: dead or alive? In J. Rutherford (ed.), *Identity*. London: Lawrence & Wishart, 28–42.
Sydie, R. 1987: *Natural Women, Cultured Men*. Milton Keynes: Open University Press.
Tahlin, M. 1993: Class inequality and post-industrial employment in Sweden. In G. Esping-Andersen (ed.), *Changing Classes*. London: Sage, 80–108.
Tang Nain, G. 1991: Black women, sexism and racism: black or anti-racist. *Feminist Review*, 37, 1–22.
Taylor, B. 1983: *Eve and the New Jerusalem*. London: Virago.
Tester, K. 1993: *The Life and Times of Post-modernity*. London: Routledge.
Therborn, G. 1989: The two-thirds, one-third society. In S. Hall and M. Jacques (eds), *New Times*. London: Lawrence & Wishart, 103–116.
Theroux, P. 1992: *The Happy Isles of Oceania*. Harmondsworth: Penguin.
Thomas, K. 1976: Age and authority in early modern England. *Proceedings of the British Academy*, 62(2), 205–48.
Thompson, K. 1976: *Auguste Comte: the founder of sociology*. London: Nelson.
Thompson, K. 1992: Social pluralism and postmodernity. In S. Hall, D. Held and A. McGrew (eds), *Modernity and Its Futures*. Cambridge: Polity, 221–72.
Thompson, P. 1993: Postmodernism: fatal distraction. In J. Hassard and M. Parker (eds), *Postmodernism and organizations*. London: Sage, 183–203.
Thomson, D. 1989: The welfare state and generation conflict: winners and adults. In P. Johnson, C. Conrad and D. Thomson (eds), *Workers Versus Pensioners: intergenerational justice in an ageing world*. Manchester: Manchester University Press, 35–56.
Tocqueville, A. de 1968: *Democracy in America*. London: Fontana.
Tong, R. 1989: *Feminist Thought*. London: Unwin Hyman.
Touraine, A. 1971: *The Post-industrial Society*. New York: Random House.
Townsend, P. 1979: *Poverty in the United Kingdom*. Harmondsworth: Penguin.
Townsend, P. 1981: The structured dependency of the elderly: a creation of social policy in the twentieth century. *Ageing and Society*, 1(1), 5–28.
TUC 1994: *Ethnic Minorities in the Labour Market*. Preliminary report.
Turner, B. 1988: *Status*. Milton Keynes: Open University Press.
Turner, B. 1990: *Theories of Modernity and Postmodernity*. London: Sage.
Useem, M. 1984: *The Inner Circle*. New York: Oxford University Press.
Van den Berghe, P. 1978: *Race and Racism: a comparative perspective*. New York: Wiley.
Van der Pijl, K. 1989: The international level. In T. Bottomore and R. Brym (eds), *The Capitalist Class*. Hemel Hempstead: Harvester Wheatsheaf, 237–66.
Walby, S. 1986: *Patriarchy at Work*. Cambridge: Polity.
Walby, S. 1990: *Theorizing Patriarchy*. Oxford: Blackwell.
Walby, S. 1992: Post-post-modernism? Theorizing social complexity. In M. Barrett and A. Phillips (eds), *Destabilizing Theory*. Cambridge: Polity, 31–52.
Walby, S. 1993: 'Backlash' in historical context. In M. Kennedy, C. Lubelska and V. Walsh (eds), *Making Connections*. London: Taylor & Francis, 79–89.

Walker, A. 1981: Towards a political economy of old age. *Ageing and Society*, 1(1), 73–94.
Walker, A. 1989: The social division of early retirement. In M. Jefferys (ed.), *Growing Old in the Twentieth Century*. London: Routledge, 73–94.
Walker, A. 1990: Poverty and inequality in old age. In J. Bond and P. Coleman (eds), *Ageing in Society: an introduction to social gerontology*. London: Sage, 229–49.
Walker, A. 1992: The poor relation: poverty among older women. In C. Glendinning and J. Millar (eds), *Women and Poverty in Britain in the 1990s*. London: Harvester Wheatsheaf, 176–92.
Walker, A. 1993: Older people in Europe: perceptions and realities. In P. Kaim-Caudle, J. Keithley and A. Mullender (eds), *Aspects of Ageing*. London: Whiting & Birch, 8–24.
Walker, M. 1995: All the King's forces. *Guardian*, 16 January.
Wallace, C. and Cross, M. (eds) 1990: *Youth in Transition*. London: Falmer.
Wallace, C. and Pahl, R. 1986: Polarization, unemployment and all forms of work. In S. Allen, A. Waton, K. Purcell and S. Wood (eds), *The Experience of Unemployment*. London: Macmillan, 116–35.
Wallace, M. 1990: *Black Macho and the Myth of the Superwoman*. London: Verso.
Wallerstein, I. 1974: *The Modern World System*. New York: Academic Press.
Weber, M. 1926: *General Economic History*. London: Allen & Unwin.
Weber, M. 1938: *The Protestant Ethic and the Spirit of Capitalism*. London: Unwin.
Weber, M. 1949: *The Methodology of the Social Sciences*. Glencoe, Ill.: Free Press.
Weber, M. 1964: *The Theory of Social and Economic Organization*. London: Macmillan.
Weber, M. 1968: *Economy and Society*. New York: Bedminster Press.
Weeks, J. 1990: The value of difference. In J. Rutherford (ed.), *Identity*. London: Lawrence & Wishart, 88–100.
Weis, L. 1990: *Working Class Without Work*. New York: Routledge.
West, C. 1994: *Race Matters*. Vintage: New York.
Westergaard, J. 1994: Amnesia over the upper class. Paper presented at Conference in celebration of Richard Brown's contribution to British Sociology. Durham, September 1994.
Westergaard, J. and Resler, H. 1975: *Class in a Capitalist Society*. London: Heinemann.
Westwood, S. 1984: *All Day, Every Day*. London: Pluto.
Westwood, S. 1990: Racism, black masculinity and the politics of space. In J. Hearn and D. Morgan (eds), *Men, Masculinities and Social Theory*. London: Unwin Hyman, 55–71.
Wetherell, M., Stiven, H. and Potter, J. 1987: Unequal egalitarianism: a preliminary study of discourses concerning gender and employment opportunities, *British Journal of Social Psychology*, 26, 59–71.
Wheelock, J. 1990: *Husbands at Home*. London: Routledge.
Wihtol de Wenden, C. 1991: Immigration policy and the issue of nationality. *Ethnic and Racial Studies*, 14(3), 319–32.
Williams, C. and Thorpe, B. 1992: *Beyond Industrial Sociology*. Sydney: Allen & Unwin.
Williams, P. 1987: Images of age and generation among older Aberdonians. In A. Bryman, B. Bytheway, P. Allatt and T. Keil (eds), *Rethinking the Life Cycle*. London: Macmillan, 88–102.

Williamson, B. 1993: Broken dreams: the sociology of inter-generational relations in Europe. In P. Kaim-Caudle, J. Keithley and A. Mullender (eds), *Aspects of Ageing*. London: Whiting & Birch, 59–70.
Willis, P. 1977: *Learning to Labour*. Aldershot: Gower.
Willis, P. 1978: *Profane Culture*. London: Routledge & Kegan Paul.
Willis, P., Jones, S., Canaan, J. and Hurd, G. 1990: *Common Culture*. Milton Keynes: Open University Press.
Wilson, E. 1977: *Women and the Welfare State*. London: Tavistock.
Wilson, W. J. 1987: *The Truly Disadvantaged*. Chicago: Chicago University Press.
Wilson, W. J. (ed.) 1993: *The Ghetto Underclass*. London: Sage.
Wilton, T. 1993: Queer subjects: lesbians, heterosexual women and the academy. In M. Kennedy, C. Lubelska and V. Walsh (eds), *Making Connections*. London: Taylor & Francis, 167–79.
Witz, A. 1992: *Professions and Patriarchy*. London: Routledge.
Wolpe, A. 1988: *Within School Walls*. London: Routledge.
Wollstonecraft, M. 1982: *A Vindication of the Rights of Woman* (1st edn 1792). Harmondsworth: Penguin.
Wood, J. 1984: Groping towards sexism: boys' sex talk. In A. McRobbie and M. Nava (eds), *Gender and Generation*. London: Macmillan, 54–84.
Wrench, J. and Lee, G. 1978: A subtle hammering – young black people in the labour market. In B. Troyna and D. Smith (eds), *Racism, School and the Labour Market*. Leicester: National Youth Bureau, 29–45.
Wright, E. O. 1976: Class boundaries in advanced capitalist societies. *New Left Review*, 98, 3–41.
Wright, E. O. 1985: *Classes*. London: Verso.
Young, I. 1981: Beyond the happy marriage: a critique of the dual systems theory. In L. Sargent (ed.), *Women and Revolution: the unhappy marriage of Marxism and feminism*. London: Pluto.
Yuval-Davis, N. 1993: Beyond difference: women and coalition politics. In M. Kennedy, C. Lubelska and V. Walsh (eds), *Making Connections*. London: Taylor & Francis, 3–10.
Zaretsky, E. 1976: *Capitalism, the Family and Personal Life*. London: Pluto.

Index